WILEY
advantage

Dear Valued Customer,

We realize you're a busy professional with deadlines to hit. Whether your goal is to learn a new technology or solve a critical problem, we want to be there to lend you a hand. Our primary objective is to provide you with the insight and knowledge you need to stay atop the highly competitive and ever-changing technology industry.

Wiley Publishing, Inc., offers books on a wide variety of technical categories, including security, data warehousing, software development tools, and networking — everything you need to reach your peak. Regardless of your level of expertise, the Wiley family of books has you covered.

- For Dummies® – The *fun* and *easy* way™ to learn
- The Weekend Crash Course® – The *fastest* way to learn a new tool or technology
- Visual – For those who prefer to learn a new topic *visually*
- The Bible – The *100% comprehensive* tutorial and reference
- The Wiley Professional list – *Practical* and *reliable* resources for IT professionals

The book you hold now, *Web Services Enhancements: Understanding the WSE for .NET Enterprise Applications*, is your hands-on guide to the tools needed for solving current problems with delivering XML Web services. You'll find this book to be a great guide to working and developing with Global XML Web Services Architecture standards. The expert author guides you through understanding XML Web services and .NET through the next steps of adding security, routing, and attachments.

Our commitment to you does not end at the last page of this book. We'd want to open a dialog with you to see what other solutions we can provide. Please be sure to visit us at www.wiley.com/compbooks to review our complete title list and explore the other resources we offer. If you have a comment, suggestion, or any other inquiry, please locate the "contact us" link at www.wiley.com.

Thank you for your support and we look forward to hearing from you and serving your needs again in the future.

Sincerely,

Richard K. Swadley

Richard K. Swadley
Vice President & Executive Group Publisher
Wiley Technology Publishing

15 HOUR WEEKEND CRASH COURSE

Visual

Bible

DUMMIES FOR

WILEY
Wiley Publishing, Inc.

Web Services Enhancements
Understanding the WSE for .NET Enterprise Applications

Web Services Enhancements

Understanding the WSE for .NET Enterprise Applications

Bill Evjen

WILEY

Wiley Publishing, Inc.

Web Services Enhancements: Understanding the WSE for .NET Enterprise Applications

Published by
Wiley Publishing, Inc.
10475 Crosspoint Boulevard
Indianapolis, IN 46256
www.wiley.com

Copyright © 2003 by Wiley Publishing, Inc., Indianapolis, Indiana
Published simultaneously in Canada

Library of Congress Control Number: 2002114852

ISBN: 0-7645-3736-9

Manufactured in the United States of America

10 9 8 7 6 5 4 3 2 1

1B/RY/QT/QT/IN

For general information on our other products and services or to obtain technical support, please contact our Customer Care Department within the U.S. at (800) 762-2974, outside the U.S. at (317) 572-3993 or fax (317) 572-4002.

Wiley also publishes its books in a variety of electronic formats. Some content that appears in print may not be available in electronic books.

 WILEY is a trademark of Wiley Publishing, Inc.

About the Author

Bill Evjen is an active proponent of the .NET technologies and community-based learning initiatives for .NET. He has been actively involved with .NET since the first bits were released in 2000 and has since become the president of the St. Louis .NET User Group (www.stlnet.org) as well as the founder and president of the International .NET Association (www.ineta.org), which represents more than 70,000 members worldwide.

Based in St. Louis, Evjen is an acclaimed author and speaker on next-generation Web Services and related technologies. Bill has written such books as the *Visual Basic .NET Bible* and *XML Web Services for ASP.NET*. He is currently authoring *ASP.NET Professional Secrets*.

In addition to working in the .NET world, Bill is a Technical Director serving in the office of the Chief Scientist for Reuters, the international news and financial services company. Bill graduated from Western Washington University in Bellingham, Washington, with a Russian language degree. When he isn't tinkering on the computer, he enjoys spending his free time in his summer place in Toivakka, Finland. You can reach Bill at evjen@yahoo.com.

Credits

SENIOR ACQUISITIONS EDITOR
Sharon Cox

PROJECT EDITOR
Neil Romanosky

TECHNICAL EDITOR
Devin Rader

DEVELOPMENT EDITOR
Kezia Endsley

COPY EDITOR
Kim Cofer

EDITORIAL MANAGER
Mary Beth Wakefield

VICE PRESIDENT & EXECUTIVE GROUP PUBLISHER
Richard Swadley

VICE PRESIDENT AND EXECUTIVE PUBLISHER
Bob Ipsen

VICE PRESIDENT AND PUBLISHER
Joseph B. Wikert

EXECUTIVE EDITORIAL DIRECTOR
Mary Bednarek

PROJECT COORDINATOR
Ryan Steffen

GRAPHICS AND PRODUCTION SPECIALISTS
Beth Brooks
Kristin McMullan

QUALITY CONTROL TECHNICIANS
John Tyler Connoley
John Greenough
Andy Hollandbeck
Carl William Pierce
Dwight Ramsey

PROOFREADING AND INDEXING
TECHBOOKS Production Services

To Tuija, for her encouragement

Preface

Web services has already started changing the way in which developers model their applications. This new model allows developers to easily expose application logic and data with relatively little work. This ease is provided on the Microsoft platform by .NET, and more importantly – ASP.NET.

Though great, the model was originally accepted in the enterprise with a little bit of worry. *Where is the security? What about sending non-XML-related items? What about routing SOAP messages?* These were some of the common questions, and rightly so, as they were good questions and pointed to where the Web services model was lacking – a common way to express security, routing, and sending attachments between disparate systems.

Companies such as IBM and Microsoft then started working on a number of specifications that addressed these needs, such as:

- WS-Security
- WS-Routing
- WS-Referral
- WS-Timestamp
- WS-Attachments

The specifications as a whole, referred to as the Global XML Web Services Architecture (GXA), were watched by Microsoft developers with great excitement, but once the specifications were introduced, these developers didn't want to wait for the next release of .NET to start using them. There was a desire to use the specifications for advanced Web services immediately, and this is what caused the birth of the tool, the Web Services Enhancements for Microsoft .NET – otherwise simply known as the WSE.

The toolkit will allow you, as either a producer or consumer of XML Web services, to use security, routing, and the ability to send attachments with your SOAP messages. The security supplied with the WSE includes the ability to send credentials and digitally sign messages, as well as apply encryption to your SOAP messages. The routing capabilities give you the ability to set up SOAP routers to control the paths of any SOAP messages you send or receive. The ability to include attachments with relative ease allows you to send non-XML-related items such as images or even compressed files.

As a technical director for Reuters, I spend a great amount of time showing financial companies how to disseminate information throughout their enterprise and amongst their partners and customers. The WSE is my number-one recommendation. The WSE is a powerful tool that is absolutely required if you plan on introducing Web services to the enterprise.

Who Should Read This Book

This book is aimed at several different types of people. First of all, this is not an introductory book on Web services on the .NET platform. Though the first chapter of the book takes you through the basics of XML Web services, you should have some familiarity and understanding of the Web services model. If you are brand-new to Web services, my suggestion is that you read my first book on Web services titled *XML Web Services for ASP.NET* (Wiley, ISBN 0-7645-4829-8) in addition to this book.

Web Services Enhancements is for

- ◆ **Web Service Developers** – If you are a Web services developer who is looking to build truly well-rounded and -thought-out XML Web services, then this book is definitely for you! If you have always wondered how you are going to apply security or add attachments to your SOAP messages, you will gain value from this book.

- ◆ **Web Service Architects** – This book will take you down the path of looking at the entire Web services picture from the creation and consumption of SOAP messages as well as the hows and whys of routing SOAP messages using SOAP routers that you can create yourself.

- ◆ **.NET Developers** – Whether you are an ASP.NET or a Windows Forms developer who will have to work with XML Web services in any manner, this book is a must as it will teach you how to manipulate and control how your SOAP messages are created, thus ensuring interoperable messages.

What Hardware and Software Do You Need?

This book is based upon a Web services toolkit, the Web Services Enhancements for Microsoft .NET (WSE), that is provided for free by Microsoft from its MSDN site. Therefore, you should download this toolkit to work through the examples in this book. This book also utilizes a great deal from the .NET Framework also provided by Microsoft. You will need to download the latest version of the .NET Framework, as well as the latest version of Visual Studio .NET. Visual Studio .NET is one of the development environments that you will use to build all the sample applications that are provided with this book. Please note, however, that you can use other IDEs for the examples here with little modification, but I highly suggest using VS.NET for your development.

Here are the minimum requirements for running the WSE, the .NET Framework, and Visual Studio .NET:

♦ Intel Pentium processor: 450MHz or equivalent processor

♦ Microsoft Windows 2000, Microsoft Windows XP Professional, or Microsoft Windows Server 2003

♦ Microsoft Internet Information Services (IIS) 5.0

♦ 128MB of available RAM

♦ 3GB of available disk space

♦ Color monitor capable of 800 x 600 resolution

♦ CD-ROM drive

♦ The WSE needs the .NET Framework 1.0 SP2 or greater

Although these are the minimum requirements, Microsoft *recommends* the following requirements:

♦ Intel Pentium processor: 733MHz or equivalent processor

♦ Microsoft Windows 2000, Microsoft Windows XP Professional, or Microsoft Windows Server 2003

♦ Microsoft Internet Information Services (IIS) 5.0

♦ 256MB of available RAM

♦ 3GB of available disk space

♦ Color monitor capable of 1024 x 768 resolution

♦ CD-ROM drive

How This Book Is Organized

This book is divided up into chapters. There are also five appendixes included in the book. The following descriptions explain what you'll find.

Chapter 1: Introduction to XML Web Services

This chapter covers an introduction to the XML Web services model and why it is so important. This chapter spends some time bringing to light this powerful new way of having remote objects communicate across boundaries to disparate systems. After an introduction, you learn how to build basic XML Web services. Throughout this chapter, you will see concrete examples.

Chapter 2: Web Services Enhancements for Microsoft .NET

The entire book concentrates on the new Web Services Enhancements for Microsoft .NET, and this chapter is a good introduction to the new toolkit. More importantly, this chapter starts off with the reason that this toolkit exists in the first place and how it answers the Web services vision that has been set out by IBM and Microsoft. In addition to the toolkit, this chapter looks at the various GXA specifications that are laid out so far and how these specifications fit into this vision. Following this, you are shown how to install the WSE and what changes this installation will make to your system.

Chapter 3: Adding Security Credentials to a SOAP Message

After introductions to XML Web services and the WSE, this chapter starts right away with one of the most requested functionalities for Web services: the ability to apply credentials. This chapter covers how you can apply credentials using usernames and passwords as well as X.509 certificates.

Chapter 4: Digitally Signing SOAP Messages

Data doesn't mean much unless it is valid. Digitally signing your SOAP messages ensures that your messages' content and values are not altered in transit. It also applies extra security in regards to credential verification. This chapter focuses on how you can easily use the WSE to digitally sign your SOAP messages and to decipher them on the receiving end.

Chapter 5: Working with Encrypted SOAP Messages

As SOAP messages get routed from one point to another with the new SOAP routing capabilities, you need a way to apply encryption to your SOAP messages so that the encryption does not rely on the wire, but instead is built into the message itself. This chapter focuses on how to apply encryption to your SOAP payloads as well as to selected parts of the SOAP header. There is also a discussion on decrypting the SOAP message on the receiving end.

Chapter 6: Using the Three Aspects of WS-Security Together

With security being a big part of the WSE story, the previous three chapters took a look at each aspect of the WSE's WS-Security implementation. This chapter looks instead at how all three aspects of the WS-Security can work together to apply one of the highest levels of security available for your XML Web services.

Chapter 7: Routing SOAP Messages

There are definite advantages to routing SOAP messages through SOAP intermediaries or SOAP routers. This chapter shows you how to construct your own SOAP router and how to use this capability to your advantage for keeping the best possible uptime for your XML Web services.

Chapter 8: Understanding WS-Attachments and DIME

When the XML Web services model was introduced, one of the first things that people wanted to use it for was to send non-XML-related items such as images and documents. Though it was possible to do this in the past, it was cumbersome and not always easy. The new WSE incorporates a better model for sending these kinds of items by using *Direct Internet Message Encapsulation* (DIME). This chapter covers DIME and how to use this new technology to send your attachments with ease.

Chapter 9: Using WSE Filters

This chapter gets into detail about how the WSE works using its various filters. The WSE is powerful in its ability to allow you as a developer to control how these filters work. Therefore, after an introduction to the filter structure, this chapter looks at how you can use or not use these filters for your advantage in building the most truly interoperable XML Web services possible.

Appendixes

The appendixes of this book are meant purely for reference. They contain short instructions on how to apply SOAP tracing to your applications as well as how to use the new Web Services Enhancements Settings Tool. In addition to this, there are references for the WSE's configuration files as well as a comprehensive list of MediaType values that you can use when sending attachments using DIME. The last appendix is a short list of Web services resources that you can use to further your education.

Conventions Used in This Book

The following sections explain the conventions used in this book.

Menu commands

When you're instructed to select a command from a menu, you see the menu and the command separated by an arrow symbol. For example, when you're asked to choose the Open command from the File menu, you see the notation File → Open.

Typographical conventions

I use *italic* to indicate new terms or to provide emphasis. I use **boldface** type to indicate text that you need to type directly on the keyboard.

Code

I use a special typeface to indicate code, as demonstrated in the following example of Visual Basic .NET code:

```
<WebMethod()> Public Function Add(ByVal a As Integer, _
    ByVal b As Integer) As Integer

    Return (a+b)
End Function
```

This special code font is also used within paragraphs to make elements such as XML tags (`</name>`) stand out from the regular text.

Navigating this book

This book is designed to be read from the beginning to the end, although if you have already been introduced to the basics of XML Web services, you can skip over the first chapter and return to it at a later time.

Tips, Cautions, Notes, and Cross-References appear in the text to indicate important or especially helpful items. Here's a list of these items and their functions:

The Note icon highlights information that requires special attention and details that are not easy to recognize.

The Caution icon highlights possible trouble spots and common mistakes.

The Tip icon highlights possible shortcuts and recommendations.

 The Cross-Reference icon highlights references to other chapters of the book.

Companion Web site

This book provides a companion Web site from which you can download the code from various chapters. All the code listings reside in a single WinZip file that you can download by going to www.wiley.com/combooks/evjen. After you download the file WSE.zip, you can open it and extract the contents by double-clicking on the file.

For Further Information

You can find help for specific problems and questions by investigating several Web sites. Microsoft's own .NET Web site is a good place to start: msdn.microsoft.com/net. I also recommend that you take a look at Appendix E for other sites.

Feel free to contact me at evjen@yahoo.com with any questions or comments. I would really like to hear anything you have to say about the book (good or bad), so I can make sure you have the information you need to write the best applications you can.

Happy coding!

Acknowledgments

As I have said before, writing books may seem like a great solo effort, but the author is just one of the contributors to what is really a team project. This book had a great team behind it and all of them worked really hard to bring you the first and the best possible book on the Web Services Enhancements product.

From this group I would like to point out Senior Acquisitions Editor Sharon Cox for allowing me to bring to light in book form this wonderful and new product that will greatly help enterprise development. If it were not for Sharon's efforts, this book would not exist.

In addition, I would like to thank the technical editor of the book, Devin Rader, one of the most knowledgeable .NET developers around. You all might have met Devin virtually since he is consistently out there helping other developers in the community at large. Devin, thanks for your concentrated help on this project.

Thanks are also due to this book's project editor, Neil Romanosky, as well as development editor Kezia Endsley and copy editor Kimberly Cofer. Your help has been invaluable for this project.

Beyond the team that helped put the book together, I would like to thank the Microsoft XML Web services team for their help with this project. This book was a challenge to write because I started writing it well before the product was released and it changed considerably during this time. I would like to point out Eric Schmidt and Yasser Shohoud from the Microsoft XML Web services team and thank them for their help and assistance — Eric especially for his advice at the conception of this project.

As a .NET developer and author, I spend a lot of my time tinkering with the latest and greatest that .NET has to offer and depend upon a circle of friends for technical advice and as a sounding board for ideas (crazy or not). From this group, I would like to thank Dan Wahlin of `www.xmlforasp.net` and Dave Wanta of `www.123aspx.com` for their help and assistance over the years. Thank you guys!

Thanks are also due to my boss at Reuters, Scott Parsons, for being supportive of my book-writing endeavors.

Most importantly, I want to thank my family. I wouldn't have the opportunity to write if my wife and children didn't provide me with the time as well as modifying their own schedules to fit mine. They actually have made this book more possible than anyone else. Thank you Tuija, Sofia, and Henri. Kiitos paljon!

Contents at a Glance

Contents

Chapter 1

Introduction to XML Web Services

IN THIS CHAPTER

- ◆ Realizing the need for XML Web services
- ◆ Understanding XML and SOAP
- ◆ Describing and discovering XML Web services
- ◆ Building simple XML Web services

BACK IN 1994 AND 1995, the world was taken over by a new wave of computing. The browser was introduced to the mass public, and people could sit in the comfort of their own homes and, over slow connections, these end users could connect to remote computers. At that moment, many of us felt that an earth-shattering change had occurred.

I, as an end user, could sit in front of a lightweight application (the browser), type in some unique address, and away my browser went on some journey to the other side of the world. It went off for me like a car on a road trip through the pipes of the Internet. Sometimes my little car had to stop and ask for directions, and other times it may have been lost somewhere "out there" never to be found again, but in most instances it brought back a whole carload of information that it displayed in the container of my browser. I was truly awed.

It was a new dawn of computing. No longer did we need to locally house information on our machines at home or in the office. Instead, we were able to venture out onto the Internet and get the information that we needed.

It wasn't long before people realized that this medium would be great to not only deliver information, but it would also be an outstanding way to provide applications to people around the world regardless of their locale. Before the Internet, if your application needed an update or a quick change, it would be a while before the end user saw the change. The Internet application answered this problem mainly because there was really only one instance of the application that was housed somewhere on a server and this single instance of the application simply dished out responses to all the requests that came its way irregardless of where the end user is in the world. If there was a change to make to the application, changes were then made to this single instance and because of this, the end user was always seeing the latest and greatest version of the application. At this point in Internet history, many people thought they were in some sort of utopia and things just simply couldn't be any better than this.

Browser-based applications became more advanced as time went on. Over time, many businesses had information about customers in thick-client applications, databases, content management servers, XML files, and tab-delimited text files, in addition to the information and functionality that was provided by the company's Web applications. Everything was scattered, and these information islands cropped up everywhere in the enterprise.

What was needed was a way for these systems, which were in many cases quite disparate, to communicate with one another so that this information could be shared. Sharing data and application logic works toward the Holy Grail of computing – *code reuse*. Instead of housing the customer's order information in three separate parts of the enterprise, the three separate applications that needed this information could share it instead from a single source ensuring that the data was always correct and up to date. However, many of these information islands were miles apart in languages and platforms and getting them to work together sometimes was difficult at best.

What Is This Internet Thing?

As the Internet started to infiltrate the enterprise, this newly spread pipeline was connecting all these data islands together. It didn't take long for various vendors (for example, Microsoft, IBM, Sun Microsystems, and others) to see that their applications and servers in the enterprise could use this pipeline for communication.

What faced each of the vendors is that they could work out ways for one entity on the Internet to communicate with another, but the problem was that there was no common-language or industry-wide standard that disparate systems could use in their desire to communicate with each other as a whole. What was needed was a common language that used a common protocol.

Instead vendors implemented proprietary solutions on their own. For example, Microsoft released DCOM as their solution, but like other solutions from other vendors, it didn't answer all the problems that the enterprises faced in getting these disparate and distant systems to talk to one another.

These solutions were in many cases using proprietary forms of communication. In some cases, such as is the case with DCOM, these solutions were dependent on specific ports to be open for application-to-application communication to occur. This was generally a problem in the enterprise space because it is not typically the developers that are controlling the opening and closing of ports within their company, but it is usually operations whose general philosophy is to lock down everything but port 80 (for surfing the Internet) for security reasons.

In the end, some of these new technologies helped, but in most cases, the basic problems still existed. There had to be an easy way for completely disparate systems (for example, a Microsoft system and an Apache system) to communicate data and business logic across the wall that stood between them. It soon became evident that no single company or proprietary system could answer these problems; instead, it would take a concerted effort on the part of the entire IT industry to find a solution. What the industry needed to do was to find a common language that everyone agreed upon and that no single company controlled.

Understanding the Beauty of XML

It came to light to all the major vendors within the IT industry that XML *(Extensible Markup Language)* was the answer for complete integration of the enterprise, regardless of the platform, language, or fashion in which data is stored. More importantly, this new XML communication would occur over HTTP.

Probably the most vital decision to come from all of this was that all the vendors understood the logic of working together in a set of common standards and protocols so that cross-platform communication could occur. The core pieces that everyone agreed upon for this new form of application communication, called simply *Web services,* involved the following three technologies:

◆ XML

◆ SOAP

◆ HTTP

XML (which will be described in more detail later in this chapter) is an ASCII-based way to describe data. It is extremely flexible and that is the power of this technology as it is easy to describe a wide-variety of data quite easily using XML. The other advantage of XML for data description is that most applications and platforms can read and understand XML, making it quite versatile.

SOAP, or *Simple Object Access Protocol,* is an XML-based way of describing an XML-encapsulated message that is being sent across the wire. The power of SOAP is that it is based upon XML, making it easily understood by the same applications and platforms that can read and use XML. Secondly, as its name suggests, it is simple and quite extensible.

HTTP is the wire in which these SOAP messages are sent from one point to another. HTTP is the Internet, and the medium that we are going to be using for our SOAP requests and responses. The great thing about SOAP using HTTP is that not only do most applications and platforms use HTTP in one manner or another, but SOAP simply flows through firewalls as regular Internet traffic over HTTP.

Microsoft's XML Web services

Based on these industry agreements, Microsoft introduced XML Web services as a core component of its new .NET platform. XML Web services in ASP.NET is a new model for exposing application logic. The entire .NET Framework has been built around this model and Microsoft provided a number of new tools and core functionality that make it quite simple to build and consume XML Web services in .NET.

One way to think of how an XML Web service works is to compare it to calling a standard function, but instead making the call over HTTP (Hypertext Transfer Protocol) by specifying a URL. This model of Web services is quite different than previous models, although it is similar to older models as well.

For example, the classic Active Server Pages model was based on the client/server technologies. The client made a request over the Internet, or HTTP, and the response, if there was one, was sent back by the same means. On the receiving end of the request, application logic or registration was applied and in most cases, a response was sent back. So, when users opened their browsers and typed a URL, a request for the page was sent to a server. Then the server made note of the page being requested and a stream of information (usually HTML) was sent back over the wire to the client. In some cases, before the requested server sent anything back over the wire, it went to another location to check another server or database for some additional information. Figure 1-1 shows how this model looks.

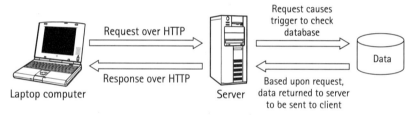

Figure 1-1: Requests/responses over HTTP using classic ASP

Working with XML Web services basically involves the same model, except that we are not using ASP or ASP.NET to build an interface that we would use to activate requests and receive responses over HTTP. There are many situations in which we would want to expose the logic or information that we are holding in a database somewhere, but we would not always want to build a visual interface to that logic or information.

For example, say that you are a large wholesaler of a wide variety of widgets and you have a number of customers who greatly depend upon your current inventory status so that their customers can place appropriate orders. The entire widget inventory is stored in a SQL Server database and you want to give access to this database to your customers. You could build a Web interface to this database in ASP.NET that would allow the users to log on to your system and gather the information that they would need.

However, what if your users want to put the information on their own Web site or extranet for their own customers? This is where you can expose your database information by offering it as an XML Web service. Doing this will allow the users to access this information in whatever fashion they choose because only the data is returned. Now within their own Web page, they can make a call to your XML Web service and get the information sent to them in an XML format where they can use it as they see fit. So instead of building separate Web interfaces for different clients to access this data, you can just provide the application logic to the users and let them deal with it in their own way.

What is outstanding about this entire process is that it doesn't matter which system the end user is using to make this request. This is not a Microsoft-proprietary message format that is being sent to the users. Instead, everything is being sent over standard protocols. The message is being sent over HTTP using SOAP, a flavor of XML. So any system that can consume XML over HTTP can use this model. Figure 1-2 shows an example.

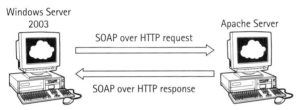

Figure 1-2: The XML Web services model: Request/response over HTTP using SOAP

Composition of XML Web services

Visual Studio .NET and the Microsoft .NET platform make building and consuming XML Web services very easy. It is important that you understand the basic structure of XML Web services in order to make your ventures into this new application model successful.

There are a few pillars of XML Web services development that will make this job a lot easier. Not all of these specifications or technologies that are used to build and consume XML Web services are required, but you should still review and understand them before you seriously start using XML Web services in any of your applications. Building XML Web services within the .NET environment allows the following:

- ◆ An industry-standard way to represent data
- ◆ A way to transfer data in a common message format
- ◆ A way to describe an XML Web service to potential consumers
- ◆ A path to discovery of XML Web services on remote servers and local machines
- ◆ A way to find XML Web services

Now let's take a look at how each of these functions plays a role in XML Web services.

Just as XML is tightly integrated throughout the .NET Framework, XML is the key technology used in Web services. Most of the Web services that are available today use XML for data representation as well as XML Schemas to describe data types. As you will see, using XML just makes sense. XML Schemas, or XSD documents, are an important part of working with XML. XSD documents support an XML document by specifying the structure of the XML document. As a replacement for Document Type Definition (DTD) documents, XSD documents are ideal as they are made up of XML themselves unlike the former DTD documents.

Introducing XML

In its short lifetime, XML has become the Internet standard in data representation. XML came to light when the W3C (World Wide Web Consortium) realized that it needed to develop a markup language to represent platform-independent data. In 1998, XML was developed and was quickly hailed as the solution for data transfer across varying systems. Not only could XML be transported over HTTP, but it could also go through firewalls, making this markup language quite fluid.

XML Web services, as its name suggests, is highly dependent on XML. Data makes the Internet go around and XML is an elementary way that data can be represented and packaged for transport to other systems.

In the past, one way to package data for transport was to place the data within a comma-, tab-, or pipe-delimited text file. Listing 1-1 shows an example of such a file.

Listing 1-1: An example of a pipe-delimited text file.

```
Bill|Evjen|Programmer|03/08/1998|Seattle, Washington|2
```

These kinds of data representations are in use today. The individual pieces of data are separated by pipes, commas, tabs, or any other characters you want to use. Looking at the collection of items in Listing 1-1, it is hard to tell what the data represents. You might be able to get a better idea based on the file name, but what do the date and the number 2 represent?

XML relates data in a self-describing manner so that any person, technical or otherwise, can decipher what the data means. Listing 1-2 shows how the same piece of data is represented using XML.

Listing 1-2: XML file example

```
<?xml version="1.0" encoding="UTF-8" ?>
<Employee>
   <FirstName>Bill</FirstName>
   <LastName>Evjen</LastName>
   <JobTitle>Programmer</JobTitle>
   <StartDate>03/08/1998</StartDate>
```

```
    <WorkLocation>Seattle, Washington</WorkLocation>
    <NumDependents>2</NumDependents>
</Employee>
```

In Listing 1-2, you can tell by just looking at the data in the file what each of the data items means and how they relate to one another. This is laid out in such a simple format that it is possible for any non-technical person to be able to understand the data.

After looking at this XML file, you may have noticed how similar XML is to HTML. Both markup languages are related, but HTML is used to mark up text for presentation purposes such as for delivering Web pages in a browser, and XML is used to mark up text for data representation purposes.

Both XML and HMTL have their roots in the Standard Generalized Markup Language (SGML), which was created in 1986. SGML is a more complex markup language that was also used for data representation. With the explosion of the Internet, the W3C realized that it needed a universal way to represent data that would be easier to use than SGML, and that brought forth the birth of XML.

Advantages of using XML for data representation

There are a number of ways to represent data, a few of which have already been addressed in this chapter. XML has a distinct advantage over other forms of data representation. The following list explains some of the reasons why XML has become as popular as it is today:

- ◆ XML is easy to read and understand.

- ◆ A large number of platforms support XML and can manage it through an even larger set of tools that are available for XML data reading, writing, and manipulation.

- ◆ XML can be used across open standards that are available today.

- ◆ XML allows developers to create their own data definitions and models of representation.

- ◆ XML is simpler to use than binary formats when sending complex data structures because there are a large number of XML tools available.

Communicating Data from an XML Web Service

XML Web services use XML for data representation. This is so that different systems and applications can quickly and easily share and consume data. XML is based on standards and any application or system that can take hold of an XML file and use it in some fashion is a candidate for dealing with an XML Web service.

To take advantage of this wide acceptance, you need to be able to transport the XML data from point A to point B. XML Web services use HTTP, and occasionally SMTP, to transport XML data from one point to another. Take a look at Figure 1-3 to understand how this works.

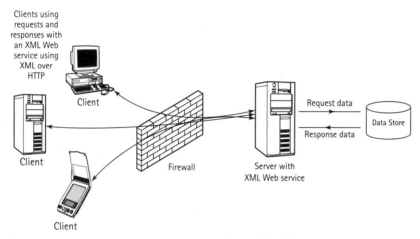

Figure 1-3: Various clients communicating with an XML Web service through a firewall using XML over HTTP

As shown in Figure 1-3, by using an XML Web service, you are making a request from some sort of client. This request then triggers a response from the server. The request message carries information about the function to be called and any parameters that are required by the function. Once the server that hosts the XML Web service receives the request message from the client, it initiates the function and returns a response message that contains information returned by the function. This response message can be just a simple message that some specific action was taken or it can contain a complete dataset. What you return is really up to you.

Using XML Web services, it is possible to communicate requests and responses using one of several common, standardized methods. They allow requests and responses to take place over HTTP-GET, HTTP-POST, and SOAP. The following sections take a look at each of these methods so you can get a better idea of which methods to use when building your own XML Web service.

XML Web services via HTTP-GET and HTTP-POST

This section takes a brief look at the HTTP-GET and HTTP-POST protocols. Each of them is discussed in more detail soon.

You may be quite familiar with using these formats in traditional client-server Web application development. In Active Server Pages 3.0, it was possible to send name/value pairs from one page to another by transmitting this information as query strings that were attached directly to the URL. This is the method that is used when working with XML Web services using HTTP-GET.

So, for example, if you called and invoked your XML Web service using HTTP-GET, you could do so in the following manner:

```
http://www.wiley.com/bookinfo/bookprice.asmx/GetBookPrice?ISBN=0764548263
```

After this request is sent to the server, ASP.NET on the server then parses the name/value pairs that were sent in the URL string, creates a `BookInfo` object, and then calls the `GetBookPrice` method passing the method the singular parameter that it needs.

Figure 1-4 shows an example of calling an XML Web service by using HTTP-GET.

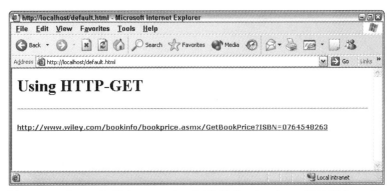

Figure 1-4: A sample Web page using HTTP-GET to invoke an XML Web service

XML Web services also accept HTTP-POST requests. HTTP-POST also passes name/value pairs similar to HTTP-GET, but it holds these name/value pairs within the actual request header rather than as query strings as it is done with HTTP-GET.

Using HTTP-POST as opposed to HTTP-GET allows you to transmit larger amounts of data because there is a 255-character limit for URLs when using HTTP-GET for some older browsers. Using HTTP-POST, you can invoke the XML Web service from your form and the form will pass the name/value pairs to the server that hosts the XML Web service. Figure 1-5 shows an example of a form that invokes an XML Web service when users press the Submit button.

The important thing to remember is that HTTP-GET and HTTP-POST are standard methods that use HTTP for encoding and passing name/value pairs. You will find using these protocols to invoke XML Web services to be easy and simple.

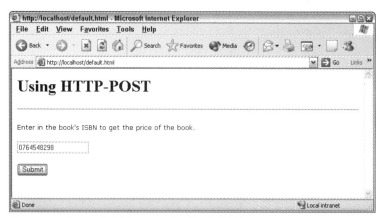

Figure 1-5: A sample Web page using HTTP-POST to invoke an XML Web service

The Simple Object Access Protocol (SOAP) is the third and most preferred way to deal with message-based communications over HTTP. SOAP is a simple, lightweight XML-based protocol for exchanging structured and type information on the Web over HTTP. There are many reasons why you would choose SOAP to deal with XML Web services, but one of the most compelling is that SOAP allows you to transmit more complex data types, such as entire datasets, rather than being limited to primitive data types.

Understanding Query Strings

Query strings are a simple and easy way to pass data from one page to the next within a Web application. Query strings are collections of name/value pairs that are appended onto the URL to be passed to the next page or a remote object.

Here is how the URL looks when passing the name of a user from one page to the next:

```
http://www.wiley.com?username=Bill
```

In this example, a variable called username with a value of Bill is appended to the URL by ending the URL string with a question mark, followed by the variable name.

It is possible to pass more than one name/value pair along with the URL by separating the name/value pairs with an ampersand (&). For example, if you were passing the username and the employee's ID number, you could do it in the following manner:

```
http://www.wiley.com?username=Bill&EmployeeID=9040777
```

Query strings are simple, but remember that they aren't the most secure ways in which to work, because everything about them is quite exposed.

SOAP uses HTTP-POST to transmit its SOAP messages to the server, unlike HTML forms, which use HTTP-POST to transmit name/value pairs within the request header. SOAP sends its requests and responses over HTTP by inserting a SOAP envelope into the payload section of HTTP-POST. Listing 1-3 shows a simple SOAP request message transmitted over HTTP-POST.

Listing 1-3: A SOAP request method transmitted over HTTP-POST

```
POST /bookinfo/bookprice.asmx HTTP/1.1
Host: www.wiley.com
Content-Type: text/xml; charset=utf-8
Content-Length: length
SOAPAction: "http://tempuri.org/GetBookPrice"

<?xml version="1.0" encoding="utf-8"?>
<soap:Envelope xmlns:xsi="http://www.w3.org/2001/XMLSchema-instance"
 xmlns:xsd="http://www.w3.org/2001/XMLSchema"
 xmlns:soapenc="http://schemas.xmlsoap.org/soap/encoding/"
 xmlns:tns="http://tempuri.org/"
 xmlns:types="http://tempuri.org/encodedTypes"
 xmlns:soap="http://schemas.xmlsoap.org/soap/envelope/">
    <soap:Body
     soap:encodingStyle="http://schemas.xmlsoap.org/soap/encoding/">
       <tns:GetBookPrice>
          <ISBN xsi:type="xsd:integer">0764548298</ISBN>
       </tns:GetBookPrice>
    </soap:Body>
</soap:Envelope>
```

This request will be sent to the XML Web service and the SOAP response will look like Listing 1-4.

Listing 1-4: The SOAP response to the SOAP request shown in Listing 1-3

```
HTTP/1.1 200 OK
Content-Type: text/xml; charset=utf-8
Content-Length: length

<?xml version="1.0" encoding="utf-8"?>
<soap:Envelope xmlns:xsi="http://www.w3.org/2001/XMLSchema-instance"
 xmlns:xsd="http://www.w3.org/2001/XMLSchema"
 xmlns:soapenc="http://schemas.xmlsoap.org/soap/encoding/"
 xmlns:tns="http://tempuri.org/"
 xmlns:types="http://tempuri.org/encodedTypes"
 xmlns:soap="http://schemas.xmlsoap.org/soap/envelope/">
```

Continued

Listing 1-4 *(Continued)*

```
<soap:Body
 soap:encodingStyle="http://schemas.xmlsoap.org/soap/encoding/">
   <tns:GetBookPriceResponse>
     <GetBookPriceResult href="#id1" />
   </tns:GetBookPriceResponse>
   <types:BookPrice id="id1" xsi:type="types:BookPrice">
     <BookPrice xsi:type="xsd:string">string</BookPrice>
   </types:BookPrice>
</soap:Body>
</soap:Envelope>
```

The main thing to point out in these two code examples is that the SOAP message is encapsulated within a SOAP envelope by using the `<soap:Envelope>` elements. Contained within the SOAP message are the SOAP body, `<soap:Body>`, and any optional headers, `<soap:header>`.

The great benefit of using SOAP is that you can transmit anything that can be represented in XML. For this reason, SOAP is the preferred transfer protocol method when working with XML Web services.

Using HTTP-GET with XML Web Services

You can use HTTP-GET to call a remote method and pass the method the parameters it needs directly in the URL. To do this, either find or deploy your own XML Web service and then link to the service from the URL in the address bar of your browser.

You then need to gain access to the XML Web service by linking to it in the following manner:

```
http://servername/vdir/webservicename.asmx/Methodname?name=value
```

You can see this in action by calling the simple `Add` WebMethod that is part of the `Calculator` XML Web service that you built earlier in this chapter. You can create a page that contains a hyperlink to the method that you want to call. Contained within the URL of the link are the values that you need to pass to the `Add()` method. The code in Listing 1-5 shows how to quickly and easily access an XML Web service using HTTP-GET.

Listing 1-5: Calling your Calculator XML Web service's Add method

```
<HTML>
   <HEAD>
      <title>WebForm1</title>
   </HEAD>
   <body>
```

```
<form id="Form1" method="post" runat="server">
   <asp:HyperLink id="HyperLink1" runat="server"
   NavigateUrl="http://localhost/Calculator/
   Service1.asmx/Add?a=5&b=5"
Font-Bold="True" Font-Names="Verdana"
Font-Size="X-Small">
      http://localhost/Calculator/service1.asmx/Add?a=5&b=5
   </asp:HyperLink>
</form>
   </body>
</HTML>
```

 The method name that you refer to in your URL is case-sensitive. Therefore, Add and add are not the same methods.

Figure 1-6 shows how your page will look with the embedded link to your XML Web service.

Figure 1-6: Using HTTP-GET to interact with an XML Web service

Clicking on the link calls the method that follows the .asmx extension in the URL, in this case, /Add. Following the method name, you insert the name/value pairs that are the parameters needed by the Add method, in this case, an integer value for a and another for b. With this full construction, you have an address for the XML Web service, the method that you are calling, and the parameters that the method needs in order to get back a return message.

In return, you get back an XML file with the value in place as shown in the following code:

```
<?xml version="1.0" encoding="utf-8" ?>
<int xmlns="http://tempuri.org/">10</int>
```

You can now use this XML in your applications as you see fit, whether they are ASP, VB6, or any .NET application. Using HTTP-GET is a quick and easy way to access XML Web services. There are, however, problems with this scenario. You can easily see what you are passing and so can everyone else. For security purposes, this might not be the best way to do things.

Using HTTP-POST with Web services

Very much like HTTP-GET, HTTP-POST works by sending name/value pairs to the XML Web service that you are calling. Therefore, you are limited by not being able to send complex data types like you can with SOAP. Unlike HTTP-GET, HTTP-POST sends these name/value pairs in the request header so they are not open to view. HTTP-GET sends the parameters in the URL and, therefore, they are open for the public to see.

To work with HTTP-POST, you must have an HTML page with a form in it. Listing 1-6 gives you a quick look at a simple form that will interact with the prior Calculator XML Web service.

Listing 1-6: Interacting with an XML Web service via HTTP-POST

```
<HTML>
    <HEAD>
        <title>Using HTTP-POST</title>
    </HEAD>
    <body>
        <form method="post"
         action="http://localhost/TestWS/Service1.asmx/Add">
            <P>
            <input type="text" name="a"></P>
            <P>
            <input type="text" name="b"></P>
            <P>
            <input type=submit value=Add></P>
            </form>
    </body>
</HTML>
```

The attributes of the <Form> tag are important. First, the method attribute needs to be set to POST. The second attribute is the action attribute. The action attribute specifies where the form will post the name/value pairs that are generated. In this case, you need to specify the location of the Calculator XML Web service. After the extension .asmx, you need to specify the method that you are going to call. In this case, it is /Add because you are calling the Add() WebMethod, but it could just as easily be /Subtract, /Multiply, or /Divide.

The form elements that collect the information that you pass on as parameters need to have a name attribute. The value of the name attribute must be the name of the parameters that the XML Web service is requesting. To determine the name of the parameters that you are going to pass to a Web service, study the WSDL document. You can look at the Calculator XML Web service's WSDL document at `http: //localhost/TestWS/Service1.asmx?wsdl`. Scroll down the document a bit and look at what the `Add()` WebMethod is asking for. The code in Listing 1-7 is from the WSDL document of the Calculator XML Web service.

Listing 1-7: Part of the WSDL document from the Calculator XML Web service

```
<s:element name="Add">
   <s:complexType>
      <s:sequence>
         <s:element minOccurs="1" maxOccurs="1" name="a"
          type="s:int" />
         <s:element minOccurs="1" maxOccurs="1" name="b"
        type="s:int" />
      </s:sequence>
   </s:complexType>
</s:element>
```

In this WSDL document, the `Add` method is asking for just two parameters, a and b, both of the type `integer`.

Running your `POST` sample, you get an XML response from the XML Web service as shown in the following code:

```
<?xml version="1.0" encoding="utf-8" ?>
<int xmlns="http://tempuri.org/">10</int>
```

This is a quick and convenient way to pass information to an XML Web service to get back some simple results. Using HTTP-POST is also a bit better than using HTTP-GET because HTTP-GET limits the number of characters that can be sent to the XML Web service. The URL of an HTTP-GET call can only handle 255 characters in some older browsers; this seriously limits the scope of the name/value pairs that you can use. If you use HTTP-POST, you can place as many name/value pairs as you need. In addition, because these name/value pairs are stored in the request header, they are hidden from the user.

As you work with XML Web services more and more, you may want to pass more complex data structures. These types of transactions are presently only possible using SOAP. So, the following section takes a quick look at SOAP and how you can use it with XML Web services.

Using SOAP (Simple Object Access Protocol) with Web services

SOAP is a lightweight XML-based protocol for exchanging more complex data structures over HTTP. You also gain the capability to specify data types in SOAP, something that isn't possible when using HTTP-GET or HTTP-POST. Using SOAP as the transport protocol is the default way in which the .NET applications communicate with XML Web services.

 You can find more information on SOAP at www.w3c.org/TR/soap.

A SOAP message is made up of three main parts – the SOAP envelope, the SOAP header, and the SOAP body, described as follows:

◆ The SOAP envelope defines the overall framework of the SOAP message and forms the root element of the packet that is sent. The SOAP envelope encapsulates the SOAP message, including any headers and the body.

◆ The SOAP header is an optional element that enables you to place information that you wouldn't put in the body part of the SOAP packet, such as authentication, transaction management, and more. Throughout this book, you'll be working with SOAP headers quite extensively in working with the GXA specifications.

◆ The SOAP body is where all the action is and is where the information is passed to the XML Web service. The code in Listing 1-8 shows an ASP.NET Web application that calls your Calculator XML Web service's Add() method.

Listing 1-8: AddMethod.aspx

```
<%@ Page Language="vb" AutoEventWireup="false"
    Codebehind="WebForm1.aspx.vb"
    Inherits="WebApplication1.WebForm1"%>
<HTML>
  <HEAD>
    <title>SOAP AddMethod</title>
  </HEAD>
  <body>
    <form id="Form1" method="post" runat="server">
      <P>
      <asp:TextBox id="TextBox1" runat="server"></asp:TextBox></P>
      <P>
      <asp:TextBox id="TextBox2" runat="server"></asp:TextBox></P>
      <P>
      <asp:Button id="Button1" runat="server"
```

```
        Text="Add"></asp:Button></P>
        <P>
        <asp:Label id="Label1" runat="server"></asp:Label></P>
      </form>
   </body>
</HTML>
```

The code-behind page that calls the Calculator's Add method is shown in Listing 1-9.

Listing 1-9: AddMethod.aspx (NOTE: Only part of the file is displayed)

[VB]

```
Private Sub Button1_Click(ByVal sender As System.Object, ByVal e As
               System.EventArgs) Handles Button1.Click

   Dim CalcWS As New Calc.Calculator()
   Label1.Text = CalcWS.Add(TextBox1.Text, TextBox2.Text)
End Sub
```

[C#]

```
private void Button1_Click(object sender, System.EventArgs e)
{
   CalcWS.Calculator ws = new CalcWS.Calculator();
   label1.Text = CalcWS.Add(int.Parse(textbox1.Text),
      int.Parse(textbox2.Text));
}
```

In this example, you created an ASP.NET application, and within this application you created an instance of the Calculator class and called the Add() method directly from your code. The call to the Add() method is quite simple because the class takes care of marshaling the call over SOAP for you. It then takes what is sent back to you in return, deserializes this data, and gets it back as an object.

The SOAP request that is sent to the Calculator XML Web service looks like the code in Listing 1-10.

Listing 1-10: The SOAP request sent from the client application to the Calculator XML Web service

```
POST /TestWS/Service1.asmx HTTP/1.1
Host: localhost
Content-Type: text/xml; charset=utf-8
Content-Length: {length}
```

Continued

Listing 1-10 *(Continued)*

```
SOAPAction: "http://www.xmlws101.com/Add"

<?xml version="1.0" encoding="utf-8"?>
<soap:Envelope xmlns:xsi="http://www.w3.org/2001/XMLSchema-instance"
 xmlns:xsd="http://www.w3.org/2001/XMLSchema"
 xmlns:soap="http://schemas.xmlsoap.org/soap/envelope/">
  <soap:Body>
    <Add xmlns="http://www.xmlws101.com">
      <a>5</a>
      <b>10</b>
    </Add>
  </soap:Body>
</soap:Envelope>
```

Right away you will notice that your SOAP request is simply an ASCII file as specified by the Content-Type value of text/xml. Encapsulating the SOAP body is the SOAP envelope. The envelope is specified by the element <soap:Envelope>. Within the <soap:Envelope> element are various namespace attributes. The SOAP envelope contains only the SOAP body because the example does not have a SOAP header. The SOAP body is specified with a <soap:Body> element.

The <soap:Body> element encapsulates the parameters that you are passing as XML elements:

```
<Add xmlns="http://www.xmlws101.com">
    <a>5</a>
    <b>10</b>
</Add>
```

Here, you are specifying the method that you are working with and the parameters that are required by this method. The parameter names are turned into elements that contain the values that you are passing between the elements. So, for instance, for the a parameter, you are passing the value of 5; and for the b parameter, you are passing the value of 10.

In return you get back a SOAP response that the application deserializes and turns into an object (see Listing 1-11).

Listing 1-11: The SOAP response from the XML Web service

```
HTTP/1.1 200 OK
Content-Type: text/xml; charset=utf-8
Content-Length: {length}

<?xml version="1.0" encoding="utf-8"?>
```

```
<soap:Envelope xmlns:xsi="http://www.w3.org/2001/XMLSchema-instance"
xmlns:xsd="http://www.w3.org/2001/XMLSchema"
xmlns:soap="http://schemas.xmlsoap.org/soap/envelope/">
  <soap:Body>
    <AddResponse xmlns="http://www.xmlws101.com">
      <AddResult>15</AddResult>
    </AddResponse>
  </soap:Body>
</soap:Envelope>
```

As in the SOAP request, you are dealing with a text file as specified in the Content-Type. Just as with the SOAP request, the response has a SOAP envelope and a SOAP body. The body of the SOAP packet contains the response from the Add method:

```
<AddResponse xmlns="http://www.xmlws101.com">
  <AddResult>15</AddResult>
</AddResponse>
```

The response is always constructed as an element with the method's name immediately followed by the word Response. For instance, you are working with the Add() method and, therefore, the element that contains the response is the <AddResponse> element. This element in the example contains a value of h.

SOAP uses the payload section of the HTTP-POST to hold the encoded SOAP envelope as it is transmitted over HTTP. The fact that you can build a complex data structure to send over HTTP gives SOAP a distinct advantage over using HTTP-GET and HTTP-POST.

Describing an XML Web service

When you find an XML Web service that you want to include in your application, you need to determine which parameters the service requires in order for it to work. After you pass the parameters to the XML Web service, you need to know what is returned so you can properly use the passed information within your own application. Without this information, using the Web service would prove rather difficult.

Just as there are standard ways within XML Web services to represent data and standard ways to move this data over the Internet, there is a standard way to get a description of the Web service that you are trying to consume. XML Web services use the Web services Description Language (WSDL) to describe the Web service. WSDL is a language that uses XML to describe XML Web services and defines the format of messages the XML Web service understands.

Listing 1-12 is a sample WSDL file that describes a simple calculator XML Web service.

Listing 1-12: A sample WSDL file

```xml
<?xml version="1.0" encoding="utf-8"?>
<definitions xmlns:s="http://www.w3.org/2001/XMLSchema"
 xmlns:http="http://schemas.xmlsoap.org/wsdl/http/"
 xmlns:mime="http://schemas.xmlsoap.org/wsdl/mime/"
 xmlns:tm="http://microsoft.com/wsdl/mime/textMatching/"
 xmlns:soap="http://schemas.xmlsoap.org/wsdl/soap/"
 xmlns:soapenc="http://schemas.xmlsoap.org/soap/encoding/"
 xmlns:s0="http://tempuri.org/"
 targetNamespace="http://tempuri.org/"
 xmlns="http://schemas.xmlsoap.org/wsdl/">
  <types>
    <s:schema attributeFormDefault="qualified"
     elementFormDefault="qualified"
     targetNamespace="http://tempuri.org/">
      <s:element name="Calculator">
        <s:complexType>
          <s:sequence>
            <s:element minOccurs="1" maxOccurs="1" name="a"
             type="s:int" />
            <s:element minOccurs="1" maxOccurs="1" name="b"
             type="s:int" />
          </s:sequence>
        </s:complexType>
      </s:element>
      <s:element name="CalculatorResponse">
        <s:complexType>
          <s:sequence>
            <s:element minOccurs="0" maxOccurs="1"
             name="CalculatorResult" type="s:string" />
          </s:sequence>
        </s:complexType>
      </s:element>
      <s:element name="string" type="s:string" />
    </s:schema>
  </types>
  <message name="CalculatorSoapIn">
    <part name="parameters" element="s0:Calculator" />
  </message>
  <message name="CalculatorSoapOut">
    <part name="parameters" element="s0:CalculatorResponse" />
  </message>
  <message name="CalculatorHttpGetIn">
    <part name="a" type="s:string" />
    <part name="b" type="s:string" />
```

```
</message>
<message name="CalculatorHttpGetOut">
  <part name="Body" element="s0:string" />
</message>
<message name="CalculatorHttpPostIn">
  <part name="a" type="s:string" />
  <part name="b" type="s:string" />
</message>
<message name="CalculatorHttpPostOut">
  <part name="Body" element="s0:string" />
</message>
<portType name="Service1Soap">
  <operation name="Calculator">
    <input message="s0:CalculatorSoapIn" />
    <output message="s0:CalculatorSoapOut" />
  </operation>
</portType>
<portType name="Service1HttpGet">
  <operation name="Calculator">
    <input message="s0:CalculatorHttpGetIn" />
    <output message="s0:CalculatorHttpGetOut" />
  </operation>
</portType>
<portType name="Service1HttpPost">
  <operation name="Calculator">
    <input message="s0:CalculatorHttpPostIn" />
    <output message="s0:CalculatorHttpPostOut" />
  </operation>
</portType>
<binding name="Service1Soap" type="s0:Service1Soap">
  <soap:binding transport="http://schemas.xmlsoap.org/soap/http"
   style="document" />
  <operation name="Calculator">
    <soap:operation soapAction="http://tempuri.org/Calculator"
     style="document" />
    <input>
      <soap:body use="literal" />
    </input>
    <output>
      <soap:body use="literal" />
    </output>
  </operation>
</binding>
```

Continued

Listing 1-12 *(Continued)*

```
<binding name="Service1HttpGet" type="s0:Service1HttpGet">
  <http:binding verb="GET" />
  <operation name="Calculator">
    <http:operation location="/Calculator" />
    <input>
      <http:urlEncoded />
    </input>
    <output>
      <mime:mimeXml part="Body" />
    </output>
  </operation>
</binding>
<binding name="Service1HttpPost" type="s0:Service1HttpPost">
  <http:binding verb="POST" />
  <operation name="Calculator">
    <http:operation location="/Calculator" />
    <input>
      <mime:content type="application/x-www-form-urlencoded" />
    </input>
    <output>
      <mime:mimeXml part="Body" />
    </output>
  </operation>
</binding>
<service name="Service1">
  <port name="Service1Soap" binding="s0:Service1Soap">
    <soap:address
     location="http://localhost/webservice1/service1.asmx" />
  </port>
  <port name="Service1HttpGet" binding="s0:Service1HttpGet">
    <http:address
     location="http://localhost/webservice1/service1.asmx" />
  </port>
  <port name="Service1HttpPost" binding="s0:Service1HttpPost">
    <http:address
     location="http://localhost/webservice1/service1.asmx" />
  </port>
</service>
</definitions>
```

Using this WSDL document, you can build a proxy class that will expose the methods of the XML Web service to your consuming application.

Pointing users to your XML Web service

After you build an XML Web service, you want users to be able to find your WSDL documents so that they can learn how to interact with your service. In order to do that you need to provide a way for users to discover your XML Web services by pointing users to your WSDL documents.

You may not always want to provide the means of users being able to find your XML Web service in order to consume the service. XML Web services that are private Web services do not need to have a discovery mechanism built into them. XML Web services that you do want to provide to the public need to have the means for users to locate them. You do this by providing a .disco file that points to any Web service description documents (such as the WSDL document). You need to be aware that the .disco file has nothing to do with a popular dance from the 1970s, but instead refers to the discovery process used in finding XML Web services.

An available Web services Discovery Document (.disco) file enables programmatic discovery of an XML Web service. This .disco file is a simple XML file that is made up of links to resources that describe the particular XML Web service, such as its WSDL document. Listing 1-13 shows the structure of a typical .disco document.

Listing 1-13: Example of a .disco file

```
<?xml version="1.0" encoding="utf-8" ?>
   <discovery xmlns:xsi="http://www.w3.org/2001/XMLSchema-instance"
    xmlns:xsd="http://www.w3.org/2001/XMLSchema"
    xmlns="http://schemas.xmlsoap.org/disco/">
   <contractRef
    ref="http://localhost/WebService1/Service1.asmx?wsdl"
    docRef="http://localhost/WebService1/Service1.asmx"
    xmlns="http://schemas.xmlsoap.org/disco/scl/" />
   </discovery>
```

By having a .disco file pointing to your WSDL file, users can use Visual Studio .NET or various other tools to locate your Web service. In Visual Studio .NET this works by having the development environment use an algorithm designed to interrogate a Web reference. The development environment attempts to locate the .disco file, which points to the XML Web services WSDL. Figure 1-7 shows the Add Web Reference dialog box in Visual Studio .NET, which you can use to interact with your local server's .disco files in order to find local XML Web services.

Discovering an XML Web service provider

Say that you are in the market to consume an XML Web service. For example, you might need a mortgage calculator on your site. You decide that instead of building the calculator yourself, you will take a look around and see if anyone is providing a mortgage calculator online, exposed as an XML Web service, that you can consume within your site.

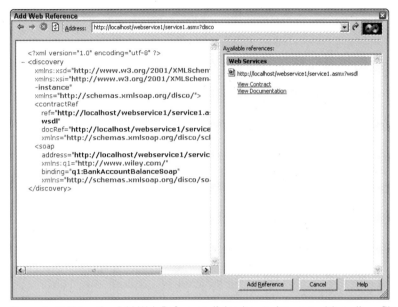

Figure 1-7: Using the Add Web Reference dialog box to interact with a .disco file

How do you find a particular XML Web service among the billions of Web sites that are available on the Internet today? It could be a daunting task to manually search the Internet for such a service.

To get through this task, various companies such as Microsoft and IBM have worked to create an online search engine of Web services: the UDDI (Universal Description, Discovery and Integration) Web site located at http://www.uddi.org. Similar to search engines on the Internet, UDDI allows you to search through the growing list of Web services that are available for public consumption.

The UDDI Web site (see Figure 1-8) is a Web service in itself and it uses UDDI specifications to define a standard way to publish and discover information about XML Web services. The XML Schemas associated with UDDI define four types of information that enable a developer to use a published XML Web service. Table 1-1 lists the types of information that UDDI provides.

TABLE 1-1 TYPES OF INFORMATION DEFINED IN UDDI

Information Provided	Description
Business Details	UDDI provides the business contact information for the person or company that is providing the particular Web service.
Service Detail	A name and description of the Web service.

Information Provided	Description
Bindings	Details the specific access points for this service instance and allows display of additional instance-specific details.
Service Classifications	Classifications classify the field of operation of a business or a service (for example, a geographic location or an industry sector). These enable users of the registry to confirm the importance of a particular Web service.

Figure 1-8: Microsoft's UDDI home page

Building a Simple XML Web Service

There are software and hardware requirements for building XML Web services. You need to make sure that everything is in place before you can actually start constructing your services. Here is a list of what you need to get started:

◆ An operating system that is capable of running IIS. You must have Windows .NET Server, Windows XP Professional, Windows 2000 Advanced Server, Windows 2000 Professional, or Windows NT 4.0 (with service pack 6a or higher).

- ◆ You must install *Internet Information Server* (IIS) on this operating system (if it is not already installed).

- ◆ A version of the .NET Framework. You need to install the .NET Framework on top of the operating system.

- ◆ It is highly suggested, but not required, that you install Visual Studio .NET. This is the IDE of the .NET Framework, and it makes building XML Web services seem like a breeze.

Building the service

To truly understand the fundamentals of XML Web services, you are not going to use Visual Studio .NET to build your first XML Web service. Instead, you'll use the ever-popular Notepad.

To do this, open Notepad and enter the code from Listing 1-14 into the document.

 Remember that you can modify the code listings and use any language that is targeted at the .NET Framework for these examples.

Listing 1-14: Service1.asmx — A simple XML Web service

[VB]

```vb
<%@ WebService Language="VB" class="Calculator" %>

Imports System.Web.Services

Public Class Calculator
    <WebMethod()> Public Function Add(ByVal a As Integer,
                ByVal b As Integer) As Integer
        Return a + b
    End Function
    <WebMethod()> Public Function Subtract(ByVal a As
                Integer, ByVal b As Integer) As Integer
        Return a - b
    End Function
    <WebMethod()> Public Function Multiply(ByVal a As
                Integer, ByVal b As Integer) As Integer
        Return a * b
    End Function
    <WebMethod()> Public Function Divide(ByVal a As Integer,
                ByVal b As Integer) As Integer
```

```
        Return a / b
    End Function
End Class
```

[C#]

```csharp
<%@ WebService Language="C#" class="Calculator" %>

using System.Web.Services;

class Calculator {
    [WebMethod]
    public int Add(int a, int b) {
        return a + b;
    }
    [WebMethod]
    public int Subtract(int a, int b) {
        return a - b;
    }
    [WebMethod]
    public int Multiply(int a, int b) {
        return a * b;
    }
    [WebMethod]
    public int Divide(int a, int b) {
        return a / b;
    }
}
```

After you type this code and save it to your system, take a quick look at what the code is doing. The first line of code in your XML Web service file is the page directive, as shown here:

[VB]

```
<%@ WebService Language="VB" Class="Calculator" %>
```

[C#]

```
<%@ WebService Language="C#" Class="Calculator" %>
```

The page directive is always enclosed within a pair of <% tags and starts with an @ sign. The page directive is the place in your pages where you can put the page attributes. Page attributes are the page-wide settings that you want to enact for your file. In this case, you are specifying that this page is going to be an XML Web service and that the language of the Web service is going to be Visual Basic .NET (specified with VB) or C#.

Specifying the WebService directive tells the compiler and the ASP.NET parser what type of component it's dealing with so that it can be compiled correctly.

After the WebService directive, you import a namespace in order to work with XML Web services:

[VB]

```
Imports System.Web.Services
```

[C#]

```
using System.Web.Services;
```

The System.Web.Services namespace is made up of the classes that enable you to build and use XML Web services.

 A namespace is the way in which .NET categorizes classes that are available for use within your applications. To gain access to the classes contained within the namespace, you have to first import that particular namespace into the page. In the following example, you want to take advantage of the System.Web.Services namespace and, therefore, you import it into the page.

After importing the namespace, you define your class. Defining a class that contains methods that you want to expose as XML Web services is no different than defining a class that doesn't have these elements. In this example, you are building the traditional Calculator class. For your first XML Web service, building a calculator has become almost the standard, just as *Hello World!* has become the standard in traditional Web-application development.

After you build the class, you add the methods that will be needed in the class. Take a look at the first method in your Calculator class:

[VB]

```
<WebMethod()> Public Function Add(ByVal a As Integer,
          ByVal b As Integer) As Integer
     Return a + b
```

```
End Function
```

[C#]

```
[WebMethod]
public int Add(int a, int b) {
    return a + b;
}
```

The first method here is the Add() method. Within this class, there are four methods (Add, Subtract, Multiply, and Delete), and you want to expose all four of these methods as Web methods that are accessible from the Calculator XML Web service. In .NET, this is as simple as adding an attribute in front of the method. In Visual Basic .NET, you do this by adding a <WebMethod()> attribute to the front of the method. In C#, you convert a regular method to a Web method by also using the Web method attribute, but C# encloses this attribute in square brackets: [WebMethod]. Now that is pretty simple!

After you have typed in the file, save it to the wwwroot folder on your computer. Follow these steps to save your file:

1. Within the wwwroot folder, create a new folder called TestWS.

2. Save the file that you created in Notepad as "Service1.asmx" in the TestWS folder. Be sure to include the quotes when saving the file, otherwise Notepad won't save the file correctly.

Notepad by default saves documents with a .txt file extension. To force Notepad to apply the .asmx extension the XML Web service file needs, you need to surround the file name with quotes in the Save As dialog box.

Although .aspx is the file extension for ASP.NET pages, XML Web services uses the file extension .asmx to instruct the ASP.NET parser that the file is an XML Web service.

Looking at a Simple XML Web Service

Now that you have built an XML Web service, you have just exposed some application logic. Anyone who knows where your application logic resides is now able to consume and use this logic.

Before you expose this logic to the public or to others within your network, it is always good to test it first.

XML Web services' Web interface: Testing your Web service

How do you look at an XML Web service? After all, it is only XML being transported over HTTP. An XML Web service is just a class that has some of its methods exposed, so how do you view that in the browser? Well, this process is one of the reasons why XML Web services on the .NET platform is so outstanding.

To view your XML Web service, open Internet Explorer and use the URL to direct the browser to the location of the service. If you saved the file according to the instructions, your XML Web service will be accessible at `http://localhost/TestWS/Service1.asmx`. Type that URL in the address bar and take a look at the results, shown in Figure 1-9.

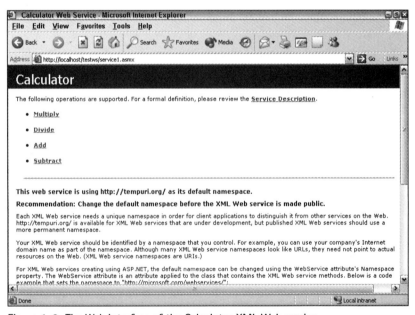

Figure 1-9: The Web interface of the Calculator XML Web service

This is how you can put a face on your XML Web services. This Web interface is automatically generated whenever someone points to the XML Web service in his or her browser.

Understanding the XML Web service interface

The Web interface provides the name of your XML Web service as well as a list of all the available methods that the consumer can use.

The solid bar at the top of the page contains the title of the XML Web service. This is taken from the name of the class. You need to give your class a meaningful name so that when users view this page and are considering consuming your XML Web service, they can understand the basic functionality of the Web service by just reading the title.

The Web interface also contains a bulleted list of all the methods that are exposed as Web methods. These methods are available for users to openly consume. All the methods that are exposed as Web methods use the WebMethod attribute. In this example, all four of the methods are exposed, and they are all listed on the Web interface.

THE WSDL DOCUMENT

In between the title and the bulleted list of methods that are available is a link to the Web services Description Language (WSDL) document. The WSDL document is the interface to the XML Web service. Clicking the link pulls up a new page that shows you the complete WSDL document.

The document is in XML, as shown in Figure 1-10. By reviewing the WSDL document, you can tell how to consume the XML Web service. Click the Back button on the browser and you are back on the Web interface page.

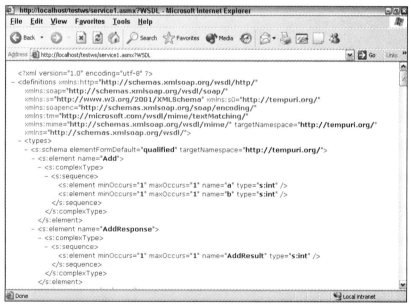

Figure 1-10: The WSDL document for the Calculator XML Web service

TESTING THE WEB METHOD

Not only does this Web interface give a description of the interface and the methods that the XML Web service exposes, but it also enables you to test your methods. Click one of the linked methods, and it takes you to a page where you can test your method and see how it performs.

Figure 1-11 shows you the page that allows you to test the Add() method. At the top of the page is the title of the XML Web service and below that is the name of the Web method. In this case, you are going to look at the Add() method and test it to make sure that it does what you want it to do.

Underneath the WebMethod title is a form that allows you to invoke the method. Below that are instructions on how to send requests to the WebMethod from your own systems or applications by using SOAP, HTTP-GET, or HTTP-POST.

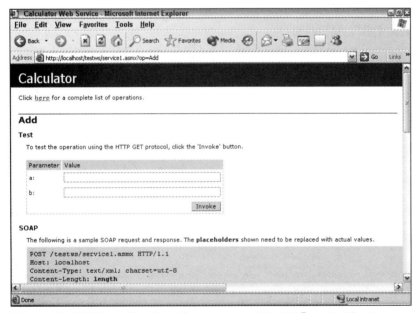

Figure 1-11: A Web interface that allows you to test the Add() method for the Calculator XML Web service

Look back at the code for the Add() WebMethod, and remember that you required two parameters to be passed with the method:

[VB]

```
<WebMethod()> Public Function Add(ByVal a As Integer,
            ByVal b As Integer) As Integer
    Return a + b
```

```
End Function
```

[C#]

```
[WebMethod]
public int Add(int a, int b) {
    return a + b;
}
```

After looking over this code, note that you are passing in an integer value that you refer to as a and another integer value that you refer to as b. Therefore, in the test page, you see the a and b parameters listed with empty text boxes next to them. Enter in values for a and b and click the Invoke button. By clicking the Invoke button, you are passing your two parameters into this remote Add() Web method, sending your parameters as XML over HTTP to the XML Web service. A listener then takes a hold of the parameters and passes them to the appropriate WebMethod. When the value is returned to the calling agent, the XML Web service passes the value (your answer) back to you as XML over HTTP.

Figure 1-12 shows the result after invoking the Add() Web method of your Calculator XML Web service.

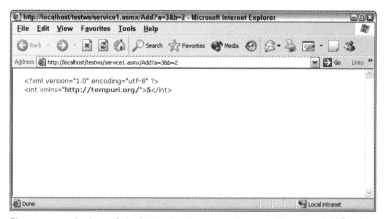

Figure 1-12: A view of the XML that is returned to you from the Add() WebMethod

In this example, you gave parameter a the value of 2 and b a value of 3. The XML returned a value of 5.

That is pretty outstanding! You just built a simple XML Web service and then tested the Add() Web method to make sure that it works. So when users interact with this Calculator XML Web service, they are basically doing the same thing that you just did in your Web interface. In the end, users get back some XML that they can consume however they please. The more you get into all this, the more you will see the magic of XML Web services.

Summary

This chapter touched on a lot of what makes up an XML Web service. It also took a look at the reasons you might want to build an XML Web service.

Microsoft's .NET Framework provides an outstanding platform to build and consume XML Web services. Because everything involved with XML Web services on the .NET platform deals with open standards such as XML, SOAP, WSDL, DISCO, and UDDI, the XML Web services that you build will be guaranteed success in integrating with any platform or system that is able to consume XML over HTTP.

Visual Studio .NET makes that construction and consumption of XML Web services simple and straightforward. Notice that there wasn't a focus in this chapter on Visual Basic .NET or C# because XML Web services is a language-neutral technology. You can build and consume your XML Web services in any .NET-compliant language, but in the end, when the XML Web service goes into action, it isn't relying on any of these languages, but instead is totally and completely using XML to do its magic!

Chapter 2 continues the journey by introducing you to the topic of this book, the Web services Enhancements for Microsoft .NET.

Chapter 2

Web Services Enhancements for Microsoft .NET

IN THIS CHAPTER

- ◆ Understanding the Global XML Web Services Architecture
- ◆ Looking at extending XML Web services
- ◆ Installing the WSE
- ◆ Understanding the future of the WSE

CHAPTER 1 TOOK a quick look at Web services in general and a closer look at XML Web services on the .NET platform. XML Web services is a powerful new application model provided with the .NET Framework. With this new model, developers make as big of a jump as they did going from the mainframe world to the client/ server world (maybe bigger!). XML Web services enables applications and data stores to go beyond their initial purposes as well as provide some of the following capabilities:

- ◆ A new and quick way to expose data stores to disparate systems
- ◆ A way to quickly expand an application's capabilities
- ◆ A simple way to expose common logic
- ◆ A system in which you are able to easily integrate with partners and customers
- ◆ New revenue models
- ◆ New ways for advertising and promotion

I could add many additional points, but let's stick with these right now. The main idea is that XML Web services changes everything. The introduction of this technology by the major players of the tech world changes many of the ways in which systems, applications, and devices function.

35

The future of XML Web services has been discussed quite extensively in books and magazines as well as on the Internet. The conclusion is that because all major devices and applications of the future will be connected to each other, they must be able to interact in ways that are easy to understand and use methods that are easy to consume. XML has been the key to both these goals. XML, as you learned in Chapter 1, is easy to understand and, because it is purely text-based, it is generally simple and easy to consume.

XML Web services technology today is new – very new. As such, it is still immature, even if it is ready to play hardball. The potential of this new technology was not realized in the first version, but it will soon be realized with the release of the Web services Enhancements 1.0 for Microsoft .NET.

Although XML Web services is an outstanding solution to many problems, it still has a lot of evolving to do. Microsoft and other vendors realize this and are working toward providing this technology with the tools it needs to grow adequately and provide end users and developers with new solutions.

Expanding on the XML Foundation

There is no doubt that the XML Web services model is here to stay. In fact, it is so popular and answers so many of the problems that developers are facing that its adoption rate is quite outstanding. However, after this model was introduced, many companies found that it was missing some core pieces in order for organizations to fully adopt this new technology as it was intended.

Most notably, after looking at the initial model, many complained of a *real* way of providing some enterprise basics such as a standard way of providing a number of different types of credentials, the routing of SOAP messages, transactions, encryption, digital signing, and more. The actual requests from the commercial space are a lot larger than this, but these were some of the requests that seemed to be common among everyone.

It is important to note that many vendors can come up with their own solutions for these problems, but this will then go against what has been accomplished thus far with the Web services model. The whole model can be pretty much summed up in one word – *interoperability.*

If you will want your Web service to work with credentials, encryption, or transactions between disparate systems, you will want common standards to be developed that have been agreed upon by the industry at large. Therefore, you can be assured that your XML Web services will work with requests coming from Unix-based systems and vice versa. So, in a sense, the XML Web services model and this book are based on the word *interoperability.* Everyone wants specifications in place that provide a common language and allow people to tie their systems together. This has been a goal of the enterprise for quite a while and it is slowly starting to be realized.

Web Services Framework: The Paper

The vendors developing their own Web services model, based on the original industry-wide agreements of XML, SOAP, and HTTP, saw the need early on for advanced functionality that would be required for enterprise-level Web services. Because of this, both Microsoft and IBM submitted a paper to the W3C in April 2001 at a Web services workshop entitled *Web Services Framework*. The purpose of the paper was to lay down a laundry list of specifications that the two companies felt were needed to bring about true enterprise-level Web services. These specifications would help deal with achieving decentralized interoperability.

The paper specified functionality that the two companies felt needed to be developed into specifications for the Web Services Framework that they were proposing. The following lists the desired functionalities specified within the paper for the companies' vision of Web services.

- ◆ **Message envelope and controlled extensibility** – The functionality needed here is a capability to tag parts of the XML message being sent. When messages start dealing with SOAP routing, it will be important to be able to tag what parts of the message can be ignored and what parts of the message cannot be ignored. This will allow SOAP intermediate processors to work with only the parts of the message that are meant for them and allow them to ignore the parts of the message that are meant for the final recipient.

- ◆ **Binary attachments** – This functionality will allow non-textual items to be sent along with the SOAP message. It is expensive to serialize and deserialize non-textual items (such as images). Therefore, a way is needed for these items to be attached to the SOAP message in their binary formats so that this serialization process is not needed.

- ◆ **Message exchange,** *a.k.a.* **routing** – Not all SOAP messages are going to be sent point-to-point. There will be instances when messages need to go through a number of intermediaries. Some of the intermediaries may need to also send a response back to the original sender. Therefore, functionality is needed that will allow this type of communication to occur.

- ◆ **Message correlation** – Messages sent may not always be able to fully encapsulate everything in a single message for an application process. Therefore, a way is needed for multiple messages to be correlated.

- ◆ **Guaranteed message exchange** – Both the sender and the receiver want some sort of message guarantee when a message is sent or received. The sender wants a guarantee or notification that a message was received. The receiver of the message wants to ensure that a message was received only once and that there aren't duplicate messages from the sender.

◆ **Digital signature** – Functionality will be required that will allow senders to digitally sign the messages that they send so that the recipients can be assured that the message is from the anticipated sender and that it has not been altered in transport.

◆ **Encryption** – It was determined early on that a way was needed to encrypt either part of the message or the entire message. The method of encryption used has to also be independent of the protocol so that the specification is not tied to any particular form of encryption.

◆ **Transactions and activities** – Functionality is needed that will allow for SOAP messages to have some sort of transactioning capabilities as well as support long-running transactions that could hours, days or weeks.

◆ **Service description** – Functionality described here specifies the need for a service description specification that would fully describe the interface of the Web service, thus letting the consumer know the details of consumption including the types of protocols used and the types and parameters required for interaction.

◆ **Process flow contract description** – This functionality will allow for enriching the service description to show the consumer the sequence that the messages need to take in order to work through the described process. There would also be a description in place for which of these messages would terminate the entire flow process.

◆ **Inspection** – The need described here details how consumers will require a way in which they can inspect a known destination for Web service endpoints, service descriptions, and process flow contracts.

◆ **Discovery** – The functionality needed for discovery is the ability to find specific Web services and their contracts based on characteristics of the services themselves.

Since this paper was released, IBM and Microsoft have released a number of specifications that address these core functions. For instance, the functionality of *discovery* has been addressed in the UDDI specification, created by Microsoft, IBM, and others.

In the end, this long list of functionality can be lumped into three distinct categories – those that deal with the wire, those that deal with description, and those that deal with discovery.

The *wire* specifications include the following functionalities from the paper:

◆ Message envelope and controlled extensibility

◆ Message exchange, *a.k.a.* routing

◆ Guaranteed message exchange

- ◆ Transactions and activities

- ◆ Digital signatures

- ◆ Encryption

The *description* specifications include:

- ◆ Service description

- ◆ Process flow contract description

The *discovery* specifications include:

- ◆ Inspection

- ◆ Discovery

In the end, this paper became the roadmap for Web services. You can rest assured that these functionality descriptions will be used by the major vendors and their partners. You also won't have to wait long, because much of what was described in the paper is here today and is the focus of this book.

Understanding the Global XML Web Services Architecture

During the year and a half following the release of the paper, Microsoft and IBM together introduced a number of specifications including WS-Security, WS-Referral, WS-Routing, WS-Transactions, WS-Coordination, and more. At times, they also worked with other companies that had a vested interest in a specification. For instance, VeriSign (a provider of X.509 certificates) helped develop WS-Security.

Microsoft refers to the sum of these new specifications as the *Global XML Web Services Architecture,* otherwise known as GXA. The GXA specifications include all the specifications that Microsoft and IBM worked on together as well as some specifications that Microsoft has worked on independently. This list presently includes:

- ◆ WS-Security

- ◆ WS-Routing

- ◆ WS-Referral

- ◆ WS-Attachments

- ◆ WS-Coordination

- ◆ WS-Transactions

- ◆ WS-Inspection
- ◆ WS-Trust
- ◆ WS-SecureConversation
- ◆ WS-SecurityPolicy
- ◆ WS-Policy
- ◆ WS-PolicyAssertions
- ◆ WS-PolicyAttachment

The following sections take a quick look at each of these specifications and the problems that they are meant to address.

WS-Security

The initial lack of a security model in XML Web services kept companies from massively adopting Web services company-wide. Many companies need a strong security model to start with when building technologies within the enterprise.

WS-Security was developed by Microsoft, IBM, and VeriSign. It addresses three main areas in order to make Web services secure – credential exchange, message integrity, and message confidentiality.

CREDENTIAL EXCHANGE
WS-Security enables two entities to exchange their security credentials from within the message. The great thing about WS-Security is that it doesn't require a specific type of credentials that are needed in the exchange, therefore it allows any type of credentials to be used.

MESSAGE INTEGRITY
Because it is possible to send messages through multiple routers and, in effect, bounce messages from here to there before they reach their final destination, you must ensure that the messages are not tampered with in transport. As messages move from one SOAP router to another, these SOAP nodes can make additions to or subtractions from the messages. If such SOAP nodes were to get into the hands of malicious parties, the integrity of the messages could be harmed. The use of WS-Security to check for message tampering will become more prevalent with the use of SOAP routers.

MESSAGE CONFIDENTIALITY
One of the most important functions that you'll need in your SOAP messages is the capability to encrypt all or part of a message. When your messages are zipping across the virtual world, there is the chance that they might be intercepted and opened for viewing by parties who shouldn't be looking at their contents.

For this reason, you will often find it beneficial to somehow scramble the contents of a message. When it reaches the intended receiver, he or she can use your encryption key and descramble the message to read the contents.

WS-Routing

The Web Service Routing protocol is a SOAP-based protocol that is used to route SOAP packets from one point to another over HTTP, TCP, or some other transport protocol. It is especially designed for use when you must route the SOAP packet through several points before it reaches its final destination.

To accomplish this routing process, the path that the SOAP message needs to travel is specified in the SOAP header along with the SOAP message. Therefore, when a SOAP message is sent, the message path will also be connected to this message.

For example, say you want to get a message from point A to point D, but in order to do this, you must route the SOAP message through points B and C along the way.

Figure 2-1 shows how this might look.

Figure 2-1: The SOAP message being routed from point A to point D

In Figure 2-1, point A is the initial SOAP sender. This is where the WS-Routing information is placed into the SOAP header and then sent on its way. Points B and C are the routing points, known as either the SOAP nodes or SOAP routers. When they receive a SOAP message with a WS-Routing specification about the final destination, these two points forward this message onto the next point. Point D is the final recipient of the SOAP message that is specified in the SOAP header.

Contained within the SOAP header itself is a forward message path, an optional reverse path, and the points through which the message must be routed. The entire message path can be described directly in the SOAP header and doesn't need to be included elsewhere. These paths can be created dynamically at runtime as well.

WS-Referral

The Web Services Referral protocol is a SOAP-based way of providing instructions about how SOAP messages should be routed. This specification only refers to the strategies that are to be used for the routing. It does not do the actual routing. The WS-Routing protocol takes care of the actual routing. WS-Referral only creates the message paths that are used within the SOAP header. These message paths can be either static paths or created dynamically.

WS-Referral can make insertions, deletions, or queries to a SOAP router. The SOAP router is the point that takes SOAP messages and forwards them to the next message path specified in the SOAP header.

This specification, which works in conjunction with WS-Routing, is based on an XML structure that describes the referral information and has similarities to a simple language. In addition to describing data, WS-Referral has a simple logic that is used to determine which paths to use for the SOAP messages that come its way.

WS-Attachments

WS-Attachments was developed by Microsoft and IBM to address the difficulty of adding file attachments to SOAP messages. SOAP is a great way to represent data as XML, but it can be difficult to represent images and documents within this structure.

It is possible to do this today with Web services, but there is significant overhead for an image to get serialized into an acceptable XML form such as base64. There is also a tremendous cost in processor power for deserializing the message on the other end.

In addition to this problem, there has been difficulty in representing other XML documents in the payload of the SOAP messages, especially if these XML documents or XML fragments don't abide by the encoding type used in the SOAP message itself.

WS-Attachments was created to address these problems, and can be used to keep other objects such as images, documents, and XML fragments from being serialized into the body of the SOAP message. This will allow for a substantial performance increase when sending these types of payloads.

WS-Coordination

As companies start developing a multitude of Web services within their enterprise, they will start to realize that many of the Web services developed have relationships with one another. For these purposes, WS-Coordination has been developed to address the description of the relationships that these Web services will have with one another.

WS-Coordination is meant to be expanded by other specifications that will further define specific coordination types. For instance, WS-Transactions will work with WS-Coordination to create a coordination type that will deal with the transactioning of Web services.

WS-Transactions

WS-Transactions uses WS-Coordination and WS-Security to allow for the definition of a Web service transaction process. Within WS-Transactions, there are two specified coordination types — *Atomic Transaction* and *Business Activity*.

Transactioning has always been an important feature to many applications in the past and this important feature is missing from Web services. The WS-Transactions specification is meant to address this need for a distributed application's coordination activities, or an applications need to work with other processes or application logic that might not be housed where message is being processed.

ATOMIC TRANSACTION

Atomic Transaction is a way of creating a transaction process that works on an all-or-nothing basis. So, if you have two Web services, *Web service A* and *Web service B,* that are related to one another using atomic transaction, both Web services are first checked to see if they will execute. If their execution is successful, both Web services are acted upon. If one of the Web services fails in its execution, they will both fail.

Atomic transactions are meant to be short lived and because of this, when you use them you are locking data resources and holding onto physical resources such as connections, threads, and memory.

BUSINESS ACTIVITY

Business activity is meant for longer lived transactions that can't have locks on data or physical resources. Business activity instead requires that these resources need to be shared. The nice thing about using business activity transactioning is that you can define business logic to determine how specific failed transactions work within an entire process. Therefore, when using business activity, an entire Web service operation will not necessarily fail when one of the transactions fails. Instead, the Business Activity process may cause another series of transactions to occur or it might just be ignored.

WS-Inspection

WS-Inspection allows you to define which services will be found at a particular site within an XML file by making pointer references to a Web service's description documents that are in place for defining the Web service's interface. This is not a new concept; the first version of Microsoft's XML Web services platform allows you to do just this using DISCO, although DISCO wasn't adopted by IBM and others and is only used by Microsoft.

WS-Inspection will allow you to selectively define the services that are offered from a site. DISCO (and other inspection means that have already been defined) is not going to disappear, but will instead be updated to work with WS-Inspection.

WS-Trust

Working in conjunction with WS-Security, WS-Trust allows for the issuance of security tokens and a way in which entities can exchange these tokens. This specification also deals with the ability of establishing trust relationships between two entities.

WS-SecureConversation

Most Web service message communication has been for a one-time request-response scenario. WS-SecureConversation works to establish a connection that will allow for entities to exchange multiple messages and maintain their established security arrangements. There is also the possibility of providing an established per-message security token using WS-SecureConversation.

WS-SecurityPolicy

Working with WS-Policy, WS-SecurityPolicy is an addendum to WS-Security that allows you to make assertions on the type of security tokens that are required, as well as on the format these security tokens need to take in transmission.

WS-Policy

With the ability to use a wide variety of specifications for your XML Web services, consumers of these Web services have reached a point where they are unsure what is actually required to consume the services. This is especially true when dealing with your Web services WS-Security implementation. WS-Policy allows you to describe to consumers exactly what is needed to consume your Web services in a standard manner.

WS-PolicyAssertions

This specification works with WS-Policy to describe some common assertions that can be used for your Web services. Some of these assertions include the version, language or encoding used.

WS-PolicyAttachment

WS-PolicyAttachment allows you to use WS-Policy with today's Web service's technologies such as WSDL and UDDI.

Extending XML Web Services

If you are going to use these specifications, you are going to have to apply the structures that are laid out in the specifications. But how is this primarily done? To understand how you can change your SOAP messages so that they can start working with these specifications, this section looks at the ways in which you can extend SOAP.

There are two primary ways in which you can extend and work with SOAP messages. One way is by placing content within the SOAP header of the SOAP message. This is one of the primary ways in which the WSE operates. The other way is to create SOAP Extensions that interact with SOAP messages at certain points within a message path.

Working with the SOAP header

Simple Object Access Protocol is an XML-based technology. It is used as a common message format in the transmission of messages from an XML Web service to any endpoint that can consume and understand these SOAP messages. This functionality is an important pillar in the XML Web services model.

SOAP is not the only means of communication available for a Web service in this multiplatform world. In fact, there are Web services on non-.NET platforms that use other means, including XML-RPC and ebXML, to structure the messages sent from the Web services that sit on those platforms.

The .NET platform uses SOAP as its common message format in the exchange of information packets from one point to another. SOAP is a lightweight, platform-neutral XML format. This means that if your platform or calling application can consume XML over HTTP, you can work with the SOAP packets that are sent and received across the wire. That's the miracle of SOAP.

You can build or consume XML Web services on the .NET platform without understanding the structure of SOAP or even knowing that it is used as the communication protocol. Still, it is a good idea to understand exactly what SOAP is. Understanding the structure of the SOAP packets that are sent across the wire will help you if you want to extend them in order to enhance the performance of your XML Web services.

Presently, the W3C is working on Version 1.2 of SOAP, but at this time, SOAP 1.1 is the latest complete specification. The biggest change from Version 1.0 to 1.1 is that SOAP 1.1 now allows SOAP packets to be sent not only via HTTP, but also via FTP and SMTP.

SOAP is not a proprietary technology, meaning that it is not run or controlled by Microsoft or IBM. It is, instead, an open standard. Therefore, you know you can use SOAP on almost any platform as long as the platform can work with XML.

The SOAP message is simple, and it was meant to be just that. The SOAP message is what is sent over the wire using HTTP, with or without the HTTP Extension Framework (HTTP-EF). SOAP messages are meant to be one-way. There is nothing built into these messages that warrants any response. SOAP does not contain any built-in functions or methods that cause specific events to be initiated.

The problem is that XML Web services require a request and response action to take place. SOAP gets around this problem by sending the SOAP message within the HTTP request and response messages.

The typical SOAP message consists of a SOAP envelope, header, and body section. The SOAP envelope is a mandatory element that is the root element of the entire package. Within the SOAP envelope element is an optional header element and a mandatory body element. Figure 2-2 shows an example of the structure of a SOAP message.

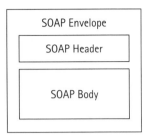

Figure 2-2: The SOAP Envelope holding a SOAP Header and Body element

You can modify how SOAP messages work by placing custom information within the SOAP header of the SOAP message. The SOAP header element is an optional element used to provide information that is related to what is contained within the SOAP body element. The convenient thing about the SOAP header is that you are not required to inform the end user beforehand about the information you place there. Basically, the SOAP header is used to transmit supporting information about the payload that is contained within the SOAP Body.

The SOAP specification doesn't make any rules about what the SOAP header must contain, and this lack of restriction makes the SOAP header a powerful tool. Basically the SOAP header is a container that is sent along with the SOAP body and therefore, we can place whatever types of information we want within it. For instance, in working with requiring credentials with each SOAP message, the user-name and password of the sender can be included within the SOAP header along with any other type of identifying information.

SOAP Extensions

SOAP Extensions is a way in which you can intercept a SOAP message and work with it before it is sent past certain points.

In .NET, there are specific points in the short life of a SOAP message being sent and received when you are able to jump in and interact with it. Figure 2-3 shows you where, in the process of sending a SOAP message, you can work with it.

Serialization is the process whereby an object is converted into a format that enables it to be readily transported. When you serialize an object within ASP.NET in the context of XML Web services, it is formatted into XML and then sent via a SOAP packet. From the SOAP packet, the XML payload can be deserialized. The process of *deserialization,* as you would expect, is the conversion of an XML pay-load back into the object that was originally sent.

ASP.NET provides these means of interacting with the SOAP message process before or after serialization and deserialization in order for you to be able to inspect or modify the SOAP message. The capability to inspect the SOAP message through-out its journey gives you quite a bit of power. On either the client or server, you can manipulate SOAP messages to perform specific actions based on items found in the SOAP payload. These points of interaction include `BeforeSerialize`, `AfterSerialize`, `BeforeDeserialize`, and `AfterDeserialize`.

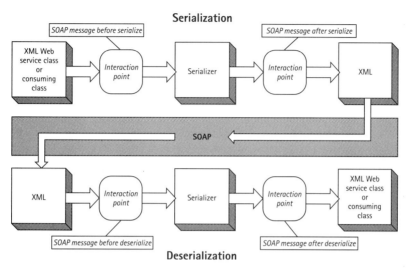

Figure 2-3: The four points to interact with a SOAP message as it is being sent

Introducing the WSE (Web Services Enhancements)

Microsoft is not in the business of making specifications; they're in the business of making software. With the specifications for some advanced features for Web services now developed, Microsoft needed to get these specifications implemented within their XML Web services model and allow .NET Web service developers to start building XML Web services today using these features. The capabilities of the Web services you can build are defined and established within the .NET Framework. The problem is that there are many capabilities defined by these new specifications that people want to use today. The .NET Framework is not going to be released in such a quick manner that it will be able to keep up with the new specifications that are being pumped out by Microsoft, IBM, and others. The new versions of the .NET Framework are planned to be years apart — *not months* — and people are not going to want to wait that long to start working with these specifications.

Therefore with the Web Services Enhancements 1.0 for Microsoft .NET (WSE), Microsoft has decided to release the capabilities to work with these specifications in a quicker fashion than would be possible by waiting for the release of the next version of the .NET Framework.

The first version of the WSE was released as a beta in the summer of 2002 and although it was not a full implementation of GXA, it included a number of classes that allow developers to build advanced Web services using selected specifications from the GXA specs.

The WSE's contents

The first release of the WSE is not a full implementation of GXA, but instead represents a smaller subset of specifications from the GXA protocols. The WSE version 1.0 includes some of the most important GXA specifications. Many customers will consider these their number one priorities when looking at the breadth of specifications available.

This first version of WSE includes the capabilities of working with the following:

- WS-Security
- WS-Timestamp
- WS-Routing
- WS-Referral
- WS-Attachments

Keep in mind that what is defined in this first version of the WSE is a full implementation of these particular specifications. There are no half-implementations within the WSE.

Functionality provided by the WSE

The rest of this book takes a look at the functionality that is provided to you with the WSE and what you can expect to accomplish by using these implementations of the GXA specifications.

The WS-Security implementation is by far the largest and most exciting aspect of the WSE. It is also the most requested implementation from all of the GXA specifications. The WSE allows you to use this implementation to provide credentials with your XML Web services. You can send in usernames and passwords in the SOAP header of the SOAP messages that are sent onto the XML Web service provider. The passwords that are sent in with the SOAP messages are encrypted, thereby providing you with a higher level of security. An additional feature that goes with the ability to provide credentials for verification with your SOAP messages is the ability to use X.509 certificates in addition to usernames and passwords.

You can also digitally sign your SOAP messages so that the receiver can be assured that the message was not altered in transport by some entity.

The last thing provided with the WS-Security implementation is the ability to encrypt and decrypt SOAP messages. This is an important feature when you start dealing with SOAP routing, because your SOAP messages will go beyond point-to-point services and will need to hop off of paths that are protected by SSL.

The WS-Routing and WS-Referral implementation will allow you to route SOAP messages through any intermediaries that you specify within routing configuration files. You will find this to be an important feature, especially when it comes to maintaining and upgrading your XML Web services. It is also possible to provide content-based routing scenarios to the SOAP messages that are sent to intermediaries for processing.

The WS-Attachments implementation works with *Direct Internet Message Encapsulation,* otherwise simply known as *DIME*. DIME allows you to send items, such as images, that are expensive to serialize into XML for SOAP message transport.

How the WSE works

The WSE is a powerful collection of classes that allow you to work with the advanced GXA specifications. WSE does this by intercepting all SOAP requests and SOAP responses and running these requests through various WSE filters.

So, for instance, your XML Web service will receive SOAP messages (incoming requests) through a WSE input filter. Any SOAP messages that are sent from the XML Web service (outgoing requests) will be sent through a WSE output filter.

On the client-side of things, the client application that is working with an XML Web service will send out all SOAP messages to the XML Web service through a WSE output filter. Then all SOAP responses that come from the XML Web service will be intercepted and run through a WSE input filter. This entire process is shown in Figure 2-4.

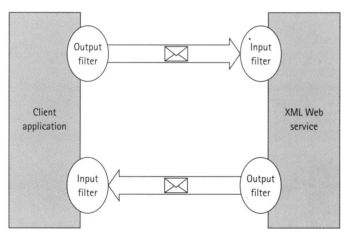

Figure 2-4: A client application and an XML Web service working with the input and output filters of the WSE

The XML Web service automatically uses these input and output filters from the WSE because of settings you make in the web.config file. The client application automatically uses the WSE's input and output filters because of changes you make to the proxy class. These filters give you the powerful ability to build GXA specifications into your SOAP messages whether you are working on the client-side, the server-side, or both.

The output filters take the SOAP messages and in most cases apply element constructions to the SOAP header of the SOAP message. In some cases, there is also the need to work with the SOAP body of the SOAP message, as it is possible to apply encryption to the body of a SOAP message. The input filters are doing the reverse as they have the ability to take incoming SOAP messages and analyze the SOAP headers and any encrypted SOAP bodies and make sense of its construction in an automatic fashion.

Installing the WSE

You can find the WSE for free on the Microsoft site at `http://msdn.microsoft.com/webservices/`. It is a small download of only 2.7MB. Once you have it downloaded to your server you are going to want to run through the installation process. Before you do, make sure that you have everything that the WSE requires.

To install the WSE, you need the following:

◆ Windows 2000 Server, Windows XP Professional, or Windows .NET Server 2003

◆ IIS 5.0 or better

◆ .NET Framework version 1.0 with at least Service Pack 2 or better

INSTALLATION PROCESS

To install the WSE onto your server, follow the steps that are laid out here.

1. Double-click on the downloaded file `web services enhancements for microsoft .net.msi`. This will start the installation process shown in Figure 2-5.

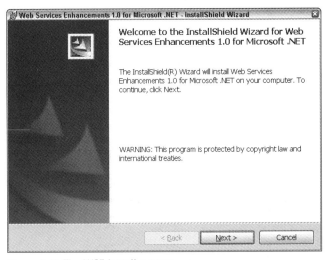

Figure 2-5: The WSE install process

2. The next step is simply the License Agreement. Select that you accept the terms and click on the Next button.

The next screen presented asks for the type of setup that you want to accomplish. The first option is the Runtime Only option. This is the default option that is selected. This option will only install the necessary assemblies required. This is shown in Figure 2-6.

For the purposes of this book, you are going to want to select the Complete option. This will install all the assemblies as well as the documentation and samples that can come with the install.

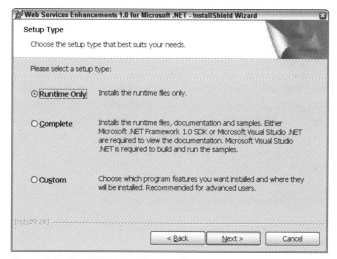

Figure 2-6: The WSE Setup Type options

3. Press the Next button and the installation process will complete.

If you are installing a newer version of the WSE on your machine, you will need to first uninstall the older version in order to properly install the newer version.

Microsoft has also released a tool that plugs into Visual Studio .NET called the Web services Enhancements Settings Tool which greatly simplifies the WSE configuration process for your WSE projects. To learn more about this tool, please refer to Appendix B of this book.

FINDING THE WSE

After installing the WSE, you will find the support documentation listed under Start → All Programs → Microsoft WSE 1.0. There is nothing about the WSE that you can look at; it is just a collection of classes that will give you these advanced XML Web services capabilities.

WHAT IS INSTALLED WITH THE WSE

The WSE installs `Microsoft.Web.Services.dll` into `C:\Program Files\ Microsoft WSE\v1.0.0000` (though your version number might be different than what is provided here) along with any help files and QuickStart applications that were specified in the installation. This DLL, `Microsoft.Web.Services.dll`, is also installed into the GAC (Global Assembly Cache).

You can see this file in the GAC by navigating to `C:\WINDOWS\assembly`. Once open, you can scroll down and see a listing for the `Microsoft.Web.Services.dll` in the GAC.

Changes that are also made to the .NET Framework's `machine.config` file by the installation process. The main change is to the end of the `machine.config` file. Here, as is shown in Listing 2-1, the `<mscorlib>` node is added to the configuration file. Microsoft states that this addition to the `machine.config` file is necessary to re-map the SHA1 algorithm implementation to allow for greater stability under stress conditions. Because of this, this entry into the `machine.config` file is not required, but is strongly recommended.

Listing 2-1: An automatic change made to the machine.config file

```
<mscorlib>
    <cryptographySettings>
        <cryptoNameMapping>
            <cryptoClasses>
                <cryptoClass
                Sha1="System.Security.Cryptography.SHA1Managed" />
            </cryptoClasses>
            <nameEntry name="SHA1" class="Sha1" />
            <nameEntry name="System.Security.Cryptography.SHA1"
            class="Sha1" />
        </cryptoNameMapping>
    </cryptographySettings>
</mscorlib>
```

The next change that you can make to the `machine.config` file is not a required change, but is highly recommended if you are going to be working with the WSE frequently in your applications. This is not a change that is made automatically for you to the `machine.config` file, but instead is something that you will need to accomplish yourself. If you don't make this change to the `machine.config` file, then you will have to make this change to either the `app.config` or `web.config` file. This addition is shown in Listing 2-2.

Listing 2-2: Adding a configuration of the WSE specific configuration handlers in the machine.config file

```
<configSections>

  <!-- Rest of the configSections node is here -->

  <section name="microsoft.web.services"
  type="Microsoft.Web.Services.Configuration.
WebServicesConfiguration, Microsoft.Web.Services, Version=1.0.0.0,
    Culture=neutral, PublicKeyToken=31bf3856ad364e35" />
</configSections>
```

 The <section> node that is shown in Listing 2-2 should appear on a single line within any of the configuration files or order to work properly. It is shown here on multiple lines only for the purposes of this book.

If you are not going to place this <section> node within the machine.config file, then you are most likely going to want to put it in the web.config file of the application that you are working on. If placed in the web.config file, you are going to want to make it appear as it does in Listing 2-3.

Listing 2-3: Adding a configuration of the WSE specific configuration handlers in the web.config file

```
<configuration>
  <configSections>

    <!-- Rest of the configSections node is here -->

    <section name="microsoft.web.services"
    type="Microsoft.Web.Services.Configuration.
WebServicesConfiguration, Microsoft.Web.Services,
      Version=1.0.0.0, Culture=neutral,
      PublicKeyToken=31bf3856ad364e35" />
  </configSections>

  <system.web>

    <!-- Rest of the standard web.config file is here -->

  </system.web>
</configuration>
```

Whether you place this register in the `machine.config` file or elsewhere is up to you. Just keep in mind that you'll need to have this configuration specified in one of these locations.

MODIFYING, REPAIRING, AND REMOVING THE WSE

After you have installed the WSE, you always have to option to modify, repair, or remove the installation. You can do this by reinitiating the `web services enhancements 1.0 for microsoft .net.msi` file. Once done, you will be presented with three options in a Program Maintenance dialog box, as shown in Figure 2-7.

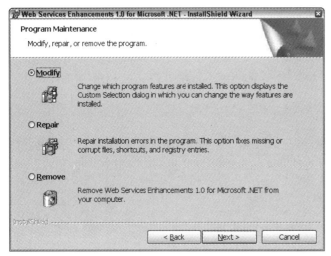

Figure 2-7: Modifying, repairing, or removing the WSE installation

Modifying the WSE will allow you to return to a custom option of selecting which pieces of the WSE you want on the machine. Therefore, if you wanted to remove the documentation for any reason, you could choose to uninstall the other components by choosing this option.

The Repair option will run the installation process again so that the installation can correct any corrupt or missing files. Finally, the Remove option will remove the WSE and any related documentation.

The future of the WSE

You might be wondering about the other specifications and the reasons that they weren't implemented in the WSE. The reason for this is that some of the specifications might not have "baked" long enough to justify implementation at this point. Also, the specifications are being released in a haphazard fashion and this makes it difficult to plan on which specifications to implement and when a WSE release should occur.

The Web Services Interoperability Group (WS-I.org)

For the purposes of having truly interoperable Web services from all the IT vendors, an organization has been formed to address interoperability related issues as it relates to the specifications defined in the GXA. The Web services Interoperability group, WS-I.org (quite conveniently found at http://www.ws-i.org) is a group made up of major vendors including Microsoft, IBM, and BEA and a number of global corporate customers including Reuters, Rational, NEC, Borland, Hewlett-Packard, and others.

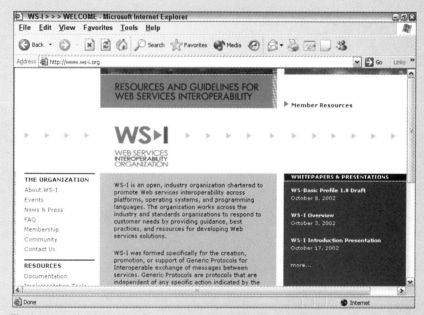

The home page of the Web Services Interoperability Organization

This group's mission is to test and address interoperability of the GXA specifications between the different vendors' platforms. They do this by creating a number of different tests that work to provide the best means of testing this interoperability as well as providing leadership and guidance on interoperability.

The idea is to get as many implementations of the specifications out there as fast as possible. From the list of available specifications that are possible to implement, Microsoft works through them to choose the specifications that are the most important to implement first.

Therefore, because all the specifications can't be implemented at once and we will see additional GXA specifications come to the scene, there will be multiple releases of the WSE over time as well. The plan from Microsoft is to release a new version of the WSE about every six months. Although the first version of the WSE contains implementations of four of the GXA specifications, the next version will add additional GXA implementations to this list.

Even though there will be additional specifications implemented in future versions of the WSE, the core specifications provided by the first version, which are vital to enterprise-level Web services development, will be used by other specifications that come down the road.

It is important to note that future versions of the .NET Framework will include what is being provided by the WSE, so you can be assured that what is being implemented here in this Web services toolkit will become part of Microsoft's .NET vision. This is just a quick way of getting the pieces out there early to developers that want to start building with these technologies today.

Summary

The GXA specifications that are being created that extend the Web services model and allow enterprises to build these advanced Web services are truly outstanding. The IT community is demanding the ability to start using these new specifications today in creating their enterprise-level Web services. Many corporations have been unable to implement a wide level of Web services because this new model did lack many important features, such as security and the capability to properly encrypt messages.

The implementation of these specifications has started with this first release of the WSE. Businesses can now take a new, fresh look at the Web services model and determine how it can play in their distributed application environment.

Chapter 3 will take a look at one of the most requested features in working with Web services – having the ability to apply credentials to XML Web services.

Chapter 3

Adding Security Credentials to a SOAP Message

IN THIS CHAPTER

◆ Making your XML Web services secure

◆ Using standards in expressing credentials

◆ Working with usernames and passwords

◆ Working with X.509 certificates

◆ Understanding how timestamps affect your SOAP messages

SECURING WEB SERVICES is one of the most important things that developers can do when exposing sensitive data or vital application logic. There are going to be instances when credentials will be required in order to consume an XML Web service. You will need to know how to apply different types of security measures to your SOAP packets before they are sent to the provider. This chapter takes a look at how you can apply various authentication and authorization techniques to your SOAP messages to help guard the information you are exposing.

Making XML Web Services Secure

When building any sort of application or operation that is working with Web services, you have to first ask yourself whether security is required. Some Web services might not need security.

For instance, if you have a simple XML Web service that is converting temperatures from Celsius to Fahrenheit, it might not be critical to build elaborate security measures around it.

However, if you have an XML Web service that exposes critical data or one that people pay to gain access to your Web site, you must think through the possible security options at your disposal. You can then apply one or more of the possible choices in order to protect your information and systems.

Just like other system applications, XML Web services can be implemented so that only authorized users receive access to its data or logic. Security measures within XML Web services are similar, in some ways, to security for applications that you have built in the past: You must apply an authorization and authentication process. There is one big difference between securing XML Web services and securing other applications, such as Web sites. When you apply authentication and authorization to a Web site, you are authorizing actual users. With XML Web services, you are applying authentication and authorization to computers, applications, or businesses.

As you have learned so far in this book, a Web service call is simply an HTTP request and response. Therefore, an XML Web service has all the HTTP security mechanisms available, including Basic, Digest, and Windows authentication.

Before you learn about the different ways in which you can apply security to your XML Web services, you should have a good understanding of both authentication and authorization. All security models are based upon these two principles. The following sections look at these two principles and discuss how they can fit into your security processes.

Authentication

Authentication is the process of determining the identity of the user (or consuming application) based upon credentials that the user or application presents. As the reviewer of these credentials, you need to be able to validate the credentials against some source.

There are many modes of authentication you can use within your applications. These modes include Basic authentication, Digest authentication, Forms authentication, Passport, Integrated Windows authentication (such as NTLM or Kerberos), or authentication methods that you develop yourself.

Internet Information Services (IIS) authentication is one possibility for authenticating end users or the consuming applications that want to gain access to your XML Web services. Using IIS or Windows-based authentication is usually a good way to authenticate your end users because it is fully integrated within the Windows operating system. IIS supports a number of different models for authentication that are built right in, such as Integrated Windows authentication, Basic authentication, Digest authentication and others.

Integrated Windows authentication was previously known as NTLM or Windows NT Challenge/Response authentication. Integrated Windows authentication has limited uses within your XML Web services. Integrated Windows authentication has the client prove its identity by sending a hash of its credentials to the server that is hosting the XML Web service.

Basic authentication is another technique in applying a username and password in order to become authenticated. The plus about Basic authentication is that it is part of the HTTP specification and, therefore, is supported by most browsers. Unfortunately, Basic authentication passes the username and passwords as clear text and, therefore, can be read if intercepted.

Digest authentication is the latest authentication model to be introduced. This authentication model alleviates the Basic authentication problem of passing credentials as clear text. Digest authentication uses an encryption algorithm to encrypt the credentials before they are sent to the server. Though, in order to use Digest authentication, you are required to have a Windows domain controller.

One of the more standard ways to authenticate users is to ask for a username and password. For instance, if you're building an XML Web service for a select group that wants to allow only members to have access, you can authenticate each user by requiring that every member supply a username and password to access the XML Web service. Another method you can use is to designate a password that everyone uses to gain access. Either way is fine, as long as the user is authenticated. However, you need to be aware that each option you choose changes the level of security for your application. For instance, a single password is not as secure as giving each user their own individual password that is put through a forced change every so often. The level of security that you are comfortable with will emerge in your applications. Just remember that nothing is foolproof.

Regardless of the method you choose, you should never allow a user to proceed to the resource if you haven't applied an authentication program to the process. Although some methods of authentication are better than others, the ones you use within your applications should directly reflect the level of security that you want to achieve. Keep in mind is that usually developing more security for your applications results in an associated hit in performance and an increased chance of errors.

Authorization

Authorization is the process of determining whether a consuming application or user, after its credentials have been authenticated, is allowed to access specific parts of the application. Authorization allows you to further categorize your users or services and limit access to certain areas or to certain users. If you have a large number of WebMethods in your XML Web service, authorization techniques are helpful, because they allow you to control access to certain WebMethods.

If you do this, you then categorize your authenticated end users into roles or groups and provide access to specific areas based upon those roles.

For example, imagine a large building with many floors. Each employee at this large building is provided with an access key to the building. The process of the employee using a key to access the building illustrates authentication. Employees can't just go to any floor in the building that they choose, however; they can only go to the floors of the building to which they are authorized (based on the keys they have). This is the authorization process.

Securing Web Services Before WS-Security

Before WS-Security came to the scene, it was always possible to secure your Web services using a wide variety of means. One of the most popular ways of accomplishing this was using SOAP headers.

Requiring credentials in a SOAP header

As you remember from earlier in the book, a SOAP message is made up of two parts, a SOAP header and a SOAP body. The SOAP body is where the message contents are held, but the SOAP header is really open for anything else that you might want to put in there. One logical thing to use the SOAP header for is to authenticate the consumers of the XML Web service. You can do this by forcing the consumer of the Web service to provide authentication credentials (for example, a username and password) within the SOAP header. Then on the XML Web service server side, you can pull those credentials from the SOAP header and authenticate or deny the users from consuming the WebMethod. Listing 3-1 shows you how to write a simple XML Web service that requires authentication credentials from a SOAP header.

Listing 3-1: An XML Web service that requires a SOAP header for authentication

[VB]

```
Imports System.Web.Services
Imports System.Web.Services.Protocols

Public Class myAuthenticationHeader
    Inherits SoapHeader

    Public AccessLogin As String
    Public Password As String
End Class

<WebService(Namespace:="http://www.wiley.com/")> _
Public Class BankAccountBalance
    Inherits System.Web.Services.WebService

    Public userLoginInfo As myAuthenticationHeader

    <WebMethod(), SoapHeader("userLoginInfo")> _
    Public Function GetBalance(ByVal AccNum as Integer) As Double
        userLoginInfo.MustUnderstand = True

        If userLoginInfo.AccessLogin = "getin12345" _
```

```
                and userLoginInfo.Password = "password" Then
                    userLoginInfo.DidUnderstand = True
           Else
                    userLoginInfo.DidUnderstand = False
           End If

           Dim AcctBalance as Double = 124.25

           Return AcctBalance
        End Function

End Class
```

[C#]

```
using System;
using System.Collections;
using System.ComponentModel;
using System.Data;
using System.Diagnostics;
using System.Web;
using System.Web.Services;
using System.Web.Services.Protocols;

namespace WebService1
{

  public class myAuthenticationHeader: SoapHeader
  {
   public string AccessLogin;
   public string Password;
  }

 [WebService(Namespace="http://www.wiley.com")]
 public class BankAccountBalance: System.Web.Services.WebService
 {
   public myAuthenticationHeader userLoginInfo;

   [WebMethod]
   [SoapHeader("userLoginInfo")]
   public double GetBalance(int AcctNum)
   {
```

Continued

Listing 3-1 *(Continued)*

```
    userLoginInfo.MustUnderstand = true;

    if (userLoginInfo.AccessLogin == "getin12345" &&
        userLoginInfo.Password == "password")
    {
     userLoginInfo.DidUnderstand = true;
    }
    else
    {
     userLoginInfo.DidUnderstand = false;
    }

    double AcctBalance;
    AcctBalance = 124.25;

    return AcctBalance;
  }
 }
}
```

In order to use SOAP headers for authentication, you import the `System.Web.Services.Protocol` namespace into your XML Web service. After this, you create the class `myAuthenticationHeader`. This class derives from `SoapHeader`:

```
Public Class myAuthenticationHeader
    Inherits SoapHeader

    Public AccessLogin As String
    Public Password As String
End Class
```

You then add a field of type `myAuthenticationHeader` to the class that implements the `BankAccountBalance` class:

```
Public userLoginInfo As myAuthenticationHeader
```

After this, you apply the `SoapHeader` to the `GetBalance` WebMethod, giving it a reference of `userLoginInfo`:

```
<WebMethod(), SoapHeader("userLoginInfo")>
```

Within the WebMethod itself, you can force the requirement that your WebMethod must understand the SOAP header that is passed to it, by using the `MustUnderstand` property:

```
GetClientInfo.MustUnderstand = True
```

After you have specified that the WebMethod is required to understand the SOAP Header that is passed to it, next you assign the `DidUnderstand` property to either `True` or `False` depending on whether the user passed in the correct information. In this case, `True` means the user passed in the correct login credentials.

If you set the `DidUnderstand` property to `False`, the rest of the method is not processed and the user receives a SOAP fault or exception.

Now that you have the XML Web service in place, you should change the `web.config` file to disable any other type of authentication mode specified so that you can use this custom authentication mechanism. This is shown here in Listing 3-2.

Listing 3-2: Allowing custom authentication in the web.config file

```xml
<?xml version="1.0" encoding="utf-8" ?>
<configuration>
   <system.web>
      <authentication mode="None" />

      <!-- The rest of the web.config file -->

   </system.web>
</configuration>
```

Your XML Web service should now be in place with the proper SOAP header definitions established. After you have changed your `web.config` file by specifying that no authentication is to be processed by the system (because you are doing this at the application level), You are now ready for others to consume the WebMethod that you have exposed.

Consuming a Web service that requires credentials

Suppose you are a potential consumer of the XML Web service that requires login credentials in order to make the WebMethod call. You have to construct the SOAP header and associate this SOAP header to the request being made in the SOAP body.

You can actually see the requirement for the SOAP header and what is required by reviewing the WSDL file for the Web service. Listing 3-3 shows a snippet of code from the WSDL file.

TIP You can see the WSDL from the XML Web service test page (type the .asmx file directly into the address bar of the browser) by clicking the Service Description link.

Listing 3-3: A piece of the WSDL document that specifies the required SOAP header

```
<s:element name="myAuthenticationHeader"
    type="s0:myAuthenticationHeader" />
<s:complexType name="myAuthenticationHeader">
    <s:sequence>
      <s:element minOccurs="0" maxOccurs="1" name="AccessLogin"
         type="s:string" />
      <s:element minOccurs="0" maxOccurs="1" name="Password"
         type="s:string" />
    </s:sequence>
</s:complexType>
```

After finding the WSDL document, the end user simply needs to make a Web reference to the XML Web service, create a proxy class, and then use the code in Listing 3-4 to access the XML Web service programmatically. In the following example, the localhost Web reference was renamed Finance. Assume, for demonstration purposes, that there is a simple ASP.NET page in place with a single Label control on the page with the ID of Label1. Executing this simple example on an ASP.NET page should return an account balance into the Label control.

Listing 3-4: The code-behind for consuming the AccountBalance XML Web service

[VB]

```
Public Class WebForm1
    Inherits System.Web.UI.Page

    Private Sub Page_Load(ByVal sender As System.Object, ByVal e As
                      System.EventArgs) Handles MyBase.Load

        Dim ws As New Finance.AccountBalance()
        Dim wsAuth As New Finance.AuthenticationHeader()

        wsAuth.Login = "getin12345"
        wsAuth.Password = "password"

        ws.AuthenticationHeaderValue = wsAuth
```

```
        Label1.Text = ws.GetBalance(1234).ToString()

    End Sub

End Class
```

[C#]

```csharp
using System;
using System.Collections;
using System.ComponentModel;
using System.Data;
using System.Drawing;
using System.Web;
using System.Web.SessionState;
using System.Web.UI;
using System.Web.UI.WebControls;
using System.Web.UI.HtmlControls;

namespace WebApplication1
{
    public class WebForm1 : System.Web.UI.Page
    {
        protected System.Web.UI.WebControls.Label Label1;

        private void Page_Load(object sender, System.EventArgs e)
        {
            Finance.AccountBalance ws = new Finance.AccountBalance();
            Finance.AuthenticationHeader wsAuth =
                new Finance.AuthenticationHeader();

            wsAuth.Login = "getin12345";
            wsAuth.Password = "password";

            ws.AuthenticationHeaderValue = wsAuth;

            Label1.Text = ws.GetBalance(1234).ToString();
        }
    }
}
```

An excellent way to monitor the action during the XML Web service execution is to use the SOAP Toolkit Trace Utility. To use this tool, modify the Reference.vb or Reference.cs files so that the SOAP request and response messages run through port 8080.

More information on using the SOAP Toolkit Trace Utility to monitor SOAP messages appears in Appendix A.

After you have compiled and run the application, you should see your SOAP messages within the SOAP Toolkit Trace Utility, as shown in Figure 3-1.

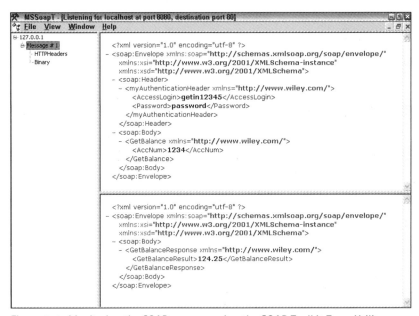

Figure 3-1: Monitoring the SOAP message using the SOAP Toolkit Trace Utility

As seen in the Trace Utility, the user sends in an appropriate SOAP message with a SOAP header containing proper credentials (using the `<myAuthenticationHeader>` element) containing the proper credentials. These are accepted in the Web service itself. A response SOAP message that contains the payload the end user is looking for is then returned.

Congratulations, you have successfully created an XML Web service that requires credentials and passes them in the proper format to an XML Web service. If invalid credentials are passed, an exception will inform the user of the error.

You have also created an XML Web service client that passes in the credentials in the format required by the XML Web service. Now, try running the consuming application again — but this time, do so without proper credentials.

For example, if you change the login to something that the XML Web service doesn't recognize, you get back a SOAP exception or an error that informs you that it was unable to process the XML Web service (see Figure 3-2).

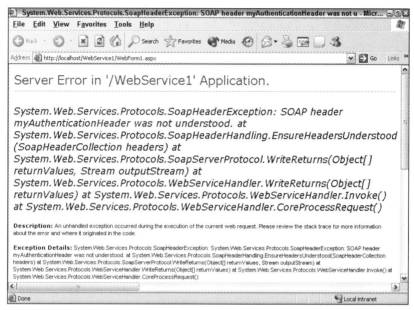

Figure 3-2: The message received when the credentials are not correct

Problems with using SOAP headers

Although using the methods described thus far will give you some basic ways to apply authentication and authorization to your Web services, this is not necessarily the best way to apply them

First, as you saw in the SOAP trace of the messages being sent from the Web service consumer to the Web service provider, the credentials were sent in clear text, which means that they would be exposed to anyone who could intercept the messages. This is obviously not a good situation if the data or application logic that you are exposing is sensitive.

Second, and more importantly, the credential structure that you provide when creating your own SOAP headers is proprietary to your own application. The means that how you structure your SOAP headers is specific to your application and may not be the same on other systems, applications, or platforms.

What is needed then is a means providing security credentials that are based upon a standard. By creating your SOAP messages' security credentials based on standards, you are ensuring more secure SOAP messages and, more importantly, interoperability. This is what the Web Services Enhancements 1.0 (WSE) provides – a cross-platform way of working with the authorization process that is based upon industry-wide standards.

Using the WSE's WS-Security Implementation

The WSE provides you with an implementation of WS-Security that you can use in the construction of your XML Web service consumers and providers. WS-Security provides you with a number of security implementations including credential exchange, encryption, and digital signing. This chapter focuses on the first aspect of WS-Security mentioned here – credential exchange.

By working with the WSE's WS-Security implementation, both the consumer and the provider of the Web service are working toward verifying credentials from a trusted source. The request for the credential verification and the token that is generated from the request are placed directly in the SOAP message. Therefore, wherever the message is sent, you are ensured that the security credentials for the request are always with the message. The great value of adding security credentials to the message itself (in most cases the security credentials and related tokens are placed directly in the SOAP header) is that you are ensured that even if the SOAP message is transported through a number of intermediaries, the security credentials or the related authorization token are always included with the message. You will see this later in the book when working with the routing and referral of SOAP messages.

One of the great things about the WSE implementation of WS-Security is that not only can you work with username and password combinations in providing authentication and authorization to your XML Web services, but you are also able to work with other security credential mechanisms such as using X.509 certificates along with your SOAP messages.

The rest of this chapter takes a look at how to work with the WSE to apply security credential authentication and authorizations to SOAP messages.

Building an XML Web service that works with usernames and passwords

To demonstrate everything that needs to be done to use the WSE to apply credential exchange, the following section works through an example that will verify credentials from Microsoft's SQL Server before authorizing use of a particular XML Web service.

CREATING A DATABASE
The first step in the process is to create a database and a table to work from. In SQL Server, you need to create a database called WSE. Once you have created a new SQL Server database called WSE, you should then open up the query analyzer and execute the table from Listing 3-5 within the WSE database.

Listing 3-5: SQL Script for the WSE_Auth table in the WSE database

```
if exists (select * from dbo.sysobjects where id =
object_id(N'[dbo].[WSE_Auth]')
and OBJECTPROPERTY(id, N'IsUserTable') = 1)
drop table [dbo].[WSE_Auth]
GO

CREATE TABLE [dbo].[WSE_Auth] (
   [UserID] [int] IDENTITY (1, 1) NOT FOR REPLICATION  NOT NULL ,
   [Username] [varchar] (10) COLLATE SQL_Latin1_General_CP1_CI_AS
    NOT NULL ,
   [Password] [varchar] (10) COLLATE SQL_Latin1_General_CP1_CI_AS
    NOT NULL ,
   [LastAccessed] [datetime] NULL
) ON [PRIMARY]
GO

ALTER TABLE [dbo].[WSE_Auth] WITH NOCHECK ADD
   CONSTRAINT [PK_WSE_Auth] PRIMARY KEY  CLUSTERED
   (
      [UserID]
   ) ON [PRIMARY]
GO
```

This script creates a table called WSE_Auth within the WSE database that stores the usernames and passwords of the entities that will be able to access the Web service. Next, open the table and populate it with some usernames and passwords. For the code samples in this chapter, I have populated the WSE_Auth table with the following usernames and passwords:

```
Username              Password
BillEvjen             Bubbles
George                Howdy
WSE_Man               LetMeIn
```

CREATING A CLASS THAT VERIFIES CREDENTIALS

Now that there is a database table in place that you can use to validate users, you can build a third-party credential verifier that will validate any incoming credentials to the Web service. If the credentials are valid, this third-party credential verifier will provide a token that will be used by the Web service.

The WSE provides the UsernameToken class for working with credential exchanges that involve usernames and passwords. To work with the UsernameToken class, you need to use a credential verifier source that will implement the

IPasswordProvider interface. For this example, you'll create a separate class that implements this interface. Once this class is in place, you need to configure the web.config file that is contained within the XML Web service's application root to work with this class. Finally, you can program your XML Web service to work with this new class.

The first step is to create an XML Web service project within Visual Studio .NET in either Visual Basic .NET or C#. Once this project is created you need to add a new class file. Within the project, right-click on the project's name and select Add New Item. You are going to want to add a class to the Web Service project and name the file myPasswordProvider.

Next you need to make a reference to some of the WSE's classes within your project. To do this, right-click on the References folder and select Add Reference.

The Add Reference dialog box will open on the .NET tab by default. From this section of the dialog box, you will make reference to the Microsoft.Web. Services.dll. To make reference, highlight this DLL and click the Select button. You will then see the reference to the assembly in the Selected Components box, as shown in Figure 3-3.

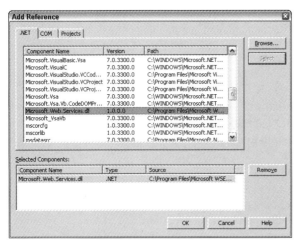

Figure 3-3: Making a reference to the Microsoft.Web.Services.dll in the Add Reference dialog box

Once this is in place, click OK and you will see that a reference to the Microsoft.Web.Services.dll has been added to your project's Reference folder. Now you can start building the myPasswordProvider class.

This class needs to derive from IPasswordProvider in order to use everything that this interface offers you. Use the code in Listing 3-6 to get at the usernames and passwords that are contained within SQL Server.

Listing 3-6: The myPasswordProvider class that will review all credentials received

[VB]

```
Imports Microsoft.Web.Services
Imports Microsoft.Web.Services.Security
Imports System.Data.SqlClient

Public Class myPasswordProvider
    Implements Microsoft.Web.Services.Security.IPasswordProvider

Public Function GetPassword(ByVal clientUsernameToken As _
            UsernameToken) As String Implements _
            IPasswordProvider.GetPassword
    Dim connStr As String = "Data Source=localhost; Initial
        Catalog=WSE; User id=sa"
    Dim conn As New SqlConnection(connStr)
    conn.Open()

    Dim cmd As New SqlCommand("Select Password From WSE_Auth " &

        "Where Username=@Username", conn)
    Dim UsernameParam As SqlParameter = _
        cmd.Parameters.Add("@Username", SqlDbType.VarChar, 10,

        "Username")
    UsernameParam.Value =
clientUsernameToken.Username.ToString()

    Dim myDataReader As SqlDataReader
    myDataReader = _
        cmd.ExecuteReader(CommandBehavior.SingleResult)

    If myDataReader.Read() Then
        Return myDataReader(0).ToString()
    Else
        Throw New Exception("Username is not present in " & _
            "system.")
    End If

    conn.Close()
```

Continued

Listing 3-6 *(Continued)*

```
      End Function

End Class
```

[C#]

```csharp
using System;
using System.Data;
using System.Data.SqlClient;
using Microsoft.Web.Services;
using Microsoft.Web.Services.Security;

namespace WebService1
{
    public class myPasswordProvider : IPasswordProvider
    {
        public string GetPassword(UsernameToken clientUsernameToken)
        {
            string connStr = "Data Source=localhost; Initial
                Catalog=WSE; User id=sa";
            SqlConnection conn = new SqlConnection(connStr);
            conn.Open();

            SqlCommand cmd = new SqlCommand("Select Password From
                WSE_Auth Where Username=@Username", conn);
            SqlParameter UsernameParam =
                cmd.Parameters.Add("@Username", SqlDbType.VarChar, 10,
                "Username");
            UsernameParam.Value =
                clientUsernameToken.Username.ToString();

            SqlDataReader myDataReader;
            myDataReader =
                cmd.ExecuteReader(CommandBehavior.SingleResult);

            if (myDataReader.Read())
            {
                return myDataReader[0].ToString();
            }
                else
            {
                throw new Exception("Username is not present in
                    system.");
            }
```

```
        conn.Close();

    }
  }
}
```

 For reasons of security, you should not hardcode connection strings directly into your code. It is considered best practice to store connection strings to a data store from within the `web.config` file. You should not have your command strings in the code either; it's better to create stored procedures. This will help prevent SQL scripting attacks on your SQL Server. Hardcode examples are shown in this and other code examples for clarity only.

CREATING THE WEB.CONFIG FILE

Now that you have your `myPasswordProvider` class in place, you have to make reference to the WSE from within the `web.config` file, which is found in the application's root (if you haven't yet made this reference in the `machine.config` file as defined in Chapter 2).

Within the `<configuration>` node but outside of the `<system.web>` node of the `web.config` file, add the code snippet in Listing 3-7 if you don't want to add it to either the `machine.config` or the `app.config` files. For any application that is going to use the WSE, you are going to have to make this reference in one of the configuration files.

Listing 3-7: Adding references to the WSE in the web.config file

```
<configuration>

    <configSections>
        <section name="microsoft.web.services"
        type="Microsoft.Web.Services.Configuration.
        WebServicesConfiguration, Microsoft.Web.Services,
        Version=1.0.0.0, Culture=neutral,
        PublicKeyToken=31bf3856ad364e35" />
    </configSections>

    <system.web>

        <!-- The rest of the web.config file -->

    </system.web>

</configuration>
```

You have to place the entire <section> node on a single line in the configuration file. It is shown here on multiple lines for readability purposes.

Once the <configSections> node is in place in one of the configuration files, you need to define the WSE SoapExtension that is used in the processing of SOAP requests and responses. Any XML Web service you build that is going to use any aspect from the WSE needs to include the definition shown in Listing 3-8 in the web.config file.

Listing 3-8: Defining the WSE SoapExtension

```
<system.web>
   <webServices>
      <soapExtensionTypes>
         <add type="Microsoft.Web.Services.WebServicesExtension,
            Microsoft.Web.Services, Version=1.0.0.0, Culture=neutral,
            PublicKeyToken=31bf3856ad364e35" priority="1" group="0"/>
      </soapExtensionTypes>
   </webServices>

   <!-- The rest of the web.config file -->

</system.web>
```

You need to place the entire <add> node on a single line in the configuration file. It is shown here on multiple lines for readability purposes.

Once this is in place, you need to add reference to the class that you created, myPasswordProvider, within the web.config file. Use the code from Listing 3-9 for this.

Listing 3-9: Adding reference to the myPasswordProvider class in the web.config file.

```
<microsoft.web.services>
   <security>
      <passwordProvider type="WebService1.myPasswordProvider,
         WebService1" />
   </security>
   <diagnostics>
```

```
    <trace enabled="true" input="ClientRequest.xml"
      output="ServiceResponse.xml" />
  </diagnostics>
</microsoft.web.services>
```

The WSE classes look for settings within the `web.config` file that are contained in between the `<microsoft.web.services>` nodes. The example in Listing 3-9 accomplishes several things. First, there is an association being made between the Web service, `WebService1`, and the `myPasswordProvider` class from within the `<security>` node.

The next step associates the `WebService1.myPasswordProvider` type. This is done so that whenever a Web service is called and the consumer is using the `UsernameToken` class, the value of the `type` is used:

```
<passwordProvider type="WebService1.myPasswordProvider,
 WebService1" />
```

It is important that the `passwordProvider` element follows the following structure:

```
<passwordProvider type=
 "MyNamespace.PasswordProvider, MyAssemblyName,
 Version=1.0.0.0,
 Culture=neutral,
 PublicKeyToken=81f0828a1c0bb867" />
```

The `Version`, `Culture`, and `PublicKeyToken` are optional. When the changes are made, save the `web.config` file in the root of your XML Web service application.

 It is important that the `<passwordProvider>` element's information is on a single line in the `web.config` file. It is shown here on separate lines for clarity and because of this book's page-width restrictions.

Although not vital for the security credential verification process to work, the `<diagnostics>` node has been added to the `web.config` file in order to trace the SOAP messages for this example. This setting traces all requests to the XML Web service and stores them in the `ClientRequest.xml` file, and all responses from the XML Web service provider will be traced and stored in the `ServerResponse.xml` file. More information on the WSE trace capability is shown in Appendix A. If you were going to have this XML Web service in production, you would turn this feature off because it will lead to performance degradation.

CREATING THE XML WEB SERVICE

Now that you have your security credential verifier class in place and all the changes made to the `web.config` file, you are ready to create your XML Web service that will work with these items. Within your project, create a Web service file named `WSE_Auth.asmx` and use the code from Listing 3-10 in the code-behind.

Listing 3-10: WSE_Auth.asmx.vb or WSE_Auth.asmx.cs

[VB]

```vb
Imports System.Web.Services
Imports System.Web.Services.Protocols
Imports Microsoft.Web.Services
Imports Microsoft.Web.Services.Security


<WebService(Namespace:="http://wiley.com/")> _
Public Class WSE_Auth
    Inherits System.Web.Services.WebService

    <WebMethod()> Public Function HelloAuthenticatedUser() As String
        Dim requestContext As SoapContext = _
            HttpSoapContext.RequestContext()

        Dim userToken As UsernameToken
        Dim returnValue As String = ""

        If requestContext Is Nothing Then
            Throw New ApplicationException("Non-SOAP request.")
        End If

        For Each userToken In requestContext.Security.Tokens

        If userToken.PasswordOption = PasswordOption.SendHashed Then
                returnValue = "Hello Authenicated User!. Your " & _
                    "username value Is " & userToken.Username
            Else
                Throw New SoapException("You must provide a " & _
                    "hashed password.", SoapException.ClientFaultCode)
        End If

        Next
        Return returnValue
    End Function

End Class
```

[C#]

```csharp
using System;
using System.Collections;
using System.ComponentModel;
using System.Data;
using System.Diagnostics;
using System.Web;
using System.Web.Services;
using System.Web.Services.Protocols;
using Microsoft.Web.Services;
using Microsoft.Web.Services.Security;

namespace WebService1
{
    public class WSE Auth : System.Web.Services.WebService
    {
        public WSE_Auth()
        {
            InitializeComponent();
        }

        [WebMethod]
        public string HelloAuthenticatedUser()
        {
            SoapContext requestContext = HttpSoapContext.RequestContext;

            string returnValue = "";

            if (requestContext == null)
            {
                throw new ApplicationException("Non-SOAP request.");
            }

            foreach (UsernameToken userToken in
                requestContext.Security.Tokens)
            {
                if (userToken.PasswordOption ==
                    PasswordOption.SendHashed)
                {
                    returnValue = "Hello Authenicated User! Your username
                        value Is " + userToken.Username;
                }
            }
```

Continued

Listing 3-10 *(Continued)*

```
        else
        {
            throw new SoapException("You must provide a hashed
                password.", SoapException.ClientFaultCode);
        }
    }

    return returnValue;
    }
}
}
```

EXAMINING THE CODE
One of the first steps required of your XML Web service is to import the appropriate namespaces. This will give you access to their functionality.

```
Imports System.Web.Services
Imports System.Web.Services.Protocols
Imports Microsoft.Web.Services
Imports Microsoft.Web.Services.Security
```

Import the System.Web.Services.Protocols namespace to get access to the SoapContext class and import both the Microsoft.Web.Services and the Microsoft.Web.Services.Security namespaces in order to work with WSE's WS-Security implementation.

After this, within your WebMethod, you need to create a SOAP context object:

```
Dim requestContext As SoapContext = HttpSoapContext.RequestContext()
```

Once an instance of the SoapContext class is created, you need to assign it the value of the WS-Security information that is contained within the SOAP header. This SOAP header is retrieved from the SOAP message that the WebMethod is receiving.

Next you need to create an instance of a UsernameToken object. You also need to create an instance of what you're returning to the consumer. In this case, you are returning a simple string:

```
Dim userToken As UsernameToken
Dim returnValue As String = ""
```

Then you need to check whether the request that the XML Web service is receiving is a SOAP request and whether it contains information in the SOAP header. If the message is not a SOAP request, the SOAP header will not be present in the SOAP envelope. If no SOAP header is present, the consumer cannot provide security credentials required by the WS-Security specification. If the request is not a SOAP request, the application will throw an application exception that specifies the error:

```
If requestContext Is Nothing Then
    Throw New ApplicationException("Non-SOAP request.")
End If
```

The consumer can send the XML Web service more than one pair of credentials. Therefore, you need to work through each instance of credentials supplied. You can do this by checking each UsernameToken instance in the SoapContext instance to see if the password is included and verifying that the password is hashed. If appropriately hashed using SHA1 hashing, the XML Web service will return the result, which, in this case, is a string value that includes the Username of the consumer.

```
For Each userToken In requestContext.Security.Tokens
   If userToken.PasswordOption = PasswordOption.SendHashed Then
       returnValue = "Hello Authenicated User! Your " & _
          username value Is " & userToken.Username
   Else
       Throw New SoapException("You must provide a hashed " & _
          password.", SoapException.ClientFaultCode)
   End If
Next

Return returnValue
```

Now you should have your security credential verification class in place, as well as all the alterations that you made to the web.config file along with your new Web service that works with these items. You now need to build a consumer that uses your XML Web service.

Building a consumer that uses usernames and passwords according to the WSE

Creating an XML Web service that works according to the WS-Security specifications requires a little extra work, but you will find that it is well worth it. Now that you have an XML Web service that needs to accept SOAP headers that abide by WS-Security, you need to have consumers that follow these rules and construct their SOAP headers accordingly. For this example, create an ASP.NET page that has two Textbox server controls, a Button server control, and a Label server control. The goal of the page is to call the XML Web service after the user enters in their username and password into the textboxes and presses the Button control. If successful, the results from the XML Web service call will then be displayed within the Label control.

Before you start building this page, you have to make a reference to the XML Web service and make some changes to the default proxy class that is created after the reference is made.

MAKING A REFERENCE TO THE XML WEB SERVICE AND APPLYING CHANGES TO THE PROXY CLASS

A proxy class is a local class that mimics the interface of the XML Web service that it is in reference to. The proxy class exposes all the WebMethods of the XML Web service and allows you to call these methods locally. Once a method is called, the proxy class takes care of all the marshalling of the arguments back and forth across HTTP using SOAP. This proxy class in essence builds the messages that you are sending to an XML Web service and parses the messages that are then received back from the Web service.

You have probably already become accustomed to all the outstanding wizards and tools that are in the .NET Framework and Visual Studio .NET that make doing much of the mundane tasks obsolete. And as you would have expected, it is no different when dealing with the proxies that you need in your applications to interface with the XML Web services that you want to consume. To create a proxy class for your XML Web service client, you need to use one of the following:

- In Visual Studio .NET, you create a Web Reference, thereby creating a proxy class

- Use the `wsdl.exe` utility that is available in the .NET Framework

To use Visual Studio .NET to create your reference and proxy class, right-click on the project where you are creating your ASP.NET page and select Add Web Reference. Then type in the URL path of the WSDL file of the XML Web service or to an `.asmx` file in the Add Web Reference dialog's address bar. When you have done this, if the dialog box has found the XML Web service's endpoint, you will be able to click on the Add Reference button, thereby creating a reference to this remote object.

After you make a reference to the `WSE_Auth` XML Web service, Visual Studio .NET will review and validate the WSDL document, and then make a proxy class directly in your project. Once complete, you will notice that the Web Reference folder in your project has expanded and is either showing `localhost` (meaning that the XML Web service is local on your server), or showing the root URL of where the XML Web service is located (but backwards!); for example, `com.wiley.www`. This is just how Visual Studio automatically names the proxy classes it creates for you.

The name of this reference is important and my recommendation is to change it to something more meaningful, which you can do by right-clicking the name and choosing Rename, so that you can understand your code a little better. This will have even more meaning if you are consuming multiple XML Web services. This name is how you make reference to the Web service in your code.

By creating an instance of this proxy class, you will have programmatic access to the methods of the XML Web Service.

So what did Visual Studio .NET actually create for you? If you click the plus sign next to the `localhost` reference, you will then notice three files contained within this folder. `Reference.map` and `WSE_Auth.wsdl`. If you do not see a third file, click the Show All Files button at the top of the Solution Explorer. You will then see a plus sign next to the `Reference.map` file. Expanding this will expose the `Reference.vb` or `Reference.cs` file – this is the proxy class that Visual Studio .NET created.

To get your consuming application to work with an XML Web service that will use SOAP headers that end up using GXA constructs as provided by the WSE, you need to make changes to this file. Therefore, double-click the file to open it up in Visual Studio .NET.

Scroll down the file until you see the code shown in Listing 3-11.

Listing 3-11: Code to look for in the Reference.vb or Reference.cs file

`[VB]`

```
Namespace localhost

    '<remarks/>
    <System.Diagnostics.DebuggerStepThroughAttribute(), _
     System.ComponentModel.DesignerCategoryAttribute("code"), _

System.Web.Services.WebServiceBindingAttribute(Name:="WSE_AuthSoap"
, [Namespace]:="http://wiley.com/")> _
    Public Class WSE_Auth
        Inherits System.Web.Services.Protocols.SoapHttpClientProtocol
```

`[C#]`

```
[System.Diagnostics.DebuggerStepThroughAttribute()]
[System.ComponentModel.DesignerCategoryAttribute("code")]
[System.Web.Services.WebServiceBindingAttribute(Name="WSE_AuthSoap",
Namespace="http://www.wiley.com")]
    public class WSE_Auth :
        System.Web.Services.Protocols.SoapHttpClientProtocol {
```

You need to change the last line of code in this example to make the proxy class inherit from `Microsoft.Web.Services.WebServicesClientProtocol` instead of `System.Web.Services.Protocols.SoapHttpClientProtocol`, as shown in Listing 3-12. Doing this will cause your application to run the requests and responses through the classes of the WSE.

Listing 3-12: Changing the class that the proxy inherits from

[VB]

```
Namespace localhost

    '<remarks/>
    <System.Diagnostics.DebuggerStepThroughAttribute(), _
     System.ComponentModel.DesignerCategoryAttribute("code"), _

System.Web.Services.WebServiceBindingAttribute(Name:="WSE_AuthSoap"
, [Namespace]:="http://wiley.com/")> _
    Public Class WSE_Auth
        Inherits Microsoft.Web.Services.WebServicesClientProtocol
```

[C#]

```
/// <remarks/>
[System.Diagnostics.DebuggerStepThroughAttribute()]
[System.ComponentModel.DesignerCategoryAttribute("code")]
[System.Web.Services.WebServiceBindingAttribute(Name="WSE_AuthSoap",
Namespace="http://www.wiley.com")]
    public class WSE_Auth :
     Microsoft.Web.Services.WebServicesClientProtocol {
```

Save the file and compile your application by selecting Build → Build Solution from the menu of Visual Studio .NET. When this is all in place, you're ready to build your consuming application.

BUILDING THE CONSUMING APPLICATION

Now that you have your proxy class in place and with the proper inheritance, you are ready to create an application that will consume the XML Web service that will work with the security credential requirements that the XML Web service requires.

First, you have to make reference to the WSE in the web.config file like you did for the XML Web service as shown here in the following code snippet as shown here in Listing 3-13. Remember that you are not required to keep this reference in the web.config file; you can also put this in the machine.config or app.config file. Storing the reference in the machine.config file is the simplest solution because you don't need to alter every web.config file for every application that you build on that computer.

The next step is to create a new ASP.NET page called WSE_Consumer.aspx in your chosen language. Listing 3-14 shows the HTML code for this page and Listing 3-15 shows the code-behind for this page.

Listing 3-13: Adding a reference to the WSE in the web.config file.

```
<configuration>

   <configSections>
      <section name="microsoft.web.services"
       type="Microsoft.Web.Services.Configuration.
       WebServicesConfiguration, Microsoft.Web.Services,
       Version=1.0.0.0, Culture=neutral,
       PublicKeyToken=31bf3856ad364e35" />
   </configSections>

   <system.web>

      <!-- The rest of the web.config file -->

   </system.web>

</configuration>
```

Once this is in place, you are ready to build the consumer. Remember that the entire <section> element should be placed on a single line in the web.config file. It is shown here on multiple lines just for presentation purposes within this book.

Listing 3-14: WSE_Consumer.aspx.

```
<%@ Page Language="vb" AutoEventWireup="false"
 Codebehind="WSE_Consumer.aspx.vb"
 Inherits="WebApplication1.WSE_Consumer"%>
<!DOCTYPE HTML PUBLIC "-//W3C//DTD HTML 4.0 Transitional//EN">
<HTML>
   <HEAD>
      <title>WSE_Consumer</title>
   </HEAD>
   <body>
      <form id="Form1" method="post" runat="server">
      <P>
      Username<BR>
      <asp:TextBox id="TextBox1" runat="server"></asp:TextBox>
      </P>
      <P>Password<BR>
      <asp:TextBox id="TextBox2" runat="server"
       TextMode="Password"></asp:TextBox></P>
      <P>
```

Continued

Listing 3-14 *(Continued)*

```
      <asp:Button id="Button1" runat="server"
       Text="Login to XML Web Service"></asp:Button>
      </P>
      <P>
      <asp:Label id="Label1" runat="server"></asp:Label></P>
      </form>
   </body>
</HTML>
```

Listing 3-15: WSE_Consumer.aspx.vb and WSE_Consumer.aspx.cs

[VB]

```
Imports Microsoft.Web.Services
Imports Microsoft.Web.Services.Security

Public Class WSE_Consumer
    Inherits System.Web.UI.Page
    Protected WithEvents Label1 As System.Web.UI.WebControls.Label
Protected WithEvents TextBox1 As
        System.Web.UI.WebControls.TextBox
Protected WithEvents TextBox2 As
        System.Web.UI.WebControls.TextBox
    Protected WithEvents Button1 As System.Web.UI.WebControls.Button

Private Sub Button1_Click(ByVal sender As System.Object, ByVal e
            As System.EventArgs) Handles Button1.Click
        Dim ws As New localhost.WSE_Auth()
        Dim userToken As UsernameToken
        userToken = New UsernameToken(TextBox1.Text.ToString(), _
            TextBox2.Text.ToString(), _
            PasswordOption.SendHashed)

        ws.RequestSoapContext.Security.Tokens.Add(userToken)
        Label1.Text = ws.HelloAuthenticatedUser()
    End Sub
End Class
```

[C#]

```
using System;
using System.Collections;
using System.ComponentModel;
using System.Data;
```

```
using System.Drawing;
using System.Web;
using System.Web.SessionState;
using System.Web.UI;
using System.Web.UI.WebControls;
using System.Web.UI.HtmlControls;
using Microsoft.Web.Services;
using Microsoft.Web.Services.Security;

namespace WebService1
{

    public class WSE_Consumer : System.Web.UI.Page
    {
        protected System.Web.UI.WebControls.TextBox TextBox1;
        protected System.Web.UI.WebControls.TextBox TextBox2;
        protected System.Web.UI.WebControls.Button Button1;
        protected System.Web.UI.WebControls.Label Label1;

        private void Button1_Click(object sender, System.EventArgs e)
        {
            localhost.WSE_Auth ws = new localhost.WSE_Auth();
            UsernameToken userToken;
            userToken = new UsernameToken(TextBox1.Text.ToString(),
                TextBox2.Text.ToString(), PasswordOption.SendHashed);

            ws.RequestSoapContext.Security.Tokens.Add(userToken);
            Label1.Text = ws.HelloAuthenticatedUser();
        }
    }
}
```

Compiling and running this application will give you two textboxes that ask for your username and password. Entering proper credentials and clicking the Login XML Web Service button will send a SOAP request that is routed directly to the security credential verifier (the myPasswordProvider class), where the credentials are verified. The class passes the result of the credential lookup to the XML Web service. Because the security credential verifying source (in this case the SQL Server database) is a trusted source, you can accept the results and authenticate or deny access to the response of the XML Web service dependent upon what this source gives us. Hence, there is no need to send off another request anywhere for security credential verification and a network request is thus saved. Figure 3-4 shows the screen of the ASP.NET consuming application with a successful request to the XML Web service.

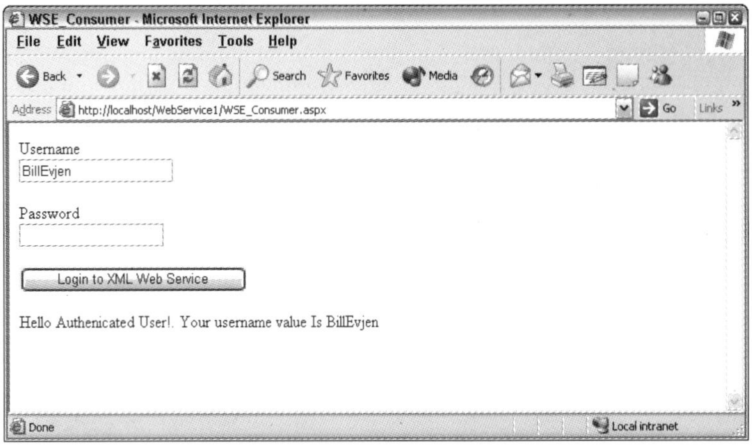

Figure 3-4: After a successful request to the XML Web service

Take a look at the code to understand what is happening on the consuming side of the application. Besides the proxy class changes that you need to make, you are working with an XML Web service in much the same manner as you would have in any previous programming techniques.

The first step is to make an instantiation of the proxy class that you have created. You need to remember that this proxy class now inherits itself from `Microsoft.Web.Services.WebServicesClientProtocol` instead of `System.Web.Services.Protocols.SoapHttpClientProtocol`.

```
Dim ws as New localhost.WSE_Auth()
```

After that you create an instance of the `UsernameToken` object that will be used to populate your username and password into the SOAP header. This `UsernameToken` object reference is called `userToken`, so don't get confused.

```
Dim userToken as UsernameToken
```

Now that you have these objects in place, the next step is to give `userToken` a value. In this case, you are assigning it the value equal to what is placed into the two textboxes, `Textbox1` and `Textbox2`. You also need to send the password in a hashed format because this is an XML Web service requirement. In this case the password is sent in a SHA1hash format.

```
userToken = New UsernameToken(TextBox1.Text.ToString(),
TextBox2.Text.ToString(), PasswordOption.SendHashed)
```

It is important to note that you need to pass the username and password into the `UsernameToken` object in a specific order. The username is specified first and the password is second, followed by a setting that indicates how the password is sent in the message. After you have given your application-side UsernameToken object the appropriate values, you assign the UsernameToken object to the SOAP request that the consuming application will send off to the XML Web service:

```
ws.RequestSoapContext.Security.Tokens.Add(userToken)
```

Now, you are done constructing the SOAP header that will be used in the request. You can continue to work with the XML Web service in the same manner as you did before the WSE. You simply need to call the particular WebMethod you are interested in working with and pass it any needed parameters. In this case, there are no parameters needed and you are assigning the value of the instantiation to a Label control that is on the ASP.NET page:

```
Label1.Text = ws.HelloAuthenticatedUser()
```

THE RESULT OF THE EXCHANGE

So, in the end, what happens in the request and response to the XML Web service? This is the important part of the entire discussion and the reason that you use the WSE for building the XML Web services in the first place. Listing 3-16 shows the request from the consumer to the provider.

Listing 3-16: The SOAP request from the consumer to the provider

```
<soap:Envelope
xmlns:soap="http://schemas.xmlsoap.org/soap/envelope/"
 xmlns:xsi="http://www.w3.org/2001/XMLSchema-instance"
 xmlns:xsd="http://www.w3.org/2001/XMLSchema">
   <soap:Header>
     <wsrp:path
      soap:actor="http://schemas.xmlsoap.org/soap/actor/next"
      soap:mustUnderstand="1"
      xmlns:wsrp="http://schemas.xmlsoap.org/rp">
        <wsrp:action>http://www.wiley.com/HelloAuthenticatedUser
        </wsrp:action>
        <wsrp:to>http://localhost/WSE1/WSE_Auth.asmx</wsrp:to>

<wsrp:id>uuid:b5615126-54f8-4ef9-8ec2-758b8d8bf1ab</wsrp:id>
     </wsrp:path>
     <wsu:Timestamp
      xmlns:wsu="http://schemas.xmlsoap.org/ws/2002/07/utility">
        <wsu:Created>2002-11-27T19:21:31Z</wsu:Created>
        <wsu:Expires>2002-11-27T19:26:31Z</wsu:Expires>
```

Continued

Listing 3-16 *(Continued)*

```
        </wsu:Timestamp>
        <wsse:Security soap:mustUnderstand="1"
         xmlns:wsse="http://schemas.xmlsoap.org/ws/2002/07/secext">
            <wsse:UsernameToken
             xmlns:wsu="http://schemas.xmlsoap.org/ws/2002/07/utility"
             wsu:Id="SecurityToken-2b0d1c08-23e3-45c1-aecc-
             78e8ff90859e">
                <wsse:Username>BillEvjen</wsse:Username>
                <wsse:Password Type="wsse:PasswordDigest">
                 /Lu04quntDDJ43okuIye/ZciQRg=</wsse:Password>
                <wsse:Nonce>JAp/b8mphxGSXUAoiS13Uw==</wsse:Nonce>
                <wsu:Created>2002-11-27T19:21:31Z</wsu:Created>
            </wsse:UsernameToken>
        </wsse:Security>
    </soap:Header>
    <soap:Body>
        <HelloAuthenticatedUser xmlns="http://www.wiley.com" />
    </soap:Body>
</soap:Envelope>
```

It seems that there is a lot to this message, but if you look at the actual SOAP body, the instantiating of the SOAP WebMethod is all that takes place:

```
<soap:Body>
    <HelloAuthenticatedUser xmlns="http://wiley.com/" />
</soap:Body>
```

All the real action takes place in the SOAP header. There is quite a bit of information here that is concentrated into three areas. The first section is the `<wsrp:path>` node, which deals with the routing of SOAP messages. The second section is the `<wsu:Timestamp>` node, which deals with the time stamping of SOAP messages. The last section in this SOAP header example is the `<wsse:Security>` node. This is where the SOAP request security credentials are represented. This is the area of the SOAP header that we will concentrate on for the purposes of this chapter.

```
<wsse:Security soap:mustUnderstand="1"
 xmlns:wsse="http://schemas.xmlsoap.org/ws/2002/07/secext">
    <wsse:UsernameToken
     xmlns:wsu="http://schemas.xmlsoap.org/ws/2002/07/utility"
     wsu:Id="SecurityToken-2b0d1c08-23e3-45c1-aecc-78e8ff90859e">
        <wsse:Username>BillEvjen</wsse:Username>
        <wsse:Password Type="wsse:PasswordDigest">
         /Lu04quntDDJ43okuIye/ZciQRg=</wsse:Password>
```

```
      <wsse:Nonce>JAp/b8mphxGSXUAoiS13Uw==</wsse:Nonce>
      <wsu:Created>2002-11-27T19:21:31Z</wsu:Created>
   </wsse:UsernameToken>
</wsse:Security>
```

The first thing to note is the XML in the SOAP header, which is an XML representation of the UsernameToken object created on the consuming side and which is passed to the XML Web service provider. Within the <wsse:UsernameToken> node is a unique ID given to the UsernameToken instance to differentiate it from other requests.

More importantly, there is a representation of the username and password that the user entered into the application represented in the SOAP header. Because there was a specification on the consuming side that the password needed to be hashed, you will notice that it has indeed been hashed and that there is a type definition in the password node of the SOAP header that specifies this.

```
<wsse:Password Type="wsse:PasswordDigest">
 /Lu04quntDDJ43okuIye/ZciQRg=</wsse:Password>
```

The <wsse:Nonce> node, which is generated from cryptographic random number generators, uniquely identifies the request. Then there is also a timestamp placed on the request with the <wsu:Created> node. The chapter will later take a look at working with this timestamp in the Web service to add extra security.

After the credentials are verified and accepted by the XML Web service, the response is sent back to the client, as shown in Listing 3-17.

Listing 3-17: The SOAP response from the provider to the consumer

```
<soap:Envelope
xmlns:soap="http://schemas.xmlsoap.org/soap/envelope/"
 xmlns:xsi="http://www.w3.org/2001/XMLSchema-instance"
 xmlns:xsd="http://www.w3.org/2001/XMLSchema">
   <soap:Header>
      <wsu:Timestamp
       xmlns:wsu="http://schemas.xmlsoap.org/ws/2002/07/utility">
         <wsu:Created>2002-11-27T19:21:33Z</wsu:Created>
         <wsu:Expires>2002-11-27T19:26:33Z</wsu:Expires>
      </wsu:Timestamp>
   </soap:Header>
   <soap:Body>
      <HelloAuthenticatedUserResponse xmlns="http://www.wiley.com">
         <HelloAuthenticatedUserResult>Hello Authenicated User! Your
          username value Is BillEvjen</HelloAuthenticatedUserResult>
      </HelloAuthenticatedUserResponse>
   </soap:Body>
</soap:Envelope>
```

In this simple response, there is a small amount of information in the SOAP header that deals with the SOAP message's timestamp and validity (this is discussed later in the chapter). Beyond this bit of information, there isn't anything else needed in the SOAP header.

Besides the SOAP header, the SOAP body contains a return value that includes the username of the entity being authenticated.

Password options

In the previous example, the password was hashed. The hashed version of the password was sent to the security credential verifier. Other ways to send the password in the SOAP header are discussed in this section.

First, Listing 3-18 reviews how to provide a username and a hashed password for an application that is a consumer of an XML Web service that requires usernames and passwords constructed in such a manner.

Listing 3-18: Constructing a username and hashed password for an XML Web service consumer

[VB]

```
userToken = New UsernameToken(TextBox1.Text.ToString(),
    TextBox2.Text.ToString(), PasswordOption.SendHashed)
```

[C#]

```
userToken = new UsernameToken(TextBox1.Text.ToString(),
    TextBox2.Text.ToString(), PasswordOption.SendHashed);
```

You are normally going to use the specific hash option required by the XML Web service provider. If you are constructing the provider, you can require consumers to hash their passwords. The code in Listing 3-19 shows how you can do this.

Listing 3-19: Forcing passwords to be hashed

[VB]

```
If userToken.PasswordOption = PasswordOption.SendHashed Then
    ' code here
End If
```

[C#]

```
if (userToken.PasswordOption == PasswordOption.SendHashed)
{
    // code here
}
```

Another option for encoding a password in the SOAP message is to not include any password option on the consuming end. This would look like Listing 3-20.

Listing 3-20: Using no password to consume an XML Web service (VB)

```
userToken = New UsernameToken(TextBox1.Text.ToString(),
TextBox2.Text.ToString())
```

You could have your XML Web service consumer constructed in the following manner if the XML Web service provider didn't require a password for consumption. You would construct your XML Web service exactly the same, but without the If Then check to see how the password was included in the SOAP header. Without this check, it is therefore possible for the consumer to provide an appropriate username with any sort of password and they would still be validated as long as the username worked.

This is also the same as using the code shown in Listing 3-21.

Listing 3-21: Another example of using no password to consume an XML Web service (VB)

```
userToken = New UsernameToken(TextBox1.Text.ToString(),
TextBox2.Text.ToString(), PasswordOption.SendNone)
```

The last option is to send the password in clear text format. This is shown in Listing 3-22.

Listing 3-22: Sending a password as clear text

```
userToken = New UsernameToken(TextBox1.Text.ToString(),
TextBox2.Text.ToString(), PasswordOption.SendPlainText)
```

In the end, this will send your XML Web service requests so that the username and password are both readable if intercepted in the stream. A sample SOAP request from such a construction is shown in Listing 3-23.

Listing 3-23: A SOAP request when the PasswordOption is set to SendPlainText

```
<soap:Envelope
 xmlns:soap="http://schemas.xmlsoap.org/soap/envelope/"
 xmlns:xsi="http://www.w3.org/2001/XMLSchema-instance"
 xmlns:xsd="http://www.w3.org/2001/XMLSchema">
    <soap:Header>
      <wsrp:path
       soap:actor="http://schemas.xmlsoap.org/soap/actor/next"
       soap:mustUnderstand="1"
       xmlns:wsrp="http://schemas.xmlsoap.org/rp">
      <wsrp:action>http://wiley.com/HelloAuthenticatedUser
```

Continued

Listing 3-23 *(Continued)*

```
      </wsrp:action>
      <wsrp:to>http://localhost/webservice16/WSE_Auth.asmx
      </wsrp:to>
      <wsrp:id>uuid:da501d8b-1819-4b14-92ce-901237e289dc</wsrp:id>
      </wsrp:path>
      <wsu:Timestamp
       xmlns:wsu="http://schemas.xmlsoap.org/ws/2002/07/utility">
        <wsu:Created wsu:Id="Id-36f2b9a4-8dc5-4a6d-8f68-
         b002eb14a66a">2002-10-16T23:58:39Z</wsu:Created>
        <wsu:Expires wsu:Id="Id-962c3578-be34-4e50-abf8-
         b92f47dcc01e">2002-10-17T00:03:39Z</wsu:Expires>
      </wsu:Timestamp>
      <wsse:Security soap:mustUnderstand="1"
       xmlns:wsse="http://schemas.xmlsoap.org/ws/2002/07/secext">
        <wsse:UsernameToken Id="SecurityToken-15b1002d-9b69-40f3-
         af23-9cb7d435213b">
         <wsse:Username>BillEvjen</wsse:Username>
         <wsse:Password
          Type="wsse:PasswordText">Bubbles</wsse:Password>
         <wsse:Nonce>5n6hE5iFhLbGNQJldWc1Ww==</wsse:Nonce>
         <wsu:Created
          xmlns:wsu="http://schemas.xmlsoap.org/ws/2002/07/utility">
          2002-10-16T23:58:39Z</wsu:Created>
        </wsse:UsernameToken>
      </wsse:Security>
    </soap:Header>
    <soap:Body>
      <HelloAuthenticatedUser xmlns="http://wiley.com/" />
    </soap:Body>
  </soap:Envelope>
```

You will notice from this request that the password is quite visible to anyone that intercepts this SOAP message on its path. If you are going to interact with XML Web services in this format, you should always be aware of the security implications. Sending the actual passwords in SOAP messages, as opposed to sending a hashed version of the password, should be done only when you are performing your SOAP requests over SSL and there is no routing of SOAP messages occurring that will take the SOAP message from the SSL-protected line. Also, you might use this format if the entire SOAP request is occurring within a controlled environment and the extra cost of hashing the password is something that you want to avoid.

Within the XML Web service itself, you can use the `PasswordOption` property to determine how the password was sent from the consumer of the Web service. This allows you to code your Web service to react differently based on how the password was sent to you, if the password was sent at all. Listing 3-24 shows how this might work in your XML Web service.

Listing 3-24: An XML Web service that checks for all possible scenarios of how the password was sent from the consumer

[VB]

```
Imports System.Web.Services
Imports System.Web.Services.Protocols
Imports Microsoft.Web.Services
Imports Microsoft.Web.Services.Security

<WebService(Namespace:="http://wiley.com/")> _
Public Class WSE_Auth
    Inherits System.Web.Services.WebService

    <WebMethod()> Public Function HelloAuthenticatedUser() As String
        Dim requestContext As SoapContext = _
            HttpSoapContext.RequestContext()

        Dim userToken As UsernameToken
        Dim returnValue As String = ""

        If requestContext Is Nothing Then
            Throw New ApplicationException("Non-SOAP request.")
        End If

        For Each userToken In requestContext.Security.Tokens
            If userToken.PasswordOption = _
                    PasswordOption.SendHashed Then
                returnValue = "Hello Authenicated User!. Your " & _
                    "username value Is " & userToken.Username
            ElseIf userToken.PasswordOption = _
                    PasswordOption.SendNone Then
                returnValue = "You need to send in a " & _
                    "password of some kind."
            ElseIf userToken.PasswordOption = _
                    PasswordOption.SendPlainText Then
                returnValue = "PlainText is not the best " & _
                    "option you know!"
            Else
                Throw New SoapException("You must provide a " & _
                    "hashed password.", _
```

Continued

Listing 3-24 *(Continued)*

```
                    SoapException.ClientFaultCode)
            End If
        Next
        Return returnValue
    End Function

End Class
```

[C#]

```csharp
using System;
using System.Collections;
using System.ComponentModel;
using System.Data;
using System.Diagnostics;
using System.Web;
using System.Web.Services;
using System.Web.Services.Protocols;
using Microsoft.Web.Services;
using Microsoft.Web.Services.Security;

namespace WebService1
{
    public class WSE_Auth : System.Web.Services.WebService
    {
        public WSE_Auth()
        {
            InitializeComponent();
        }

        [WebMethod]
        public string HelloAuthenticatedUser()
        {
            SoapContext requestContext = HttpSoapContext.RequestContext;

            string returnValue = "";

            if (requestContext == null)
            {
                throw new ApplicationException("Non-SOAP request.");
            }

            foreach (UsernameToken userToken in
                requestContext.Security.Tokens)
```

```
      {
        if (userToken.PasswordOption ==
            PasswordOption.SendHashed) {
          returnValue = "Hello Authenicated User!. Your username
            value Is " + userToken.Username;    }
        else if (userToken.PasswordOption ==
            PasswordOption.SendNone)    {
          returnValue = "You need to send in a password of some
            kind.";      }
        else if (userToken.PasswordOption ==
            PasswordOption.SendPlainText)    {
          returnValue = "PlainText is not the best option you
            know!";      }
        else    {
          throw new SoapException("You must provide a hashed
            password.", SoapException.ClientFaultCode);
        }
      }

      return returnValue;
      }
    }
}
```

With this code, you can determine how the password is sent to the XML Web service, and alter the returned value based on how the password was sent. This is vital if you want to make sure that your XML Web services are as secure as possible.

Sending in more than one set of credentials

You have been working with passing in a single username and password combination to an XML Web service by constructing a UsernameToken construct and passing that construct to the XML Web service, which then reads it in from the SoapContext request. It is also possible to pass in more than one UsernameToken object with each request. This might play in nicely with your Web services or it might be something that you want to guard against.

CREATING THE CONSUMER

Let's take a look at a consuming application that consumes the XML Web service from Listing 3-9, but instead of passing in one set of username and password combinations, let's pass in two and see what happens.

In the XML Web service consumer, you can actually create as many UsernameToken objects as you want and include those in the header. One approach to accomplishing this task is shown in Listing 3-25.

Listing 3-25: Creating two UsernameToken objects to pass into the SOAP header

[VB]

```vb
Private Sub Button1_Click(ByVal sender As System.Object, ByVal e As
    System.EventArgs) Handles Button1.Click
        Dim ws As New localhost.WSE_Auth()
        Dim userToken1 As UsernameToken
        userToken1 = New UsernameToken("BillEvjen ", "Bubbles",
            PasswordOption.SendHashed)
        ws.RequestSoapContext.Security.Tokens.Add(userToken1)

        Dim userToken2 As UsernameToken
        userToken2 = New UsernameToken("WSE_Man", "LetMeIn",
            PasswordOption.SendHashed)
        ws.RequestSoapContext.Security.Tokens.Add(userToken2)
        Label1.Text = ws.HelloAuthenticatedUser()
End Sub
```

[C#]

```csharp
private void Button1_Click(object sender, System.EventArgs e)
{
    localhost.WSE_Auth ws = new localhost.WSE_Auth();
    UsernameToken userToken1;
    userToken1 = new UsernameToken(TextBox1.Text.ToString(),
        TextBox2.Text.ToString(), PasswordOption.SendHashed);
    ws.RequestSoapContext.Security.Tokens.Add(userToken1);

    UsernameToken userToken2;
    userToken2 = new UsernameToken(TextBox1.Text.ToString(),
        TextBox2.Text.ToString(), PasswordOption.SendHashed);
    ws.RequestSoapContext.Security.Tokens.Add(userToken2);

    Label1.Text = ws.HelloAuthenticatedUser();
}
```

The code's construction is quite simple. In the button click event, you simply create two instances of the UsernameToken object, userToken1 and userToken2. Each of these UsernameToken objects have separate credentials and are passed into the SOAP header using the Add() method of the SoapContext class. Once complete, the request SOAP message from the XML Web service consumer will contain both sets of credentials, as shown in Listing 3-26.

Listing 3-26: The SOAP request that contains two sets of credentials   .

```
<soap:Envelope
 xmlns:soap="http://schemas.xmlsoap.org/soap/envelope/"
 xmlns:xsi="http://www.w3.org/2001/XMLSchema-instance"
 xmlns:xsd="http://www.w3.org/2001/XMLSchema">
    <soap:Header>
     <wsrp:path
      soap:actor="http://schemas.xmlsoap.org/soap/actor/next"
      soap:mustUnderstand="1"
      xmlns:wsrp="http://schemas.xmlsoap.org/rp">
       <wsrp:action>http://wiley.com/HelloAuthenticatedUser
       </wsrp:action>
       <wsrp:to>http://localhost/webservice1/WSE_Auth.asmx
       </wsrp:to>
       <wsrp:id>uuid:d104d16f-6de0-4658-80f2-c06da6757776</wsrp:id>
     </wsrp:path>
     <wsu:Timestamp
      xmlns:wsu="http://schemas.xmlsoap.org/ws/2002/07/utility">
       <wsu:Created wsu:Id="Id-b312038e-6ed6-46fa-95da-
       4e710b8eb2c4">2002-10-19T19:21:23Z</wsu:Created>
       <wsu:Expires wsu:Id="Id-210bdee9-bf83-48c3-9841-
        25a120d387dc">2002-10-19T19:26:23Z</wsu:Expires>
     </wsu:Timestamp>
     <wsse:Security soap:mustUnderstand="1"
      xmlns:wsse="http://schemas.xmlsoap.org/ws/2002/07/secext">
       <wsse:UsernameToken Id="SecurityToken-6572ce76-9500-4f49-
        adec-16839ddbc93d">
        <wsse:Username>BillEvjen</wsse:Username>
        <wsse:Password Type="wsse:PasswordDigest">
         6ZOay5k5HI5Ce5+JhaovAZjyAOk=</wsse:Password>
        <wsse:Nonce>kU5hp0Qon7pNSbnjqbzuIQ==</wsse:Nonce>
        <wsu:Created
        xmlns:wsu="http://schemas.xmlsoap.org/ws/2002/07/utility">
        2002-10-19T19:21:23Z</wsu:Created>
       </wsse:UsernameToken>
       <wsse:UsernameToken Id="SecurityToken-e1e0cff0-a5f1-41b9-
        8606-7f21410d06b9">
        <wsse:Username>WSE_Man</wsse:Username>
        <wsse:Password Type="wsse:PasswordDigest">
         yPmOeTep3ZpRRefFcxX2KlgGKe8=</wsse:Password>
        <wsse:Nonce>nCjlIECBSFS105MDkulIsQ==</wsse:Nonce>
        <wsu:Created
```

Continued

Listing 3-26 *(Continued)*

```
        xmlns:wsu="http://schemas.xmlsoap.org/ws/2002/07/utility">
        2002-10-19T19:21:23Z</wsu:Created>
      </wsse:UsernameToken>
    </wsse:Security>
  </soap:Header>
  <soap:Body>
    <HelloAuthenticatedUser xmlns="http://wiley.com/" />
  </soap:Body>
</soap:Envelope>
```

GUARDING AGAINST MULTIPLE CREDENTIALS

In your XML Web service, you might not care whether there are more than one set of credentials being sent into the Web service, just as long as one of the credentials sent in is valid. For added security, however, you might want to check the number of credentials being sent into the XML Web service and only allow requests that contain a single UsernameToken object, regardless of whether a request with multiple UsernameToken objects contained a valid set of credentials or not.

In this case, you simply need to use an If Then statement that checks for the number of credentials. An example of this is shown in Listing 3-27.

Listing 3-27: Checking on the number of UsernameToken objects in the SOAP header

[VB]

```
If requestContext.Security.Tokens.Count = 1 Then
' Process request here
End If
```

[C#]

```
if (requestContext.Security.Tokens.Count == 1)
{
// Process request here
}
```

This check will ensure that only requests that contain a single instance of the UsernameToken object are acted on.

Putting a timestamp on SOAP requests

It is always possible that some entity will intercept your request and alter or replace the message with their own before sending it to the XML Web service. To guard against such an action, an automatic five-minute timestamp is placed within the SOAP header of the request. This is shown in Listing 3-28.

Listing 3-28: The default timestamp of five minutes within the SOAP header

```
<wsu:Timestamp
 xmlns:wsu="http://schemas.xmlsoap.org/ws/2002/07/utility">
   <wsu:Created wsu:Id="Id-e7d3aa6c-5112-412d-8d93-
   2b377511b38a">2002-10-19T19:18:49Z</wsu:Created>
   <wsu:Expires wsu:Id="Id-3675ebeb-f4e1-4a27-814b-
   f9957f0c5182">2002-10-19T19:23:49Z</wsu:Expires>
</wsu:Timestamp>
```

The timestamp information placed into the SOAP header include when the SOAP message was created and the time for when the SOAP message should expire and be rejected irregardless of whether the security information contained within the message is valid or not. Receiving messages outside these time restraints could mean that the SOAP message is being replayed.

If the request's timestamp has expired, the XML Web service will not process the request. If you feel you need to shorten or lengthen the requests, change the timestamp from the default of five minutes. The sample code for this is shown in Listing 3-29.

Listing 3-29: Changing the timestamp on the XML Web service consumer

[VB]

```
Private Sub Button1_Click(ByVal sender As System.Object, ByVal e As
    System.EventArgs) Handles Button1.Click
        Dim ws As New localhost.WSE_Auth()
        Dim userToken As UsernameToken
        userToken = New UsernameToken(TextBox1.Text.ToString(),
            TextBox2.Text.ToString(), PasswordOption.SendHashed)

        Dim myRequestContext As SoapContext = ws.RequestSoapContext
        myRequestContext.Timestamp.Ttl = 30000

        ws.RequestSoapContext.Security.Tokens.Add(userToken)

        Label1.Text = ws.HelloAuthenticatedUser()
End Sub
```

[C#]

```
private void Button1_Click(object sender, System.EventArgs e)
{
    localhost.WSE_Auth ws = new localhost.WSE_Auth();
    UsernameToken userToken;
```

Continued

Listing 3-29 *(Continued)*

```
    userToken = new UsernameToken(TextBox1.Text.ToString(),
        TextBox2.Text.ToString(), PasswordOption.SendHashed);

    SoapContext myRequestContext = ws.RequestSoapContext;
    myRequestContext.Timestamp.Ttl = 30000;

    ws.RequestSoapContext.Security.Tokens.Add(userToken);

    Label1.Text = ws.HelloAuthenticatedUser();
}
```

This code example from the Listing 3-29 creates an instance of the `SoapContext` object, called `myRequestContext`, which will represent the SOAP request made to the XML Web service:

```
Dim myRequestContext as SoapContext = ws.RequestSoapContext
```

Then you can assign the timestamp value by assigning a value to the `Timestamp.Ttl` property:

```
myRequestContext.Timestamp.Ttl = 30000
```

The value given to the `Timestamp.Ttl` property is the length of time that the request will be valid. The time in the value is recorded as milliseconds. In this case, the timestamp value assigned to the request is 30,000 milliseconds or 30 seconds. This will result in a SOAP header with a timestamp heading as shown in Listing 3-30.

Listing 3-30: The modified timestamp in the SOAP header

```
<wsu:Timestamp
  xmlns:wsu="http://schemas.xmlsoap.org/ws/2002/07/utility">
        <wsu:Created wsu:Id="Id-5c42e588-3ea2-4b63-bce7-
        5c473dad3687">2002-10-19T20:35:38Z</wsu:Created>
        <wsu:Expires wsu:Id="Id-fbd2107d-2fa5-49df-bf57-
        50e66a9fdf99">2002-10-19T20:36:08Z</wsu:Expires>
</wsu:Timestamp>
```

As you can see from the timestamp that is placed in the SOAP header of the SOAP request, there is a 30 second period during which the request is valid. In this case, there is a start time and an end time. It is important to note that this can be a problem if the correct times are not set on the server of the XML Web service consumer or on the server of the XML Web service provider.

Putting a timestamp on SOAP responses

Just as you can control the timestamp on SOAP requests to an XML Web service provider, you can also control the timestamp of the SOAP responses. Similar to requests made to an XML Web service provider, there is a default setting of five minutes for the response.

You can control this as simply as you were able to with the SOAP request. Listing 3-31 shows how you can give the SOAP response any timestamp value that you choose.

Listing 3-31: Changing the timestamp value on the SOAP response.

[VB]

```
For Each userToken In requestContext.Security.Tokens
If userToken.PasswordOption = PasswordOption.SendHashed Then
    Dim responseContext as SoapContext =
        HttpSoapContext.ResponseContext()
    responseContext.Timestamp.Ttl = 30000
        returnValue = "Hello Authenicated User!. Your " & _
            username value Is " & userToken.Username
  Else
        Throw New SoapException("You must provide a hashed " & _
            password.", SoapException.ClientFaultCode)
  End If
Next
```

[C#]

```
foreach (UsernameToken userToken in
    requestContext.Security.Tokens)
{
    if (userToken.PasswordOption == PasswordOption.SendHashed)
    {
        SoapContext responseContext = HttpSoapContext.ResponseContext;
        responseContext.Timestamp.Ttl = 30000;
        returnValue = "Hello Authenicated User!. Your username
            value Is " + userToken.Username;
    }
    else
    {
        throw new SoapException("You must provide a hashed
            password.", SoapException.ClientFaultCode);
    }
}
```

In this example, you create an instance of the `SoapContext` object called `responseContext`, which is a representation of the SOAP response that is going to be sent to the consumer of the XML Web service. Then you assign the `Timestamp`. `Ttl` property of the `responseContext` object to 30 seconds (30,000 milliseconds). Just as it did in the SOAP request example, this change will then assign a time-stamp within the SOAP header of the SOAP response that makes the response valid for 30 seconds.

Choose a timeframe with good consideration on the length of time requesters will need to consume your WebMethods and remember that having a span of time that is too great could create a security hole that might be hard to live with.

Building an XML Web service that works with X.509 certificates

The WS-Security specification not only allows you to work with username/pass-word combinations, but you can also use other forms of authentication by using the `BinarySecurityToken` element that is defined in the specification.

The `BinarySecurityToken` element is designed specifically to work with X.509 certificates and Kerberos tickets. The first release of the WSE allows you to use the `BinarySecurityToken` element only with X.509 certificates. The ability to use X.509 certificates is an alternative to using username/password combinations for the authentication of XML Web services.

WHAT IS AN X.509 CERTIFICATE?

An X.509 certificate is a public key that has been signed by an entity. This public key being digitally signed by the entity is one way of providing authentication to a consumer.

X.509 certificates have been around since 1988 and three versions are available. The latest version was introduced in 1996 and supports the ability to add extensions to the certificate. The WSE supports only this last version of X.509 certificates.

Certificates work with public key encryption technologies and are made up of public and private keys. The private keys are used to digitally sign a message and the public keys are used to verify signatures.

LOOKING AT THE CERTIFICATE STORE

The .NET Framework by itself does not have the capability to look at the local cer-tificate store with any of its classes. But using the WSE, you can take a look at the local certificate store if your ASP.NET worker process has the permission to do this.

Let's create a page that will use X.509 certificates to construct a SOAP request that will let you provide credentials for authentication purposes. In order to work with certificates and certificate stores in your code, you will need to make sure that you import in the following namespaces:

```
Imports Microsoft.Web.Services
Imports Microsoft.Web.Services.Security
Imports Microsoft.Web.Services.Security.X509
```

Once these namespaces are imported, you can start working with X.509 certificates. The code in Listing 3-32 shows you how to display all the available certificates of the current user in a drop-down list on an ASP.NET page.

Listing 3-32: Displaying available certificates in a DropDownList control

[VB]

```
Private Sub Page_Load(ByVal sender As System.Object, ByVal e As
  System.EventArgs) Handles MyBase.Load
        Dim myCertStore As X509CertificateStore
        myCertStore = X509CertificateStore.
            CurrentUserStore(X509CertificateStore.MyStore)

        myCertStore.OpenRead()

        Dim Cert As X509Certificate
        For Each Cert In myCertStore.Certificates
            DropDownList1.Items.Add(Cert.GetName())
        Next
End Sub
```

[C#]

```
private void Page_Load(object sender, System.EventArgs e)
{
    X509CertificateStore myCertStore;
    myCertStore = X509CertificateStore.
        CurrentUserStore(X509CertificateStore.MyStore);

    myCertStore.OpenRead();

    foreach (X509Certificate Cert in myCertStore.Certificates)
    {
        DropDownList1.Items.Add(Cert.GetName());
    }
}
```

Now that you have access to the certificates, you can allow the consumer of the XML Web service to specify a certificate to use to send into the XML Web service as a way to provide authentication.

PROVIDING AN X.509 CERTIFICATE FROM THE CLIENT

In building an ASP.NET page that sends a SOAP request to an XML Web service provider, create a page that includes a DropDownList control, a Button control, and a Label control.

Let the user select a certificate from the drop-down list and send that in the SOAP header for verification to the XML Web service provider. Once authenticated and authorized with the XML Web service provider, the returned result will be displayed in the Label control.

In addition to the Page_Load event shown in Listing 3-32, you need to create a Button_click event handler where you will call the XML Web service using the X.509 certificate that was chosen in the drop-down list. An example of this is shown in Listing 3-33.

Listing 3-33: Calling an XML Web service using an X.509 certificate

[VB]

```
Private Sub Button1_Click(ByVal sender As System.Object, ByVal e As
    System.EventArgs) Handles Button1.Click
        Dim ws As New localhost.WSE_Auth()

        Dim myCertStore As X509CertificateStore
        myCertStore = X509CertificateStore.
            CurrentUserStore(X509CertificateStore.MyStore)
        myCertStore.OpenRead()

        Dim myCert As X509Certificate
        myCert = myCertStore.
            Certificates(DropDownList1.SelectedIndex)

        Dim myRequestContext As SoapContext = ws.RequestSoapContext
        ws.RequestSoapContext.Security.Tokens.Add(New
            X509SecurityToken(myCert))

        Label1.Text = ws.HelloAuthenticatedUser()
End Sub
```

[C#]

```
private void Button1_Click(object sender, System.EventArgs e)
{
    localhost.WSE_Auth ws = new localhost.WSE_Auth();

    X509CertificateStore myCertStore;
    myCertStore = X509CertificateStore.
```

```
        CurrentUserStore(X509CertificateStore.MyStore);
    myCertStore.OpenRead();

    X509Certificate myCert;
    myCert = myCertStore.Certificates(DropDownList1.SelectedIndex);

    SoapContext myRequestContext = ws.RequestSoapContext;
    ws.RequestSoapContext.Security.Tokens.Add(new
        X509SecurityToken(myCert));

    Label1.Text = ws.HelloAuthenticatedUser();
}
```

Once you have constructed a SOAP request that includes an X.509 certificate, the WSE abides by the WS-Security specification and uses a `BinarySecurityToken` element within the SOAP header. This is shown in Listing 3-34.

Listing 3-34: Part of the SOAP header in the request that includes the X.509 certificate

```
<wsse:Security soap:mustUnderstand="1"
 xmlns:wsse="http://schemas.xmlsoap.org/ws/2002/07/secext">
        <wsse:BinarySecurityToken ValueType="wsse:X509v3"
          EncodingType="wsse:Base64Binary" Id="SecurityToken-
          cc5af462-d054-4306-9d66-d7b1091f93eb">
MIICrTCCAhYCAQEwDQYJKoZIhvcNAQEEBQAwgZ4xIDAeBgNVBAoTF01pY3Jvc29mdCBU
cnVzdCBOZXR3b3JrMR4wHAYDVQQLExVNaWNyb3NvZnQgQ29ycG9yYXRpb24xLTArBgNV
BAsTJE1pY3Jvc29mdCBUaW1lIFN0YW1waW5nIFN1cnZpY2UgUm9vdDErMCkGA1UECxMi
Q29weXJpZ2h0ICHjKSAxOTk3IE1pY3Jvc29mdCBDb3JwLjAeFw05NzA1MTMxNjEyNT1a
Fw05OTEyMzAyMzU5NTlaMIGeMSAwHgYDVQQKExdNaWNyb3NvZnQgVHJ1c3QgTmV0d29y
azEeMBwGA1UECxMVTW1jcm9zb2Z0IENvcnBvcmF0aW9uMSOwKwYDVQQLEyRNaWNyb3Nv
ZnQgVGltZSBTdGFtcGluZyBTZXJ2aWN1IEFJvb3QxKzApBgNVBAsTIkNvcHlyaWdodCAo
YykgMTk5NyBNaWNyb3NvZnQgQ29ycC4wgZ8wDQYJKoZIhvcNAQEBBQADgYOAMIGJAoGB
ALdaOPUfN8ypQ8TcJBi+8oVStB1bXxi5C49Lbaj/zUBQbNOg01xHwrn3huTNfTUFaTcf
rz3dH/2PFTTCxHnMWXSKb4wOw+gR64Q4R5hT4fEMDeQBDPAbHiDaKno9whVSjor/ezK/
WB41mIMmy4rJxAcUJLxJntd6s4caJTO8bQhHAgMBAAEwDQYJKoZIhvcNAQEEBQADgYEA
UFvFa2+NU1sNyb2sNH0YygqHyq5MSroUpOtScJUh4LWhYE73QwJRAa8eOnDOvxi2hiiZ
Z+sI6JdAXBaC/bgl+zZvb3Y+xUyO4qdR+srBY7pegyRHC5Ny9kSazqeVOo9QEJ4dsVkW
q88+34OLx/rDa9xknOArHOUkBK5JL/bfDJE=
        </wsse:BinarySecurityToken>
</wsse:Security>
```

Now that you can send a SOAP request that contains the X.509 certificate in the SOAP header from an XML Web service consumer, let's build an XML Web service provider that works with the X.509 certificates that it receives.

BUILDING AN XML WEB SERVICE THAT WORKS WITH X.509 CERTIFICATES

You have already seen how to construct clients that can consume an XML Web service and provide an X.509 certificate in the SOAP header of the request. Now let's look at how an XML Web service provider can work with X.509 certificates sent in the SOAP header. This is shown in Listing 3-35.

Listing 3-35: An XML Web service provider that works with X.509 certificates

[VB]

```
Imports System.Web.Services
Imports System.Web.Services.Protocols
Imports Microsoft.Web.Services
Imports Microsoft.Web.Services.Security
Imports Microsoft.Web.Services.Security.X509

<WebService(Namespace:="http://wiley.com/")> _
Public Class WSE_Auth
    Inherits System.Web.Services.WebService

    <WebMethod()> Public Function HelloAuthenticatedUser() As String
        Dim requestContext As SoapContext =
            HttpSoapContext.RequestContext()

        Dim secToken As SecurityToken
        Dim returnValue As String = ""

        If requestContext Is Nothing Then
            Throw New ApplicationException("Non-SOAP request.")
        End If

        If requestContext.Security.Tokens.Count = 1 Then
            For Each secToken In requestContext.Security.Tokens
                Dim certToken As X509SecurityToken
                certToken = secToken
                returnValue = certToken.Certificate.GetName()
            Next
        End If

        Return returnValue
    End Function

End Class
```

[C#]

```csharp
using System;
using System.Collections;
using System.ComponentModel;
using System.Data;
using System.Diagnostics;
using System.Web;
using System.Web.Services;
using System.Web.Services.Protocols;
using Microsoft.Web.Services;
using Microsoft.Web.Services.Security;
using Microsoft.Web.Services.Security.X509;

namespace WebService1
{
    public class WSE_Auth : System.Web.Services.WebService
    {
        public WSE_Auth()
        {
            InitializeComponent();
        }

        [WebMethod]
        public string HelloAuthenticatedUser()
        {
          SoapContext requestContext = HttpSoapContext.RequestContext;

          string returnValue = "";

          if (requestContext == null)
          {
             throw new ApplicationException("Non-SOAP request.");
          }

          if (requestContext.Security.Tokens.Count == 1)
          {
             foreach (SecurityToken secToken in
             requestContext.Security.Tokens)
             {
                X509SecurityToken certToken;
                certToken = secToken;
```

Continued

Listing 3-35 *(Continued)*

```
                returnValue = certToken.Certificate.GetName;
        }

        return returnValue;
        }
    }
}
```

As you can see from these examples, it is just as easy to work with the SecurityToken object to pass in X.509 certificates in the SOAP request as it was to build an XML Web service that worked with the UsernameToken object.

Summary

The WS-Security implementation found within Microsoft's Web Services Enhancements 1.0 is a full implementation of the current specification and a partial implementation of the WS-Security addendum that allows X.509 certificates to be placed in the SOAP header.

This chapter focused only on part of the WS-Security implementation that you will find within the WSE 1.0. In addition to the ability to provide credentials in the SOAP header, there is also the ability to digitally sign and encrypt messages. These other WS-Security implementations are covered in chapters four and five.

In this chapter, you learned how to construct both XML Web service providers and consumers that worked with passing usernames and passwords that were placed in the SOAP header, as well as how to use X.509 certificates in place of user-names and passwords.

You also learned how to apply timestamps to either the SOAP request or the SOAP response in order to add extra security to your application logic or to data that was being delivered by SOAP over HTTP.

As stated, this is just part of the WS-Security implementation. The next few chapters take a look at the digital signing of messages and the encryption of messages.

Chapter 4

Digitally Signing SOAP Messages

THE LAST CHAPTER began to look at how to use the Web Services Enhancements 1.0 to build XML Web service consumers and providers that worked with the WS-Security specification. That specification is part of the GXA specifications defined by Microsoft, IBM, and others. You worked with applying usernames and passwords to SOAP messages for authentication purposes. You were also able to apply alternative means of working with authentication that go beyond usernames and passwords by directly applying X.509 certificates to the SOAP headers to be verified by the provider.

This chapter takes those developments one step further and uses the WSE to apply a means of digitally signing your SOAP messages.

Why Digitally Sign SOAP Messages?

Like other packets of information that travel over the Internet, SOAP packets in their transport from the SOAP consumer to the SOAP provider (and vice versa) are open to the world. Because SOAP messages are transmitted as clear text, it is easy to intercept the messages as they travel across the Internet and glean information from them.

Just as it is possible for others to intercept these messages and read their contents, it is also possible to alter the contents of the message before it's sent back on its way. This can be catastrophic if you are basing major decisions on the contents of these SOAP messages.

If you want to guard your SOAP messages against these threats, one step you need to consider adding to your application is the digital signing of your SOAP messages.

By digitally signing SOAP messages before they are sent to an XML Web service provider, you can send the signature and the signed SOAP body to consumers and they will be able to attribute a few things to your message. The consumer will be able to tell who sent the message, as well as whether the message was altered since it was signed. If the SOAP message was altered after it was signed, that means that it was intercepted in its path and changed, and therefore should be disregarded by the consumer.

Using digital signing is another step in ensuring the security of your data; therefore, if you are working with sensitive data or application logic it is highly recommended that you implement it. Although data and logic are important, of even greater importance is ensuring that you have valid data and logic.

Note that digital signing does not encrypt the SOAP message in any way. It is only meant to verify that the contents of a SOAP message have not been altered in transit. Although the term *digitally signing* appears to mean that the SOAP message is signed and sealed from others even viewing as it travels across the wire, this isn't true. The message is still in clear text and quite viewable. You'll explore different ways of encrypting the contents of SOAP messages in Chapter 5.

Applying a Digital Signature to a Simple SOAP Message

If you want to send a simple SOAP message that uses a username and password as authentication, it is simple to apply a digital signature to the message before it is sent.

To do this, you need to work with the built-in Signature class provided with the WSE. The Signature class represents a digital signature that is defined by the XML Signature specification and has been included in the WS-Security specification.

Creating the XML Web service consumer

In the example shown in Listing 4-1, the XML Web service consumer constructs a message, provides credentials, and then applies a signature to the message before sending the entire SOAP message onto the XML Web service provider. This page is the code-behind for an ASP.NET page that was used in Listing 3-13 (Chapter 3). This ASP.NET page contains a couple of TextBox controls that allow the users to enter in the appropriate username and password in order to consume the XML Web service, a Button control to initiate the XML Web service call, and a Label control to display the result of the call into the XML Web service. It is assumed that you have made the necessary corrections to the web.config file in order to have your client application work with the WSE. It is also assumed that you have made the necessary changes to the proxy class that is working with the WebMethod that you are trying to consume.

Listing 4-1: Consuming an XML Web service by providing a digital signature

[VB]

```vb
Imports Microsoft.Web.Services
Imports Microsoft.Web.Services.Security

Public Class WSE_Consumer
    Inherits System.Web.UI.Page
    Protected WithEvents Label1 As System.Web.UI.WebControls.Label
Protected WithEvents TextBox1 As _
        System.Web.UI.WebControls.TextBox
Protected WithEvents TextBox2 As _
        System.Web.UI.WebControls.TextBox
    Protected WithEvents Button1 As System.Web.UI.WebControls.Button

Private Sub Button1_Click(ByVal sender As System.Object, ByVal e _
            As System.EventArgs) Handles Button1.Click
        Dim ws As New localhost.WSE_Auth()
        Dim userToken As UsernameToken
        userToken = New UsernameToken(TextBox1.Text.ToString(), _
            TextBox2.Text.ToString(), _
            PasswordOption.SendHashed)

        ws.RequestSoapContext.Security.Tokens.Add(userToken)
        ws.RequestSoapContext.Security.Elements.Add(New _
            Signature(userToken))

        Label1.Text = ws.HelloAuthenticatedUser()
    End Sub
End Class
```

[C#]

```csharp
using System;
using System.Collections;
using System.ComponentModel;
using System.Data;
using System.Drawing;
using System.Web;
using System.Web.SessionState;
```

Continued

Listing 4-1 *(Continued)*

```
using System.Web.UI;
using System.Web.UI.WebControls;
using System.Web.UI.HtmlControls;
using Microsoft.Web.Services;
using Microsoft.Web.Services.Security;

namespace WebApplication1
{
    public class WSE_Consumer : System.Web.UI.Page
    {
        protected System.Web.UI.WebControls.TextBox TextBox1;
        protected System.Web.UI.WebControls.TextBox TextBox2;
        protected System.Web.UI.WebControls.Button Button1;
        protected System.Web.UI.WebControls.Label Label1;

        private void Button1_Click(object sender, System.EventArgs e)
        {
            localhost.WSE_Auth ws = new localhost.WSE_Auth();
            UsernameToken userToken;
            userToken = new UsernameToken(TextBox1.Text.ToString(),
                TextBox2.Text.ToString(), PasswordOption.SendHashed);

            ws.RequestSoapContext.Security.Tokens.Add(userToken);
            ws.RequestSoapContext.Security.Elements.Add(new
                Signature(userToken));
            Label1.Text = ws.HelloAuthenticatedUser();
        }
    }
}
```

As with applying usernames and passwords to the SOAP header, any application that is going to apply digital signature to the SOAP header must import the appropriate namespaces. In this case you need to import two namespaces from the WSE into your code:

```
Imports Microsoft.Web.Services
Imports Microsoft.Web.Services.Security
```

Once you have these namespaces imported into the file, you need to first create an instantiation of the proxy class that will work with the XML Web service that you are going to consume. In the case of the ASP.NET page that you are working with here, this is done within the button click event itself:

```
Dim ws as New localhost.WSE_Auth()
```

After the proxy class has been instantiated, you need to create an instance of the UsernameToken class. This object stores the credentials that you need to provide in order to consume the XML Web service. You simply pass the username and password along with the option to hash the password to the object's constructor:

```
Dim userToken as UsernameToken
userToken = New UsernameToken(Textbox1.Text.ToString(), _
  Textbox2.Text.ToString(), PasswordOption.SendHashed)
```

Now that the UsernameToken object has been created and credentials have been assigned to it, it is time to add this object to the SOAP header of the request message that is going to be sent to the XML Web service provider:

```
ws.RequestSoapContext.Security.Tokens.Add(userToken)
```

Everything is in place now as far as the username and password are concerned. Next you need to add the digital signature to the SOAP header, which you do in virtually the same manner as the username and password assignments to the SOAP header. Instead of adding a token to the SOAP header, however, you are adding a new set of elements that will represent the digital signature. The digital signature is created with a SecurityToken object and is assigned a security key that is assigned as a value of the SecurityKey property:

```
ws.RequestSoapContext.Security.Elements.Add(New _
  Signature(userToken))
```

After this step, the message is ready to be sent with its credentials and signature in place. You simply send the message by calling the WebMethod of the XML Web service. You do this in the last line of code within the button click event. The value returned from the XML Web service is assigned to the Label control on the ASP.NET page:

```
Label1.Text = ws.HelloAuthenticatedUser()
```

Once complete, the XML SOAP request message that has been sent will look like Listing 4-2.

Listing 4-2: The SOAP request sent to the XML Web service provider that is using a username and password along with a digital signature

```
<soap:Envelope
 xmlns:soap="http://schemas.xmlsoap.org/soap/envelope/"
 xmlns:xsi="http://www.w3.org/2001/XMLSchema-instance"
 xmlns:xsd="http://www.w3.org/2001/XMLSchema">
```

Continued

Listing 4-2 *(Continued)*

```
<soap:Header>
  <wsrp:path
    soap:actor="http://schemas.xmlsoap.org/soap/actor/next"
    soap:mustUnderstand="1"
    xmlns:wsrp="http://schemas.xmlsoap.org/rp">
    <wsrp:action
      xmlns:wsu="http://schemas.xmlsoap.org/ws/2002/07/utility"
      wsu:Id="Id-3cc4622c-638d-4426-9eb3-6e2b40031200">
      http://www.wiley.com/HelloAuthenticatedUser</wsrp:action>
    <wsrp:to
      xmlns:wsu="http://schemas.xmlsoap.org/ws/2002/07/utility"
      wsu:Id="Id-13b7ffd3-f588-49e8-919f-7d720a9bac25">
      http://localhost/webservice19/WSE_Auth.asmx</wsrp:to>
    <wsrp:id
      xmlns:wsu="http://schemas.xmlsoap.org/ws/2002/07/utility"
      wsu:Id="Id-bf701f6f-a72b-4837-9385-3a5541850fdd">
      uuid:4cf3cdd8-ff6c-41f8-85f9-a1d6e390c1d2</wsrp:id>
  </wsrp:path>
  <wsu:Timestamp
    xmlns:wsu="http://schemas.xmlsoap.org/ws/2002/07/utility">
    <wsu:Created wsu:Id="Id-507ddafc-ecad-46f3-a1b3-
      438787cc29b2">2002-10-21T16:14:49Z</wsu:Created>
    <wsu:Expires wsu:Id="Id-41e6a1ab-8b18-469f-acbb-
      0148c44d1b01">2002-10-21T16:19:49Z</wsu:Expires>
  </wsu:Timestamp>
  <wsse:Security soap:mustUnderstand="1"
    xmlns:wsse="http://schemas.xmlsoap.org/ws/2002/07/secext">
    <wsse:UsernameToken Id="SecurityToken-95484d27-5b89-45ee-
      b8e2-21d21887f427">
      <wsse:Username>BillEvjen</wsse:Username>
      <wsse:Password Type="wsse:PasswordDigest">
      E/uoBZ8YNK5qVFhLj7XILaP4Afo=</wsse:Password>
      <wsse:Nonce>7iRG1PKmpg9CjDedhdSEsw==</wsse:Nonce>
      <wsu:Created
      xmlns:wsu="http://schemas.xmlsoap.org/ws/2002/07/utility">
      2002-10-21T16:14:49Z</wsu:Created>
    </wsse:UsernameToken>
    <Signature xmlns="http://www.w3.org/2000/09/xmldsig#">
      <SignedInfo>
        <CanonicalizationMethod
        Algorithm="http://www.w3.org/2001/10/xml-exc-c14n#" />
        <SignatureMethod
        Algorithm="http://www.w3.org/2000/09/xmldsig#hmac-sha1"
```

```
/>
<Reference URI="#Id-7a615756-d48b-44d4-969f-
  0a12c44debd1">
  <Transforms>
    <Transform Algorithm="http://www.w3.org/2001/10/xml-
      exc-c14n#" />
  </Transforms>
  <DigestMethod
   Algorithm="http://www.w3.org/2000/09/xmldsig#sha1" />
  <DigestValue>DdczIuZ2BmYoTbKDQKnq9gOKE7c=</DigestValue>
</Reference>
<Reference URI="#Id-3cc4622c-638d-4426-9eb3-
  6e2b40031200">
  <Transforms>
    <Transform Algorithm="http://www.w3.org/2001/10/xml-
      exc-c14n#" />
  </Transforms>
  <DigestMethod
   Algorithm="http://www.w3.org/2000/09/xmldsig#sha1" />
  <DigestValue>Mz1TenZduFDocALmXRP23fo59Qo=</DigestValue>
</Reference>
<Reference URI="#Id-13b7ffd3-f588-49e8-919f-
  7d720a9bac25">
  <Transforms>
    <Transform Algorithm="http://www.w3.org/2001/10/xml-
      exc-c14n#" />
  </Transforms>
  <DigestMethod
   Algorithm="http://www.w3.org/2000/09/xmldsig#sha1" />
  <DigestValue>U6GfyQJiXnzalzUQ29pffkfg5b4=</DigestValue>
</Reference>
<Reference URI="#Id-bf701f6f-a72b-4837-9385-
  3a5541850fdd">
  <Transforms>
    <Transform Algorithm="http://www.w3.org/2001/10/xml-
      exc-c14n#" />
  </Transforms>
  <DigestMethod
   Algorithm="http://www.w3.org/2000/09/xmldsig#sha1" />
  <DigestValue>ttFrL9emij4ScKOr3EANvK/02xs=</DigestValue>
</Reference>
<Reference URI="#Id-507ddafc-ecad-46f3-a1b3-
  438787cc29b2">
```

Continued

Listing 4-2 *(Continued)*

```
                <Transforms>
                    <Transform Algorithm="http://www.w3.org/2001/10/xml-
                        exc-c14n#" />
                </Transforms>
                <DigestMethod
                    Algorithm="http://www.w3.org/2000/09/xmldsig#sha1" />
                <DigestValue>kIrW8nJxIGPBQP22zL4YF7gpOLU=</DigestValue>
            </Reference>
            <Reference URI="#Id-41e6a1ab-8b18-469f-acbb-
                0148c44d1b01">
                <Transforms>
                    <Transform Algorithm="http://www.w3.org/2001/10/xml-
                        exc-c14n#" />
                </Transforms>
                <DigestMethod
                    Algorithm="http://www.w3.org/2000/09/xmldsig#sha1" />
                <DigestValue>C7u2tx9xMDLJtMgvdrB/CHixnqA=</DigestValue>
            </Reference>
          </SignedInfo>
          <SignatureValue>
            QIBIX8E5DokLiyAitx4kEFn4SY8=</SignatureValue>
          <KeyInfo>
            <wsse:SecurityTokenReference>
                <wsse:Reference URI="#SecurityToken-95484d27-5b89-
                    45ee-b8e2-21d21887f427" />
            </wsse:SecurityTokenReference>
          </KeyInfo>
        </Signature>
      </wsse:Security>
    </soap:Header>
    <soap:Body
      xmlns:wsu="http://schemas.xmlsoap.org/ws/2002/07/utility"
      wsu:Id="Id-7a615756-d48b-44d4-969f-0a12c44debd1">
        <HelloAuthenticatedUser xmlns="http://www.wiley.com" />
    </soap:Body>
</soap:Envelope>
```

Looking at the SOAP message from the consumer

After looking at this message, you are probably concerned about the message size required to simply instantiate a remote object. It is important to understand that when applying advanced XML Web service features like those of the WSE, much of the information that is applied to the SOAP messages will be applied to the SOAP header. When applying multiple specifications or functionalities to a SOAP message, sometimes the SOAP header becomes rather lengthy.

Whether or not this is an issue really depends on what you are trying to accomplish and how important extreme performance capabilities are to what you are trying to accomplish. If you are designing and building applications that require extreme performance metrics, you might want to consider other alternatives to using XML Web services, but in most situations, XML Web services will perform more than adequately enough to fill your needs.

If you save the SOAP message in its entirety into Notepad and then look at the properties of the file, you will notice that the entire message's payload is not more than 5KB. In most cases, sending a 5KB message from one point to another, or through any intermediaries, is not going to be an issue.

Examining the SOAP Header

The message itself is doing a lot, so let's take a look at what is contained in the SOAP header and try to get a better understanding of all the pieces. You will notice at the bottom of the message that the body of this SOAP envelope is just a couple of lines. This would be the same whether or not you were using the WSE because nothing is different about the request being made to the XML Web service provider. What is different is the SOAP header, which constitutes most of the message.

Within the SOAP header is the typical WS-Routing and Timestamp information that is included with every XML Web service message using the WSE. This chapter concentrates on the `<wsse:Security>` node of the SOAP header.

```
<wsse:Security soap:mustUnderstand="1"
 xmlns:wsse="http://schemas.xmlsoap.org/ws/2002/07/secext">

   <!-- Contents here -->

</wsse:Security>
```

The first information provided within the `Security` node of the SOAP header is the description of the `UsernameToken` object that is serialized into XML. This node includes the username, password, and nonce nodes. This part is the same as shown in previous chapters.

What is different is the new `<Signature>` child node contained within the `<wsse:Security>` node. This section contains all the information about the digital signature and is broken up into numerous parts.

The `<Signature>` node contains additional child nodes such as `<SignedInfo>`, `<SignatureValue>`, and `<KeyInfo>`.

<SIGNEDINFO>

When digitally signing SOAP messages, the `<SignedInfo>` child node is a required part of the `<Signature>` node. The `<SignedInfo>` node contains what is actually being signed in the message, which in this case is the body of the SOAP message.

The reason for this is that the receiver of the SOAP message will then be able to take the actual SOAP body and make comparisons to the SOAP body that was signed into the SOAP header. If differences are found in making these comparisons, that would mean that something was altered in transport and therefore message integrity was jeopardized. This will give you the ability make sure that your SOAP message are that much more secure as they are transported through intermediaries and across the Internet.

The three important elements that are provided within the <SignedInfo> node are the <CanonicalizationMethod>, <SignatureMethod>, and the numerous <Reference> nodes.

The <CanonicalizationMethod> is the algorithm that is used to canonicalize, or relate the procedure applied for the algorithm of the <SignedInfo> element before it is digested as part of the signature operation. The <SignatureMethod> describes the algorithm that is used to convert the <SignedInfo> element into a <SignatureValue> element:

```
<SignatureMethod
 Algorithm="http://www.w3.org/2000/09/xmldsig#hmac-sha1" />
```

In this case, notice that for this digital signature, you are using a SHA1 hash to digitally sign this message.

One of the more interesting parts of the <SignedInfo> element is the numerous <Reference> elements that end up making a large part of the SOAP header. In the case of the SOAP client request that is shown in Listing 4-2, notice that are six instances of the <Reference> element contained within the <SignedInfo> element.

Here is the first <Reference> element contained within the SOAP header for the SOAP message shown in Listing 4-2:

```
<Reference URI="#Id-7a615756-d48b-44d4-969f-0a12c44debd1">
   <Transforms>
      <Transform Algorithm="http://www.w3.org/2001/10/xml-
      exc-c14n#" />
   </Transforms>
   <DigestMethod
    Algorithm="http://www.w3.org/2000/09/xmldsig#sha1" />
   <DigestValue>DdczIuZ2BmYoTbKDQKnq9gOKE7c=</DigestValue>
</Reference>
```

The <Reference> elements contained within the <SignedInfo> element define the exact information that is being signed. Notice that the <Reference> element contains a URI attribute with a long ID number as the value.

Looking at the value that is given to the URI in this instance (#Id-7a615756-d48b-44d4-969f-0a12c44debd1), notice that this value is also contained with the SOAP body element as well:

```
<soap:Body xmlns:wsu="http://schemas.xmlsoap.org/ws/2002/07/utility"
 wsu:Id="Id-7a615756-d48b-44d4-969f-0a12c44debd1">
   <HelloAuthenticatedUser xmlns="http://www.wiley.com" />
</soap:Body>
```

This means that the SOAP body and all of its contents are included in the digital signature. If you look at the other URI values in the other <Reference> elements contained within the <SignedInfo> element, you will notice that other parts of the SOAP message are included in the digital signature.

In fact, in this SOAP header the following elements are included in the digital signature:

```
<soap:Body>
<action>       <!-- Part of WS-Routing information set -->
<to>           <!-- Part of WS-Routing information set -->
<id>           <!-- Part of WS-Routing information set -->
<Created>      <!-- Part of WS-Timestamp information set -->
<Expires>      <!-- Part of WS-Timestamp information set -->
```

These six elements that are part of the entire SOAP envelope are included in the digital signature. The reason that the individual parts of the WS-Routing and WS-Timestamp elements are digitally signed and the entire <Path> and <Timestamp> sections is not is because when SOAP messages are routed through multiple intermediaries, those intermediaries will sometimes need to interject elements into these sections of the SOAP header. If they did this and the entire related portion of the element was digitally signed, then the message would be considered altered and not valid. Just digitally signing the portions inserted into these larger container nodes allows others to work with the messages and not break the signatures.

<SIGNATUREVALUE>

The <SignatureValue> contains the actual value of the digital signature. The value is encoded using a base64 MIME encoding.

<KEYINFO>

The <KeyInfo> element contains the key information that the receiver of the SOAP message will need to validate the signature. In this case, the key is included as a SecurityTokenReference object.

Verifying a Signature in a Simple SOAP Message

Now that you can send a SOAP message that is digitally signed, you would only need to do this if the recipient of the SOAP message worked with messages that were signed in the first place. It is always possible to just digitally sign all the SOAP messages that you send, but it will be of no benefit unless the recipients of the messages are actually using the digitally signed information in the SOAP message to verify the data integrity.

Creating the XML Web service provider

The SOAP message that is sent from the client application in Listing 4-1 not only includes a username and password that is hashed, but it also contains a request to instantiate the XML Web service provider's exposed WebMethod. Included in the SOAP message of the SOAP request is a digital signature from the sender of the SOAP message.

The fact that a digital signature is included with the SOAP request really doesn't mean anything if the XML Web service that is going to provide the SOAP response does not act upon the signature.

The best approach to make sure that the data contained within the SOAP messages is unaltered and to consistently require requesters to include digital signatures within their SOAP requests. Doing this will cause SOAP requests that don't include digital signatures within their SOAP messages to fail.

Listing 4-3 shows an example of an XML Web service provider that accepts and validates digital signatures that are included in SOAP requests.

Listing 4-3: An XML Web service that is working with digital signatures

[VB]

```
Imports System.Web.Services
Imports System.Web.Services.Protocols
Imports Microsoft.Web.Services
Imports Microsoft.Web.Services.Security

<WebService(Namespace:="http://wiley.com/")> _
Public Class WSE_Auth
    Inherits System.Web.Services.WebService

    <WebMethod()> Public Function HelloAuthenticatedUser() As String
        Dim requestContext As SoapContext = _
            HttpSoapContext.RequestContext()

        Dim userToken As UsernameToken
        Dim elem as Object
        Dim returnValue As String = ""

        If requestContext Is Nothing Then
```

```vb
            Throw New ApplicationException("Non-SOAP request.")
        End If

        For Each userToken In requestContext.Security.Tokens

            If userToken.PasswordOption = _
                    PasswordOption.SendHashed Then
                For Each elem In requestContext.Security.Elements
                    If TypeOf elem Is Signature Then
                        Dim clientSign As Signature = _
                            CType(elem, Signature)

                        If TypeOf clientSign.SecurityToken Is _
                            UsernameToken Then
                          returnValue = "Howdy " & _
                            CType(clientSign.SecurityToken, _
                            UsernameToken).Username
                        End If
                    End If
                Next
            Else
                Throw New SoapException("You must provide a " & _
                    "hashed  password.", SoapException.ClientFaultCode)
            End If

        Next
        Return returnValue
    End Function

End Class
```

[C#]

```csharp
using System;
using System.Collections;
using System.ComponentModel;
using System.Data;
using System.Diagnostics;
using System.Web;
using System.Web.Services;
using System.Web.Services.Protocols;
using Microsoft.Web.Services;
```

Continued

Listing 4-3 *(Continued)*

```csharp
using Microsoft.Web.Services.Security;

namespace WebService1
{
    [WebService(Namespace="http://www.wiley.com")]
    public class WSE_Auth : System.Web.Services.WebService
    {

        public WSE_Auth()
        {
            InitializeComponent();
        }

        [WebMethod]
        public string HelloAuthenticatedUser()
        {
            SoapContext requestContext =
                HttpSoapContext.RequestContext;

            string returnValue = "";

        if (requestContext == null)
        {
            throw new ApplicationException("Non-SOAP request.");
        }

        foreach (UsernameToken userToken in
            requestContext.Security.Tokens)
        {
            if (userToken.PasswordOption == PasswordOption.SendHashed)
            {
                foreach (Object elem in
                        requestContext.Security.Elements)
                {
                    if (elem is Signature)
                    {
                        Signature clientSign = (Signature)elem;

                        if (clientSign.SecurityToken is UsernameToken)
                            returnValue = "Howdy " +
                                ((UsernameToken)clientSign.
                                    SecurityToken).Username;
                    }
```

```
            }
        }
        else
        {
        throw new SoapException("You must provide a hashed
            password.", SoapException.ClientFaultCode);
        }
    }

    return returnValue;
    }
  }
}
```

 In order for your XML Web service provider to work, you need to create a class file that does your password lookups as illustrated in Listing 3-6 (Chapter 3). You also have to make the appropriate changes to the web.config file, also illustrated in Chapter 3.

Much of what you are doing in this XML Web service was illustrated in earlier chapters. The difference is that in the iteration through each of the UsernameTokens sent with the request, you are also determining whether there is a Signature object within the SOAP request. You do this by looking at each of the elements provided in the security section of the SOAP header and determining whether any of these elements is a Signature object:

```
foreach (Object elem in requestContext.Security.Elements)
{
    if (elem is Signature)
    {
        // Perform operations here
    }
}
```

If the element that is being checked from the SOAP header is of type Signature, then this generic object has the reference of elem and is then easily referenced from within the If Then block of code.

Once the object is found to be of a Signature type, it is assigned to an instance of a Security object called clientSign. Then a check is made to see if the clientSign object is a digital signature that was signed using a UsernameToken, and if true, the return value of the WebMethod is assigned a string statement that includes the username from the UsernameToken object:

```
Signature clientSign = (Signature)elem;

if (clientSign.SecurityToken is UsernameToken)
    returnValue = "Howdy " + ((UsernameToken)clientSign.
                    SecurityToken).Username;
```

Running this XML Web service provider and the consumer shown in Listing 4-1 gives you a simple result shown in Figure 4-1.

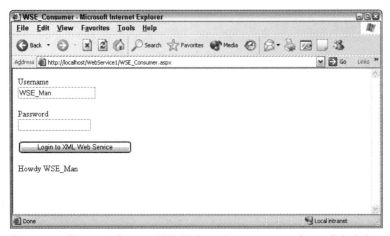

Figure 4-1: The result from an XML Web service consumer using a digital signature to call an XML Web service provider

Looking at the SOAP message from the provider

Once the WebMethod in the sample is instantiated, the XML Web service provider makes a number of appropriate checks to determine whether the SOAP message is properly constructed in order to receive a response. The XML Web service itself makes the following checks upon the incoming SOAP request:

- Does the SOAP message include a username and password constructed from a UsernameToken object?

- Has the password included in the UsernameToken object been hashed?

- Is the password correct for that particular username?

- Has the SOAP message been signed by the UsernameToken object?

Once these checks are made, the SOAP response is made. Although unlike the SOAP request, which was rather lengthy, the SOAP response is quite simple. Listing 4-4 shows the SOAP response.

Listing 4-4: The SOAP response from the XML Web service provider

```
<soap:Envelope
 xmlns:soap="http://schemas.xmlsoap.org/soap/envelope/"
 xmlns:xsi="http://www.w3.org/2001/XMLSchema-instance"
 xmlns:xsd="http://www.w3.org/2001/XMLSchema">
    <soap:Header>
     <wsu:Timestamp
      xmlns:wsu="http://schemas.xmlsoap.org/ws/2002/07/utility">
       <wsu:Created wsu:Id="Id-802c669c-4b5f-4ee6-bfe7-
        e40d71207957">2002-10-29T20:59:16Z</wsu:Created>
       <wsu:Expires wsu:Id="Id-48efac5d-1aad-4c87-93b0-
        1f85609e2996">2002-10-29T21:04:16Z</wsu:Expires>
     </wsu:Timestamp>
    </soap:Header>
    <soap:Body>
      <HelloAuthenticatedUserResponse xmlns="http://www.wiley.com">
        <HelloAuthenticatedUserResult>Hello BillEvjen
        </HelloAuthenticatedUserResult>
      </HelloAuthenticatedUserResponse>
  </soap:Body>
</soap:Envelope>
```

Besides the Timestamp object being included within the SOAP header, the message is rather simple and is what you would expect from a normal SOAP response. The power in this code is that before this SOAP response was sent out to the consumer, a number of checks were made to ensure that the SOAP request was valid.

Validating the digital signature

Another feature of digital signing is the capability to sign and check for signatures on individual parts of a SOAP message, for example, on the SOAP body. The reason for this is that it is possible to sign a number of different items from the SOAP message as a whole. You saw this earlier when the entity sending the SOAP request digitally signed the message. Not only was the SOAP body digitally signed into the SOAP header, but so was the message path and timestamp information.

Because multiple sections of the SOAP message can be digitally signed within the SOAP header, in most instances you need to make sure that not only is there a digital signature included, but that this digital signature includes a signing of the SOAP body.

For an example of this type of check, let's use the same XML Web service provider shown in Listing 4-4, but with the changes shown in Listing 4-5.

Listing 4-5: Ensuring that the SOAP body was included in the digital signature

[VB]

```vb
For Each elem In requestContext.Security.Elements
    If TypeOf elem Is Signature Then
        Dim clientSign As Signature = CType(elem, Signature)

        If clientSign.SignatureOptions.IncludeSoapBody Then
            If TypeOf clientSign.SecurityToken Is UsernameToken Then
                returnValue = "Howdy " & _
                CType(clientSign.SecurityToken, UsernameToken).Username
            End If
        End If
    End If
Next
```

[C#]

```csharp
foreach (Object elem in requestContext.Security.Elements)
{
    if (elem is Signature)
    {
        Signature clientSign = (Signature)elem;

        if (clientSign.SignatureOptions.IncludeSoapBody)
        {
            if (clientSign.SecurityToken is UsernameToken)
                returnValue = "Hello " +
                ((UsernameToken)clientSign.SecurityToken).Username;
        }
    }
}
```

Make this check when ensuring that a digital signature was included within the SOAP request. Doing this ensures that the SOAP body of the request does not include anything that could be changed or would prevent the WebMethod from executing properly.

In addition to the SOAP body, you can also check for the other five pieces of the SOAP message that might be included in the digital signature. The following list is the enumerations of the SignatureOptions property that is part of the Signature class. These enumerations check whether specific parts of the SOAP message were included in the digital signature:

```
IncludeNone
IncludePath
```

```
IncludePathAction
IncludePathFrom
IncludePathId
IncludePathTo
IncludeSoapBody
IncludeTimestamp
IncludeTimestampCreated
IncludeTimestampExpires
```

Applying a Signature to a SOAP Message Using a Certificate

Not only is it possible to create a digital signature for a SOAP message using a `UsernameToken` object, but it is also just as easy to apply a digital signature using an X.509 certificate. It is possible to build a consumer that signs the SOAP message with a certificate, but you would also need to look for this in the XML Web service.

 You can get test certificates from Verisign at `www.verisign.com`.

The first step in building an XML Web service consumer that will digitally sign a SOAP message with a certificate is to locate the certificate. Similar to the certificate examples in the last chapter, create a page that will allow users to select a certificate from a drop-down list of certificates and instantiate the XML Web service by clicking a button on the page. The result from the XML Web service WebMethod call will then be shown directly within a Label control on the ASP.NET page.

The code from the ASP.NET page, whether you are coding the project in Visual Basic .NET or in C#, should look similar to Listing 4-6.

Listing 4-6: ASP.NET page listing of available certificates for digital signing

```
<%@ Page Language="vb" AutoEventWireup="false"
 Codebehind="WSE_Consumer.aspx.vb"
 Inherits="WebApplication1.WSE_Consumer"%>
<!DOCTYPE HTML PUBLIC "-//W3C//DTD HTML 4.0 Transitional//EN">
<HTML>
   <HEAD>
      <title>CertDisplay</title>
```

Continued

Listing 4-6 *(Continued)*

```
  </HEAD>
  <body>
    <form id="Form1" method="post" runat="server">
      <P>
      <asp:DropDownList id="DropDownList1"
       runat="server"></asp:DropDownList></P>
      <P>
      <asp:Button id="Button1" runat="server"
       Text="Login to Web Service"></asp:Button></P>
      <P>
      <asp:Label id="Label1" runat="server">Label</asp:Label></P>
    </form>
  </body>
</HTML>
```

The idea is when a certificate is selected from the drop-down list and the button is clicked, the WebMethod will be instantiated, the certificate will digitally sign the entire SOAP message, and the SOAP response will be sent. To accomplish this task, you use the code in Listing 4-7 as the code-behind of this ASP.NET page.

Listing 4-7: Consuming an XML Web service by providing a digital signature signed by an X.509 certificate

[VB]

```
Imports Microsoft.Web.Services
Imports Microsoft.Web.Services.Security
Imports Microsoft.Web.Services.Security.X509


Public Class WSE_Consumer
    Inherits System.Web.UI.Page
    Protected WithEvents Button1 As System.Web.UI.WebControls.Button
Protected WithEvents DropDownList1 As _
        System.Web.UI.WebControls.DropDownList
    Protected WithEvents Label1 As System.Web.UI.WebControls.Label


Private Sub Page_Load(ByVal sender As System.Object, ByVal e As _
        System.EventArgs) Handles MyBase.Load
        Dim myCertStore As X509CertificateStore
        myCertStore = X509CertificateStore.
            CurrentUserStore(X509CertificateStore.MyStore)

        myCertStore.OpenRead()
```

```
        Dim Cert As X509Certificate
        For Each Cert In myCertStore.Certificates
            DropDownList1.Items.Add(Cert.GetName())
        Next
    End Sub

    Private Sub Button1_Click(ByVal sender As System.Object, ByVal e
        As System.EventArgs) Handles Button1.Click
        Dim ws As New localhost.WSE_Auth()

        Dim myCertStore As X509CertificateStore
        myCertStore = X509CertificateStore.
            CurrentUserStore(X509CertificateStore.MyStore)
        myCertStore.OpenRead()

        Dim myCert As X509Certificate
        myCert = myCertStore.
            Certificates(DropDownList1.SelectedIndex)

        If (myCert.SupportsDigitalSignature And _
            myCert.PrivateKeyAvailable) Then
            Dim myCertToken as X509SecurityToken = New _
                X509SecurityToken(myCert)

            ws.RequestSoapContext.Security.Tokens.Add(myCertToken)
            ws.RequestSoapContext.Security.Elements.Add(New _
                Signature(myCertToken))
            Label1.Text = ws.HelloAuthenticatedUser()
    End Sub
End Class
```

[C#]

```
using System;
using System.Collections;
using System.ComponentModel;
using System.Data;
using System.Drawing;
using System.Web;
using System.Web.SessionState;
using System.Web.UI;
using System.Web.UI.WebControls;
```

Continued

Listing 4-7 *(Continued)*

```csharp
using System.Web.UI.HtmlControls;
using Microsoft.Web.Services;
using Microsoft.Web.Services.Security;
using Microsoft.Web.Services.Security.X509;

namespace WebService1
{
    public class WSE_Consumer : System.Web.UI.Page
    {
        protected System.Web.UI.WebControls.DropDownList DropDownList1;
        protected System.Web.UI.WebControls.Button Button1;
        protected System.Web.UI.WebControls.Label Label1;

        private void Page_Load(object sender, System.EventArgs e)
        {
            X509CertificateStore myCertStore;
            myCertStore = X509CertificateStore.
            CurrentUserStore(X509CertificateStore.MyStore);

            myCertStore.OpenRead();

            foreach (X509Certificate Cert in myCertStore.Certificates)
            {
                DropDownList1.Items.Add(Cert.GetName());
            }
        }

        private void Button1_Click(object sender, System.EventArgs e)
        {
            localhost.WSE_Auth ws = new localhost.WSE_Auth();
            X509CertificateStore myCertStore;
            myCertStore = X509CertificateStore.
                CurrentUserStore(X509CertificateStore.MyStore);
            myCertStore.OpenRead();

            X509Certificate myCert;
            myCert = (X509Certificate)myCertStore.
                Certificates[DropDownList1.SelectedIndex];

            if (myCert.SupportsDigitalSignature &&
                myCert.PrivateKeyAvailable)
            {
                X509SecurityToken myCertToken = new
```

```
                X509SecurityToken(myCert);

            ws.RequestSoapContext.Security.Tokens.Add(myCertToken);
            ws.RequestSoapContext.Security.Elements.Add(new
                Signature(myCertToken));
            Label1.Text = ws.HelloAuthenticatedUser();
        }
        else
        {
            throw new ApplicationException("Your certificate must
                support digital signatures and must have a private key
                available!");
        }
    }
  }
}
```

As you can tell from this code, digitally signing a SOAP message using a certificate involves virtually the same procedure as when you are digitally signing it with a UsernameToken object.

Looking at the code from Listing 4-7, in the Button1_click event you create an instance of the XML Web service that you are going to consume after you have made that appropriate reference to this remote object that you are going to consume:

```
localhost.WSE_Auth ws = new localhost.WSE_Auth();
```

You need to create an instance of a certificate store object, in this case called myCertStore. myCertStore is populated with the current user's X.509 certificate store contents. These are read into the object by using the OpenRead method of the X509CertificateStore object:

```
X509CertificateStore myCertStore;
myCertStore = X509CertificateStore.
    CurrentUserStore(X509CertificateStore.MyStore);
myCertStore.OpenRead();
```

Once the certificate store object myCertStore is populated, you then create an instance of an X509Certificate object called myCert. This object is populated with the certificate that the user selects from the drop-down list on the ASP.NET page:

```
X509Certificate myCert;
myCert = (X509Certificate)myCertStore.
    Certificates[DropDownList1.SelectedIndex];
```

Now you have an X.509 certificate that you can work with, and can digitally sign the SOAP message. Before you do, however, it is a best practice to first make the appropriate checks on the certificate that is stored within the X509Certificate object. You need to make sure that the X.509 certificate chosen for the digital signing supports digital signatures and has a private key. By using the SupportsDigitalSignature and PrivateKeyAvailable methods of the X509Certificate object, you can make sure that the certificates are of the type that you need to perform the operation. In the following example the check is made in an If Then statement. If the certificate doesn't support either of these scenarios, an exception is thrown that informs the users that they need to select a certificate that does support these items:

```
if (myCert.SupportsDigitalSignature ||
   myCert.PrivateKeyAvailable)
{
   // Perform code execution here
}
else
{
   throw new ApplicationException("Your certificate must
      support digital signatures and must have a private key
      available!");
}
```

If the certificate makes it through the appropriate checks, then an X509SecurityToken object is created and populated with the X509Certificate. Once in place, you can add this X509SecurityToken object to the SOAP header of the request SOAP message that is going to be sent to the XML Web service provider. Once the X.509 certificate has been added to the SOAP header, the entire SOAP message is digitally signed using the same X.509 certificate and the SOAP message is ready to be sent. The final line of code then instantiates the remote method of the XML Web service provider and populates the returned result into a Label control that is on the ASP.NET page:

```
X509SecurityToken myCertToken = new X509SecurityToken(myCert);

ws.RequestSoapContext.Security.Tokens.Add(myCertToken);
ws.RequestSoapContext.Security.Elements.Add(new
      Signature(myCertToken));
Label1.Text = ws.HelloAuthenticatedUser();
```

As you can tell, it was fairly simple and straightforward to digitally sign a SOAP message with an X.509 certificate. Just remember that you first have to get a certificate from some third party (such as VeriSign) to perform these operations. Once you have a certificate store and the appropriate certificates in place, you can then apply a more advanced security program to your XML Web services that you send to consumers.

Verifying a Signature in a SOAP Message that Uses a Certificate

As with digitally signing your SOAP messages with a UsernameToken object, it doesn't do much good to digitally sign your messages with certificates if the XML Web service provider does not verify the signature of the SOAP messages that it receives. Therefore, now that you have the means of sending a digitally signed message from the consumer to the provider with certificates, let's create the XML Web service provider that will verify the integrity of these messages.

Listing 4-8 shows you how to build an XML Web service provider that ensures that the SOAP message was digitally signed by an X.509 certificate.

Listing 4-8: An XML Web service that works with digital signatures signed using an X.509 certificate

[VB]

```
Imports System.Web.Services
Imports System.Web.Services.Protocols
Imports Microsoft.Web.Services
Imports Microsoft.Web.Services.Security
Imports Microsoft.Web.Services.Security.X509

<WebService(Namespace:="http://wiley.com/")> _
Public Class WSE_Auth
    Inherits System.Web.Services.WebService

    <WebMethod()> Public Function HelloAuthenticatedUser() As String
        Dim requestContext As SoapContext = _
            HttpSoapContext.RequestContext()

        Dim userToken As SecurityToken
        Dim elem as Object
        Dim returnValue As String = ""

        If requestContext Is Nothing Then
            Throw New ApplicationException("Non-SOAP request.")
```

Continued

Listing 4-8 *(Continued)*

```
            End If

        For Each userToken In requestContext.Security.Tokens

            For Each elem In requestContext.Security.Elements
                If TypeOf elem Is Signature Then
                    Dim clientSign As Signature = _
                        CType(elem, Signature)

                    If TypeOf clientSign.SecurityToken Is _
                        X509SecurityToken Then
                      returnValue = "Howdy " & _
                        CType(clientSign.SecurityToken, _
                        X509SecurityToken).Certificate.GetName()
                    End If
                End If
            Next

        Next
        Return returnValue
    End Function

End Class
```

[C#]

```csharp
using System;
using System.Collections;
using System.ComponentModel;
using System.Data;
using System.Diagnostics;
using System.Web;
using System.Web.Services;
using System.Web.Services.Protocols;
using Microsoft.Web.Services;
using Microsoft.Web.Services.Security;
using Microsoft.Web.Services.Security.X509;

namespace WebService1
{
    [WebService(Namespace="http://www.wiley.com")]
    public class WSE_Auth : System.Web.Services.WebService
    {
```

```
        public WSE_Auth()
        {
            InitializeComponent();
        }


        [WebMethod]
        public string HelloAuthenticatedUser()
        {
            SoapContext requestContext =
                HttpSoapContext.RequestContext;

            string returnValue = "";

    if (requestContext == null)
    {
        throw new ApplicationException("Non-SOAP request.");
    }

    foreach (SecurityToken userToken in
        requestContext.Security.Tokens)
    {
        foreach (Object elem in
                requestContext.Security.Elements)
        {
            if (elem is Signature)
            {
                Signature clientSign = (Signature)elem;

                if (clientSign.SecurityToken is X509SecurityToken)
                    returnValue = "Howdy " +
                        ((x509SecurityToken)clientSign.
                            SecurityToken).Certificate.GetName();
            }
        }
    }

    return returnValue;
        }
    }
}
```

This code example is quite similar to what you saw earlier in the chapter when working with digitally signing a SOAP message using a `UsernameToken` object. There are some important differences that you should be aware of, as discussed in the following sections.

After the `SoapContext` object is populated with the request SOAP message that is sent to the XML Web service provider, all of the `SecurityToken` objects contained within the SOAP header of the request message are reviewed:

```
foreach (SecurityToken userToken in requestContext.Security.Tokens)
{
    // Perform code execution here
}
```

Then for each `SecurityToken` object, all the elements that are contained within the `<wsse:Security>` node are checked to determine whether the element is a digital signature:

```
foreach (Object elem in requestContext.Security.Elements)
{
    if (elem is Signature)
    {
        // Perform code execution here
    }
}
```

If the element found is of a type `Signature`, it is assigned to a `Signature` object. In this case, it is assigned to a `Signature` object name `clientSign`. Once this assignment is made, the object is checked to see if the `clientSign` object is an `X509SecurityToken` object. If it is, a return value for the XML Web service is assigned and included in the string that is returned is the name from the certificate:

```
Signature clientSign = (Signature)elem;

if (clientSign.SecurityToken is X509SecurityToken)
    returnValue = "Howdy " +
        ((x509SecurityToken)clientSign.
            SecurityToken).Certificate.GetName();
```

In the end, you can see that it is just as easy to work with X.509 certificates as it is to work with `UsernameTokens`.

Digitally Signing Custom SOAP Header Elements

The WSE performs its magic of building SOAP messages that are GXA compliant, whether they are for the request or for the response, by placing these WS-Security or other GXA features in the SOAP header of the messages being constructed. The

SOAP header, being as open as it is, is not the best place for the WSE when extending SOAP messages. There will also be moments where these GXA extensions of the SOAP messages work side-by-side with your own custom extensions.

If you have extended the SOAP header of either the SOAP request or the SOAP response, you'll sometimes need to apply some of the WSE features to these custom extensions. For instance, if there is a custom extension that is built in to the SOAP message, you'll need to digitally sign this extension along with the rest of the SOAP message.

The WSE makes this all possible. To show an example of this, let's create a class that extends the SOAP header and requires the consumers of the XML Web service to also include their names and email addresses in the SOAP header in order to consume it. Then the consumers will not only incorporate this addition into their SOAP request, but they will also digitally sign this addition within the SOAP header.

The XML Web service provider

The first piece to build is an XML Web service that will extend the SOAP message and require these additional elements be placed within in the SOAP header of all of the SOAP requests that the Web service receives. To do this, open Visual Studio .NET and create a new ASP.NET Web service project called ExtendSOAP with a Web service called WSE_Auth.asmx. The first step in the creation of this file is shown in Listing 4-9. This is the full listing of all the namespaces that you need to import into the XML Web service in addition to the namespaces that are automatically included by Visual Studio .NET when you create an XML Web service page.

Listing 4-9: Extending the SOAP header in the XML Web service

[VB]

```
Imports System.Web.Services
Imports System.Web.Services.Protocols
Imports System.Xml.Serialization
Imports System.Text.RegularExpressions
Imports Microsoft.Web.Services
Imports Microsoft.Web.Services.Security
```

[C#]

```
using System;
using System.Collections;
using System.ComponentModel;
using System.Data;
using System.Diagnostics;
using System.Web;
```

Continued

Listing 4-9 *(Continued)*

```
using System.Web.Services;
using System.Web.Services.Protocols;
using System.Xml.Serialization;
using System.Text.RegularExpressions;
using Microsoft.Web.Services;
using Microsoft Web.Services.Security;
```

First you need to import the `System.Web.Services.Protocols` namespace in order to create a class that extends the `SoapHeader` class. This namespace also allows you to work with SOAP exceptions. The `System.Xml.Serialization` namespace is imported so that you can work with XML attributes in the SOAP header. The `System.Text.RegularExpressions` namespace is imported in order to work with some regular expressions that will validate the email address that is supplied in the SOAP header. Finally, the `Microsoft.Web.Services` and `Microsoft.Web.Services.Security` namespaces are imported so you can work with digitally signed SOAP messages that are generated from the WSE.

After the namespaces are imported, you create a new class in your Web service page. This code for this class is shown in Listing 4-10.

Listing 4-10: The class that extends the SOAP header

`[VB]`

```
Public Class PersonalInformation
    Inherits SoapHeader

    <XmlAttribute("Id", _
    Namespace:="http://schemas.xmlsoap.org/ws/2002/07/utility")> _
    Public Id As String

    Public Name As String
    Public EmailAddress As String
End Class
```

`[C#]`

```
public class PersonalInformation: SoapHeader
 {
[XmlAttribute("Id",
Namespace="http://schemas.xmlsoap.org/ws/2002/07/utility")]
public string Id;

  public string Name;
  public string EmailAddress;
 }
```

This simple class contains three objects – two being the consumer's name and email address that will be included in the SOAP header of every SOAP request that comes into the Web service. The third object, the Id field, is the most important element to the WSE if the consumer is also going to digitally sign the PersonalInformation element and its associated child elements.

Another important thing to note is the System.Xml.Serialization. XmlAttributeAttribute class used to let the XmlSerializer know that the member Id should be serialized as an XML attribute and not as an element, which is the default. This method includes parameters that set the AttributeName property to Id and assigns a value to the Namespace property to the attribute.

If you use the PersonalInformation element within your SOAP response, you have to assign a value to the Id field before the SOAP response is sent. The value of Id needs to be a unique identifier that follows the rules for the xsd:Id type.

Once the PersonalInformation class is in place, you can then construct the Web service class. This Web service exposes a WebMethod called Hello AuthenticatedUser that returns a string containing some of the elements from the PersonalInformation class. The consumer includes these elements in the SOAP header that allows you to authenticate and authorize them to consume this XML Web service. Listing 4-11 shows you the code you need for the Web service class.

The assumption here is that you already have a class in place that verifies usernames and passwords, and that you have made all the necessary changes to the web.config file in order for you XML Web service to work properly with the WSE, as discussed in Chapter 2.

Listing 4-11: The WSE_Auth.asmx Web service

[VB]

```
<WebService(Namespace:="http://www.wiley.com")> _
Public Class WSE_Auth
    Inherits System.Web.Services.WebService

    Public PersonalInformation As PersonalInformation

<WebMethod(), SoapHeader("PersonalInformation")> _
    Public Function HelloAuthenticatedUser() As String
```

Continued

Listing 4-11 *(Continued)*

```
        PersonalInformation.MustUnderstand = True

        Dim EmailRegex As Regex = _
            New Regex("([\w-]+@([\w-]+\.)+[\w-]+)")
        Dim M As Match = _
            EmailRegex.Match(PersonalInformation.EmailAddress)

        If M.Success Then
            PersonalInformation.DidUnderstand = True
        Else
            PersonalInformation.DidUnderstand = False
        End If

        Dim requestContext As SoapContext = _
            HttpSoapContext.RequestContext()

        Dim userToken As UsernameToken
        Dim elem As Object
        Dim returnValue As String = ""

        If requestContext Is Nothing Then
            Throw New ApplicationException("Non-SOAP request.")
        End If

        For Each elem In requestContext.Security.Elements
            If TypeOf elem Is Signature Then
                Dim clientSign As Signature = CType(elem, Signature)

                If TypeOf clientSign.SecurityToken _
                  Is UsernameToken Then
                    returnValue += "Hello Authenticated User! " & _
                        "Your username value is " & _
                        CType(clientSign.SecurityToken, _
                            UsernameToken).Username & _
                        " and your email address is " & _
                        PersonalInformation.EmailAddress
                End If
            End If
        Next

        Return returnValue
    End Function
```

```
End Class
```

[C#]

```
[WebService(Namespace="http://www.wiley.com")]
 public class WSE_Auth: System.Web.Services.WebService
 {
  public PersonalInformation PersonalInformation;

  [WebMethod]
  [SoapHeader("PersonalInformation")]
  public string HelloAuthenticatedUser()
  {
   PersonalInformation.MustUnderstand = true;

   Regex EmailRegex = new Regex("([\w-]+@([\w-]+\.)+[\w-]+)");
   Match M = EmailRegex.Match(PersonalInformation.EmailAddress);

   If (M.Success)
   {
      PersonalInformation.DidUnderstand = true;
   }
   else
   {
      PersonalInformation.DidUnderstand = false;
   }

   SoapContext requestContext = HttpSoapContext.RequestContext;

   string returnValue = "";

   if (requestContext == null)
   {
      throw new ApplicationException("Non-SOAP request.");
   }

   foreach (Object elem in requestContext.Security.Elements)
   {
      if (elem is Signature)
      {
         Signature clientSign = (Signature)elem;

         if (clientSign.SecurityToken is UsernameToken)
```

Continued

Listing 4-11 *(Continued)*

```
            returnValue = "Hello Authenticated User! " +
                "Your username value is " +
                ((UsernameToken)clientSign.SecurityToken).Username +
                " and your email address is " +
                PersonalInformation.EmailAddress;
            }
        }
    }

    return returnValue;

    }
}
```

Note that an instance of the `PersonalInformation` class is created in the `WSE_Auth` class. In this case, you simply gave this instance of the class the same name:

```
Public PersonalInformation As PersonalInformation
```

Next, the WebMethod `HelloAuthenticatedUser` applies the `PersonalInformation` class to its SOAP header by using the `SoapHeaderAttribute` class:

```
<WebMethod(), SoapHeader("PersonalInformation")> _
 Public Function HelloAuthenticatedUser() As String
```

In the WebMethod, not only is the name and email address of the consumer absorbed from the SOAP header, but also the email address is checked to ensure that it has a valid email address construction. This is done using regular expressions. In this case, a regular expression is contained within an instance of the `Regex` class. Then a comparison is made between this regular expression and the email address provided in the SOAP header. Its success or failure is assigned to an instance of the `Match` class:

```
Dim EmailRegex As Regex = New Regex("([\w-]+@([\w-]+\.)+[\w-]+)")
Dim M As Match = EmailRegex.Match(PersonalInformation.EmailAddress)
```

This instance of the `Match` class is checked for success or failure. If the regular expression comparison to the email address provided by the consumer was a success, then the `DidUnderstand` property of the `PersonalInformation` class is given a value of `True`, otherwise a `False` value is assigned and the consumer will receive a SOAP fault:

```
If M.Success Then
   PersonalInformation.DidUnderstand = True
Else
   PersonalInformation.DidUnderstand = False
End If
```

Now that the email address has been verified, you can begin constructing the SOAP response. The rest of the code is the same as shown earlier in this chapter, although the big difference is that the email address that was provided in the SOAP request is also provided by using `PersonalInformation.EmailAddress`.

The XML Web service consumer

The XML Web service provider was just built to work with the extra information being provided in the SOAP header of all the SOAP requests that the provider receives. This information – the name and email address of the consumer – are required elements in order to consume the XML Web service. The SOAP request must also be digitally signed.

It is quite easy, as you saw earlier in this chapter, to digitally sign your SOAP messages. When you digitally signed the SOAP request earlier in the chapter, you should have noticed that what was digitally signed included the SOAP body, the path and all of its sub-elements, as well as the timestamp information and all of its sub-elements.

If you digitally sign your SOAP request that contains the `PersonalInformation` class in the manner shown earlier in the chapter, you will notice that this `PersonalInformation` element and all of its child elements are not included in the digital signature. This may be fine in most cases, but for the same reasons that you want to digitally sign the SOAP body, you might also want to include these custom constructions within the SOAP header in the digital signature as well.

Therefore, for the example used here now, you will construct an XML Web service consumer that uses the `PersonalInformation` class within the SOAP header of the SOAP request as is required by the provider. In addition to providing this additional information in the SOAP header, you will digitally sign this personal information.

Before you create the ASP.NET page that will perform these operations, you need to make a Web reference to the XML Web service that was just created. Remember that after you make the reference to the XML Web service, you need to change the class that the proxy class inherits from to `Microsoft.Web.Services.WebServicesClientProtocol` and recompile this class. You also need to make the appropriate changes to the `web.config` file in order to allow your XML Web service consumer application to work with the WSE.

Again, the page that you will construct for these purposes is an ASP.NET page. You can find the code for the visual aspect of this page from Listing 3-13 (Chapter 3). It is a simple page containing two textboxes, a Button control, and a Label control. When the users enter their proper credentials in the textboxes (the username and password) and click the button on the page, the XML Web service is invoked and the SOAP request is sent. Before the SOAP request is sent, you are going to work with this request in order to add in these credentials and to digitally sign the message. Listing 4-12 shows you the code-behind for this ASP.NET page that performs these operations.

Listing 4-12: Digitally signing custom SOAP header information

[VB]

```
Imports Microsoft.Web.Services
Imports Microsoft.Web.Services.Security

Public Class WSE_Consumer
    Inherits System.Web.UI.Page
    Protected WithEvents TextBox1 As
System.Web.UI.WebControls.TextBox
    Protected WithEvents TextBox2 As
System.Web.UI.WebControls.TextBox
    Protected WithEvents Button1 As System.Web.UI.WebControls.Button
    Protected WithEvents Label1 As System.Web.UI.WebControls.Label


Private Sub Button1_Click(ByVal sender As System.Object, _
        ByVal e As System.EventArgs) Handles Button1.Click
        Dim ws As New localhost.WSE_Auth()
        Dim wsHeader As New localhost.PersonalInformation()

        wsHeader.Name = "Bill Evjen"
        wsHeader.EmailAddress = "evjen@yahoo.com"
        wsHeader.Id = "Id:05d2518d-d6db-481f-846d-2e8872b6e56d"

        ws.PersonalInformationValue = wsHeader

        Dim userToken As UsernameToken
        userToken = New UsernameToken(TextBox1.Text.ToString(), _
            TextBox2.Text.ToString(), PasswordOption.SendHashed)

        Dim sig As Signature
        sig = New Signature(userToken)

        Dim digiSignRef As Reference = _
            New Reference("#Id:05d2518d-d6db-481f-846d-2e8872b6e56d")
        sig.AddReference(digiSignRef)

        ws.RequestSoapContext.Security.Tokens.Add(userToken)
```

```
        ws.RequestSoapContext.Security.Elements.Add(sig)

        Label1.Text = ws.HelloAuthenticatedUser()
    End Sub
End Class
```

[C#]

```
using System;
using System.Collections;
using System.ComponentModel;
using System.Data;
using System.Drawing;
using System.Web;
using System.Web.SessionState;
using System.Web.UI;
using System.Web.UI.WebControls;
using System.Web.UI.HtmlControls;
using Microsoft.Web.Services;
using Microsoft.Web.Services.Security;

namespace WebApplication1
{
    public class WSE_Consumer : System.Web.UI.Page
    {
        protected System.Web.UI.WebControls.TextBox TextBox1;
        protected System.Web.UI.WebControls.TextBox TextBox2;
        protected System.Web.UI.WebControls.Button Button1;
        protected System.Web.UI.WebControls.Label Label1;

        private void Button1_Click(object sender, System.EventArgs e)
        {
            localhost.WSE_Auth ws = new localhost.WSE_Auth();
            localhost.PersonalInformation wsHeader =
                new localhost.PersonalInformation();

            wsHeader.Name = "Bill Evjen";
            wsHeader.EmailAddress = "evjen@yahoo.com";
            wsHeader.Id = "Id:05d2518d-d6db-481f-846d-2e8872b6e56d";

            ws.PersonalInformationValue = wsHeader;

            UsernameToken userToken;
```

Continued

Listing 4-12 *(Continued)*

```
        userToken = new UsernameToken(TextBox1.Text.ToString(),
          TextBox2.Text.ToString(), PasswordOption.SendHashed);

        Signature sig;
        Sig = new Signature(userToken);

        Reference digiSignRef =
          new Reference("#Id:05d2518d-d6db-481f-846d-
2e8872b6e56d");
        sig.AddReference(digiSignRef);

        ws.RequestSoapContext.Security.Tokens.Add(userToken);
        ws.RequestSoapContext.Security.Elements.Add(sig);

        Label1.Text = ws.HelloAuthenticatedUser();
      }
    }
}
```

Now examine the code from this XML Web service consumer. First, when the users enter in their credentials into the textboxes and click the button, the Button1_Click event is called and an instance of the WebMethod is created. An instance of the PersonalInformation class is also created at this time:

```
Dim ws As New localhost.WSE_Auth()
Dim wsHeader As New localhost.PersonalInformation()
```

Once these two instances are created, the properties of the PersonalInformation class are assigned values. The first value assigned is the name of the consumer and the second value is the email address. You should also know since you have also built the XML Web service, that the value assigned to EmailAddress will be verified and therefore needs to be a properly formatted email address. The last value assigned is the Id property. It is important to give an Id value that is of type xsd:Id and to make sure that it is unique. The reason that this property is so important is that later in this code sample, you will use this Id to find the section of the SOAP header of a particular SOAP request that you will add to the digital signature.

Once these values are assigned, you simply assign this instance of the PersonalInformation object to the instance of the WebMethod:

```
wsHeader.Name = "Bill Evjen"
wsHeader.EmailAddress = "evjen@yahoo.com"
wsHeader.Id = "Id:05d2518d-d6db-481f-846d-2e8872b6e56d"

ws.PersonalInformationValue = wsHeader
```

After this, you create an instance of the UsernameToken object as you normally do and assign to it the values that were provided in the two textboxes. At this point, you also need to configure the password provided with the UsernameToken so that it is hashed:

```
Dim userToken As UsernameToken
userToken = New UsernameToken(TextBox1.Text.ToString(), _
    TextBox2.Text.ToString(), PasswordOption.SendHashed)
```

Then if you want to digitally sign the custom SOAP header information that you constructed using the PersonalInformation object, you have to create an instance of a Signature class called sig. Once created, the value of sig is assigned the UsernameToken object, userToken:

```
Dim sig As Signature
sig - New Signature(userToken)
```

If you use this signature at this point, it would digitally sign six elements within your SOAP request just as it did earlier in the chapter. In addition to these six items, you are also need to digitally sign the seventh element, the instance of the PersonalInformation object. To do this, you have to create an instance of the Reference class (called digiSignRef) and assign a reference to the part of the SOAP header that contains the unique ID that you gave the PersonalInformation object. Notice that the value assigned to the Reference object is this unique ID, but it is preceded with a number sign (#).

Once an instance of the Reference class is created, this instance is assigned your instance of the Signature object (sig):

```
Dim digiSignRef As Reference = _
    New Reference("#Id:05d2518d-d6db-481f-846d-2e8872b6e56d")
sig.AddReference(digiSignRef)
```

Finally, the UsernameToken is assigned to the SOAP request as well a digital signature that was created which includes a digital signature of the custom SOAP header elements that you built into the SOAP header. Once these items are in place, the XML Web service is called and its value is assigned to the text property of the Label control.

The browser will show the following results:

```
Hello Authenticated User! Your username value is BillEvjen
and your email address is evjen@yahoo.com
```

Listing 4-13 shows the SOAP request that the XML Web service consumer created and sent to the XML Web service provider. Notice that everything related to the custom SOAP header information that you placed in the SOAP header and digitally signed is in bold.

Listing 4-13: The SOAP request containing a digitally signed PersonalInformation element

```
<soap:Envelope
xmlns:soap="http://schemas.xmlsoap.org/soap/envelope/"
 xmlns:xsi="http://www.w3.org/2001/XMLSchema-instance"
 xmlns:xsd="http://www.w3.org/2001/XMLSchema">
    <soap:Header>
        <PersonalInformation d3p1:Id="Id:05d2518d-d6db-481f-846d-
        2e8872b6e56d"
         xmlns:d3p1="http://schemas.xmlsoap.org/ws/2002/07/utility"
         xmlns="http://www.wiley.com">
          <Name>Bill Evjen</Name>
          <EmailAddress>evjen@yahoo.com</EmailAddress>
        </PersonalInformation>
        <wsrp:path
         soap:actor="http://schemas.xmlsoap.org/soap/actor/next"
         soap:mustUnderstand="1"
         xmlns:wsrp="http://schemas.xmlsoap.org/rp">
          <wsrp:action wsu:Id="Id-b8485a29-eaa9-41bd-
bef4-2d24060a42f9"
            xmlns:wsu="http://schemas.xmlsoap.org/ws/2002/07/utility">
            http://www.wiley.com/HelloAuthenticatedUser</wsrp:action>
          <wsrp:to wsu:Id="Id-76dec87d-24d1-4d4e-a392-bf88b6776641"
            xmlns:wsu="http://schemas.xmlsoap.org/ws/2002/07/utility">
            http://localhost/WSE1/WSE_Auth.asmx</wsrp:to>
          <wsrp:id wsu:Id="Id-7167f64b-c4e1-443b-b753-46d824277470"
            xmlns:wsu="http://schemas.xmlsoap.org/ws/2002/07/utility">
            uuid:77693dfa-cb34-4331-97f4-471700abb170</wsrp:id>
        </wsrp:path>
        <wsu:Timestamp
         xmlns:wsu="http://schemas.xmlsoap.org/ws/2002/07/utility">
          <wsu:Created wsu:Id="Id-be2133e2-48cc-4563-8167-
          0edff8898efc">2002-11-30T21:45:14Z</wsu:Created>
          <wsu:Expires wsu:Id="Id-5ebbd9b8-49e6-425d-bfc9-
          8807071090ed">2002-11-30T21:50:14Z</wsu:Expires>
        </wsu:Timestamp>
        <wsse:Security soap:mustUnderstand="1"
         xmlns:wsse="http://schemas.xmlsoap.org/ws/2002/07/secext">
          <wsse:UsernameToken
            xmlns:wsu="http://schemas.xmlsoap.org/ws/2002/07/utility"
            wsu:Id="SecurityToken-69b5203f-
85d3-45f3-9e07-5adfa87fcd7b">
              <wsse:Username>BillEvjen</wsse:Username>
              <wsse:Password Type="wsse:PasswordDigest">
              sCfDC3pUDwjcSFi5K2MsSCxZvfU=</wsse:Password>
```

```
    <wsse:Nonce>nZxzDDPBeC6ZLN8w+7JpOA==</wsse:Nonce>
    <wsu:Created>2002-11-30T21:45:14Z</wsu:Created>
  </wsse:UsernameToken>
  <Signature xmlns="http://www.w3.org/2000/09/xmldsig#">
    <SignedInfo>
      <CanonicalizationMethod
       Algorithm="http://www.w3.org/2001/10/xml-exc-c14n#" />
      <SignatureMethod
       Algorithm="http://www.w3.org/2000/09/xmldsig#hmac-sha1"
/>
        <Reference URI="#Id:05d2518d-d6db-481f-846d-
2e8872b6e56d">
          <DigestMethod
           Algorithm="http://www.w3.org/2000/09/xmldsig#sha1" />

<DigestValue>2qCCIQSCTZNO6CDYIMISOiD39QO=</DigestValue>
        </Reference>
        <Reference URI="#Id-2069325c-10b7-49d4-a0af-
c605a62a3950">
          <Transforms>
            <Transform Algorithm="http://www.w3.org/2001/10/xml-
              exc-c14n#" />
          </Transforms>
          <DigestMethod
           Algorithm="http://www.w3.org/2000/09/xmldsig#sha1" />

<DigestValue>+n5S4MSFxszYwCOvpnByGO+tX1A=</DigestValue>
        </Reference>

        <!-- Removed an additional five <Reference> nodes for
            space reasons -->

    </SignedInfo>
    <SignatureValue>
     7VaCO65/y6VDMMICSmF6xxmNwts=</SignatureValue>
    <KeyInfo>
      <wsse:SecurityTokenReference>
        <wsse:Reference URI="#SecurityToken-69b5203f-
85d3-45f3-
          9e07-5adfa87fcd7b" />
      </wsse:SecurityTokenReference>
    </KeyInfo>
  </Signature>
```

Continued

Listing 4-13 *(Continued)*

```
            </wsse:Security>
        </soap:Header>
<soap:Body wsu:Id="Id-2069325c-10b7-49d4-a0af-c605a62a3950"
        xmlns:wsu="http://schemas.xmlsoap.org/ws/2002/07/utility">
            <HelloAuthenticatedUser xmlns="http://www.wiley.com" />
        </soap:Body>
</soap:Envelope>
```

Notice by looking over this SOAP request that the first item contained within the SOAP header is an instance of the `PersonalInformation` object. Included in the `<PersonalInformation>` element is an XML attribute named `Id`. The value of `Id` is the unique identifier that you assigned to it in the `Button1_Click` event code. The fact that this `Id` attribute is assigned as a value means that it can later be referenced in the digital signature. Included within the `<PersonalInformation>` element are the two child elements — `<Name>` and `<EmailAddress>` — along with their associated values.

In addition to the `<path>` and `<Timestamp>` elements, there is the `<UsernameToken>` element with the child elements `<Username>` and `<Password>`. Immediately following the `<UsernameToken>` element is the digitally signed parts of the SOAP message. The first signed reference in the SOAP request is the `<PersonalInformation>` element. You can tell that this is for this particular element because the value of the `URI` attribute contained within the `<Reference>` element is the same unique ID that is the value of the attribute of the `<PersonalInformation>` element displayed earlier in the SOAP header. By digitally signing the `<PersonalInformation>` element, you are also digitally signing all of the child elements of the `<PersonalInformation>` element — in this case, the `<Name>` and `<EmailAddress>` elements. Included with the `<Reference>` element is the method that was used to digitally sign the SOAP message (in this case, SHA1) and the value of the signing.

Following this signed reference to your custom SOAP header element are the additional digitally signed references that you would expect, such as the SOAP body and the other parts of the SOAP header.

Looking for digitally signed elements

Because you can digitally sign a SOAP message and not sign every element, you can program your XML Web service provider to look at each of the signed elements individually as you might only care of certain elements and child elements were digitally signed and you may not care about if the other elements were signed as well. Listing 4-14 shows you a short example of what you can do to iterate through each of the digitally signed elements.

Listing 4-14: Iterating through each of the digitally signed elements

`[VB]`

```
Dim i As Integer

For i = 1 To clientSign.SignedInfo.References.Count
    ' Code goes here
Next
```

`[C#]`

```
for(int i = 0; i < clientSign.SignedInfo.References.Count; i++)
{
    // Code goes here
}
```

In the end, not only should you apply digital signatures to your SOAP requests and SOAP responses before sending them across the wire, but you should also make sure that you digitally sign any custom constructions that might be contained within the SOAP headers of your messages. This two-pronged approach will ensure the integrity of your data.

Summary

In this section of the book, you have taken a look at how to apply usernames and passwords to SOAP messages that are being sent to XML Web services that require them. It also took this a step further and included X.509 certificates as a means of providing identification to the consumer of the SOAP message.

This chapter took this application of authentication to XML Web services and showed you how to use them to also apply a digital signature to the SOAP message that was being sent.

By digitally signing messages or by building XML Web services that only accept SOAP messages that are digitally signed, you are saying that the integrity of the data that is contained within these messages is important and vital for the purposes of the information that your XML Web service is providing.

If this is the case, then you are going to want to make this a requirement for all the messages that come into your XML Web service applications.

In the next chapter, we will take a look at one of the most requested features in the XML Web services model – encryption.

Chapter 5

Working with Encrypted SOAP Messages

IN THIS CHAPTER

♦ Apply encryption to your SOAP messages

♦ Understanding encryption and decryption within XML Web services

♦ Storing your shared secrets

♦ Understand how to encrypt SOAP messages using an X.509 certificate

♦ Using two encryption keys

THE DATA THAT IS SENT to and from XML Web services sometimes contains information that should remain private. With SOAP messages going back and forth across the Internet, some might be grabbed as they travel from one SOAP router to another. You definitely do not want some of this data exposed to people or applications for which the message payload was not intended. For instance, you do not want you credit card number, medical information, or bank account information floating around in cyberspace without any protection. You can protect this data by putting it (in a sense) under lock and key.

This chapter looks at how to encrypt and decrypt SOAP messages that are sent between the XML Web service consumer and the provider.

Encrypting SOAP Messages

The point of XML Web services is to expose data and application logic to other entities. Doing this can be cause for concern for some people, because business-related data is often sensitive and should not be exposed to the public. Therefore, when the XML Web services model was introduced, there were a lot of companies and organizations that first asked, "Where is the security?" – *and rightly so!*

When working with XML Web services on the .NET platform from the .NET Framework version 1.0, you could build XML Web services and encrypt the entire message from point-to-point by using SSL. This is a secure method that encrypts the *entire* SOAP message. Therefore, the HTTP header and the entire SOAP message, including any SOAP headers, are encrypted before they are sent across the wire.

This format is secure and safe, but it taxes the server and makes the SOAP message dependent on HTTP for message transport.

This would be a fine solution in working with XML Web services that are not going to use any of the advanced functionality found in the GXA specifications. This is because the XML Web services that you build without using any of the GXA specifications are usually point-to-point Web services and do not need to travel through any intermediaries as they are transported.

GXA specifications go beyond point-to-point Web services because they can travel through multiple SOAP routers before they reach their final destinations. In some cases, you might not even control where the messages hop to in their journeys and that would make SSL obsolete. There will also be times when you send messages through SOAP routers and want the SOAP routers to take actions on certain parts of the SOAP headers as they travel through the router. In these cases, having the entire SOAP message encrypted won't work because you would want just the SOAP body encrypted and the SOAP header left exposed for these SOAP routers to read.

As stated, XML Web services that use GXA specifications can still be kept under lock and key. With these XML Web services, the lock is *encryption* or *cryptography,* and the key is the public or private key used for encrypting and decrypting the information in the SOAP message. You can do this using DES encryption or a number of other methods. The examples in this chapter use Triple DES encryption.

Triple DES encryption

DES is a popular U.S. government algorithm, developed in the 1970s, which is used to encrypt and decrypt data. The algorithm is designed to encipher and decipher blocks of data consisting of 64 bits under control of a 64-bit key. The key consists of 64 binary digits (0s and 1s) of which 56 bits are generated randomly and then used directly by the algorithm. The other 8 bits, which are not used by the algorithm, are used for error detection.

Using DES, the person who encrypts the message has to have the same key as the person who decrypts the message. So in the end, one copy of the key locks up the message and another copy of the key unlocks it. The consumer of your XML Web service must have the algorithm key to unlock the encrypted message.

The problem with DES encryption is that it is breakable. With today's advancing technologies, it is getting easier to break something encrypted using DES encryption. Triple DES encryption is based on DES encryption, but instead of a single 64-bit encryption string, Triple DES encryption uses three separate 64-bit strings that make a key length of 192 bits. You simply need to provide the 192-bit key and then the key is broken up into three pieces. The process of encrypting data is quite similar to DES encryption, but Triple DES encryption repeats the process three times. For this reason, Triple DES encryption is slower, but it is quite a bit more secure in the data that it transmits. The WSE's use of Triple DES encryption is a great way of encrypting your SOAP messages that are sent either from the XML Web service consumer or the provider. In either case, using this encryption is a great way of locking up the secrets of your data as it travels across the wire.

Building an XML Web service consumer that encrypts the SOAP body of the SOAP message

This section starts off by building an XML Web service consumer application that will work to consume an XML Web service WebMethod using encryption in SOAP body of the SOAP message. The WebMethod that you are going to be working with is just a simple `Add()` method that takes two integers and then returns the sum of the two integers.

Start off by creating simple ASP.NET page that contains two TextBox controls, a Button control, and a Label control where the result of the WebMethod call can be displayed. Listing 5-1 shows the ASP.NET code for the page.

Listing 5-1: The ASP.NET page that will work with the Add() WebMethod

```
<%@ Page language="c#" Codebehind="Add.aspx.cs"
 AutoEventWireup="false" Inherits="WebService1.Add" %>
<!DOCTYPE HTML PUBLIC "-//W3C//DTD HTML 4.0 Transitional//EN" >
<HTML>
   <HEAD>
      <title>Add</title>
   </HEAD>
   <body>
   <form id="Add" method="post" runat="server">
      <P>
      <asp:TextBox id="TextBox1" runat="server"></asp:TextBox></P>
      <P>
      <asp:TextBox id="TextBox2" runat="server"></asp:TextBox></P>
      <P>
      <asp:Button id="Button1" runat="server"
       Text="Add"></asp:Button></P>
      <P>
      <asp:Label id="Label1" runat="server"></asp:Label></P>
   </form>
   </body>
</HTML>
```

Now that the ASP.NET page is in place, you are nearly ready to code the code-behind for this page. Before you progress with the code-behind, there are some additional changes you need to make to the application.

STORING A SHARED SECRET

In working with the encryption and subsequent decryption of the SOAP body, you as the XML Web service consumer are going to need to share a secret with the XML Web service provider that receives your encrypted SOAP message. Without sharing this secret, the XML Web service provider will be unable to decrypt the message that you send. This is called *symmetric encryption*. The WSE supports both symmetric encryption and asymmetric encryption. Both symmetric and asymmetric encryption will be covered in this chapter.

Symmetric encryption means that when you encrypt something, you do so with a shared key. When the receiving party decrypts the message, they use the same shared key. This is a great way of doing this until a third party discovers your shared secret.

With asymmetric encryption, you encrypt something with an X.509 certificate's public key, and the only way to decrypt the message is to provide the certificate's private key.

Of the two, symmetric encryption is the easiest and fastest to use, but as mentioned, it isn't as secure as asymmetric encryption and should be used with caution because you do not want your shared secrets being jeopardized.

Therefore, you are going to need to store this shared secret somewhere. One option is to store this shared secret directly in the web.config file. This also gives you the ability to easily get at the value by using the System.Web.Configuration namespace in your ASP.NET applications. Listing 5-2 shows you a sample construction of how you might place this in your web.config file.

Listing 5-2: Storing the shared secret in the web.config file

```
<?xml version="1.0" encoding="utf-8" ?>
<configuration>

    <appSettings>
        <add key="symmetricKey"
         value="BAA62349A24A7796116785784F54B149" />
    </appSettings>

    <system.web>
        <!-- The rest of the web.config file -->
    </system.web>
</configuration>
```

In the web.config file example here, you are simply storing a key/value pair directly in the <appSettings> section of the document. If you are new to this, you will not find this section in the web.config file already; you will have to create it there yourself. Just make sure that you keep it outside of the <system.web> nodes.

For this example, you have created a key called symmetricKey and have given it a value of BAA62349A24A7796116785784F54B149, which is a 32-character string created from an MD5 hash of a word. This hash is the shared secret that will be used on both the XML Web service consumer side and on the provider side.

CREATING A HASH TO USE AS YOUR SHARED SECRET

It is easy to create your own hash to use with an entity that you will be sending messages to. One option is to create a simple ASP.NET page that randomly produces an MD5 hash. Once the hash is created in the Page_Load event, it will then be populated into a Literal control that is on the page.

Listing 5-3 shows you how you can easily do this in the Page_Load event.

Listing 5-3: Easily creating a random MD5 hash to use as a shared secret

[VB]

```
Private Sub Page_Load(ByVal sender As System.Object, ByVal e As
    System.EventArgs) Handles MyBase.Load
        Literal1.Text = FormsAuthentication.
            HashPasswordForStoringInConfigFile("Bubbles", "MD5")
End Sub
```

[C#]

```
private void Page_Load(object sender, System.EventArgs e)
{
    Literal1.Text = FormsAuthentication.
      HashPasswordForStoringInConfigFile("Bubbles", "MD5");
}
```

This little bit of code takes the word Bubbles and applies an MD5 hash to it, thus creating BAA62349A24A7796116785784F54B149. To get this to work, you have to also import in the System.Web.Security namespace to work with the FormsAuthentication class.

The method HashPasswordForStoringInConfigFile is one of the leading contenders for the longest method name in .NET and takes two parameters — the word that you are going to hash, followed by the method you are going to use (in this case MD5). Use this bit of code to generate your random symmetric key that you can then use to encrypt and decrypt the SOAP messages.

CREATING THE CODE-BEHIND FOR THE XML WEB SERVICE CONSUMER APPLICATION

Now that you have your basic ASP.NET page in place and you have also made the appropriate changes to the web.config file, it is time to apply the code that will run the ASP.NET page to construct a SOAP message, encrypt the SOAP body of the message, and then send it off to the XML Web service provider. The key is not sent with the message, as it is expected that the XML Web service provider will also be storing a copy of this key somewhere in their system. Note that the XML Web service provider is not required to store this key in the same fashion as the XML Web service consumer.

For the code-behind of the ASP.NET page you are going to create a couple of methods. The first is for the button click event and the second is a method supplies the encryption key that will sign the SOAP message. Listing 5-4 is the full code-behind for the XML Web service consumer application.

Listing 5-4: An XML Web service consumer that will send the SOAP body encrypted

[VB]

```vb
Imports Microsoft.Web.Services
Imports Microsoft.Web.Services.Security
Imports System.Security.Cryptography
Imports System.Security.Cryptography.Xml
Imports System.Configuration

Public Class myAdd
  Inherits System.Web.UI.Page
  Protected WithEvents TextBox1 As System.Web.UI.WebControls.TextBox
  Protected WithEvents TextBox2 As System.Web.UI.WebControls.TextBox
  Protected WithEvents Button1 As System.Web.UI.WebControls.Button
  Protected WithEvents Label1 As System.Web.UI.WebControls.Label

  Private Sub Button1_Click(ByVal sender As System.Object, ByVal e _
  As System.EventArgs) Handles Button1.Click
      Dim ws As New localhost.Calculator()

      Dim key As EncryptionKey = GetEncryptionKey()

      ws.RequestSoapContext.Security.Elements.Add(New _
          EncryptedData(key))

      Label1.Text = ws.Add(TextBox1.Text.ToString(), _
          TextBox2.Text.ToString())
    End Sub

  Private Function GetEncryptionKey() As EncryptionKey
      Dim baseKey As String = _
          ConfigurationSettings.AppSettings("symmetricKey")

      If baseKey Is Nothing Then
         Throw New ApplicationException("Symmetric key not " & _
            "found in configuration.")
      End If

      Dim keyBytes As Byte() = Convert.FromBase64String(baseKey)
      Dim key As SymmetricEncryptionKey = New _
          SymmetricEncryptionKey(TripleDES.Create(), keyBytes)

      Dim keyName As KeyInfoName = New KeyInfoName()
      keyName.Value = "AddEncrypt"
```

```
        key.KeyInfo.AddClause(keyName)

        Return key
    End Function
End Class
```

[C#]

```
using System;
using System.Collections;
using System.ComponentModel;
using System.Configuration;
using System.Data;
using System.Drawing;
using System.Web;
using System.Web.Services;
using System.Web.Services.Protocols;
using Microsoft.Web.Services;
using Microsoft.Web.Services.Security;
using System.Security.Cryptography;
using System.Security.Cryptography.Xml;

namespace WebApplication1
{
    public class Add : System.Web.UI.Page
    {
        protected System.Web.UI.WebControls.TextBox TextBox1;
        protected System.Web.UI.WebControls.TextBox TextBox2;
        protected System.Web.UI.WebControls.Button Button1;
        protected System.Web.UI.WebControls.Label Label1;

        private void Button1_Click(object sender, System.EventArgs e)
        {
            localhost.Calculator ws = new
                localhost.Calculator();

            EncryptionKey key = GetEncryptionKey();

            ws.RequestSoapContext.Security.Elements.Add(new
                EncryptedData(key));

            Label1.Text = ws.Add(int.Parse(TextBox1.Text),
                int.Parse(TextBox2.Text)).ToString();
```

Continued

Listing 5-4 *(Continued)*

```
    }

    private EncryptionKey GetEncryptionKey()
    {

        string baseKey =
            ConfigurationSettings.AppSettings["symmetricKey"];

        if (baseKey == null)
        {
            throw new ApplicationException("Symmetric key not found
                in configuration.");
        }

        byte[] keyBytes = Convert.FromBase64String(baseKey);
        SymmetricEncryptionKey key = new
            SymmetricEncryptionKey(TripleDES.Create(), keyBytes);

        KeyInfoName keyName = new KeyInfoName();
        keyName.Value  = "AddEncrypt";
        key.KeyInfo.AddClause(keyName);

        return key;
    }
  }
}
```

There is a lot going on in this small application, so let's take a look at it closely. First of all, the end user enters one number in each of the text boxes and clicks the button on the page. Clicking the button causes the XML Web service to be remotely called, although before it is, the SOAP request is constructed by the consumer application. Similar to how you added credentials or performed digital signing on a SOAP request, a SOAP request is constructed that encrypts its payload before sending the SOAP message onto the XML Web service provider.

Looking at the code, the first step is to make the proper imports into the application:

```
using System.Configuration;
using Microsoft.Web.Services;
using Microsoft.Web.Services.Security;
using System.Security.Cryptography;
using System.Security.Cryptography.Xml;
```

The first namespace that you need to add to your XML Web service consumer application is System.Configuration. It enables programmatic access to the key value stored in the `web.config` file. Also notice that in addition to the two name-spaces from the WSE, you need to import some additional namespaces from the .NET Framework. If you have trouble finding the `System.Security.Cryptography.Xml` namespace, you have to make a reference to the `System.Security.dll` in your project. Once you make this reference, you will then be able to import this namespace into the application.

There are two methods in this class; the first method is `GetEncryptionKey`. It returns an instance of an `EncryptionKey` object.

First, the base key is retrieved from the `web.config` file:

```
string baseKey = ConfigurationSettings.AppSettings["symmetricKey"];
```

Once there is an attempt to retrieve the key that you are going to use from the `web.config` file, there is then a simple check done to see if the key was actually retrieved by checking if the value of `baseKey` is `null` or not. Once the key is retrieved, a byte array called `keyBytes` is given the value of the `baseKey`, which is converted to an array of 8-bit unsigned integers using the `Convert` class.

After the creation of the `keyBytes` byte array, a `SymmetricEncryptionKey` object is instantiated.

```
byte[] keyBytes = Convert.FromBase64String(baseKey);
SymmetricEncryptionKey key = new
    SymmetricEncryptionKey(TripleDES.Create(), keyBytes);
```

Now that you have the `SymmetricEncryptionKey` object in place with the appropriate value, you are almost ready to return this key value from the method. Before that happens, though, you should assign a value to the `KeyInfo` property of the `SymmetricEncryptionKey` class. The `KeyInfo` property is used by the XML Web service provider to identify the name of the `SymmetricEncryption` key being sent. This allows the particular key that you are using to be distinguishable from other similar keys that the provider might receive from other consumers.

To do this, first create an instance of `KeyInfoName` and then give it an appropriate value. The XML Web service provider might at times require that you not only have a specific encryption key when encrypting your SOAP messages, but you might also be asked to provide a specific `KeyInfo` property in order for the encrypted SOAP message to be accepted. In the previous code example, you are creating an instance of the `KeyInfoName` property and giving it a value of `AddEncrypt`. Once assigned, you then need to simply add this particular `KeyInfoName` to the key itself using `AddClause`:

```
KeyInfoName keyName = new KeyInfoName();
keyName.Value  = "AddEncrypt";
key.KeyInfo.AddClause(keyName);
```

Now you have a symmetric key in place that has everything this key needs. In the end, the symmetric key is returned.

The `Button1_Click` method is quite similar to the button click methods from the other chapters that worked with WS-Security. The first step is to create an instantiation of the proxy class that calls the XML Web service. Then you then need to simply get hold of the symmetric key by instantiating an `EncryptionKey` object and assigning it the value that is returned from the `GetEncryptionKey` method call:

```
EncryptionKey key = GetEncryptionKey();
```

Now that you have your encryption key in place, stored as `key`, you can assign this encryption to the SOAP message as shown in the following code snippet:

```
ws.RequestSoapContext.Security.Elements.Add(new EncryptedData(key));
```

Once this has been assigned to the SOAP message, the XML Web service is remotely called in the same manner as you are used to:

```
Label1.Text = serviceProxy.Add(int.Parse(TextBox1.Text),
    int.Parse(TextBox2.Text)).ToString();
```

In the end, this little bit of code will take your SOAP request and encrypt the SOAP body of the message before it is sent onto the XML Web service provider to consume.

LOOKING AT WHAT THE XML WEB SERVICE CONSUMER SENDS

After these methods do their little magic, you might wonder what has happened to the actual SOAP request that was sent to the XML Web service provider. This section takes a look at the SOAP request and then talks about what happened and why. Listing 5-5 shows the actual SOAP request.

Listing 5-5: The encrypted SOAP request

```
<soap:Envelope
 xmlns:soap="http://schemas.xmlsoap.org/soap/envelope/"
 xmlns:xsi="http://www.w3.org/2001/XMLSchema-instance"
 xmlns:xsd="http://www.w3.org/2001/XMLSchema">
   <soap:Header>
     <wsrp:path
      soap:actor="http://schemas.xmlsoap.org/soap/actor/next"
      soap:mustUnderstand="1"
      xmlns:wsrp="http://schemas.xmlsoap.org/rp">
       <wsrp:action>http://www.wiley.com/Add</wsrp:action>
     <wsrp:to>http://localhost/webservice1/Calculator.asmx
     </wsrp:to>
       <wsrp:id>uuid:9cc50b1d-855c-4142-9b62-608f9673a48c</wsrp:id>
     </wsrp:path>
     <wsu:Timestamp
```

```
  xmlns:wsu="http://schemas.xmlsoap.org/ws/2002/07/utility">
    <wsu:Created wsu:Id="Id-c53a4010-13a4-4a41-8590-
    0acc0220ca12">2002-11-06T03:26:53Z</wsu:Created>
    <wsu:Expires wsu:Id="Id-1416284e-9b80-4b53-b547-
    8cfa581ae08c">2002-11-06T03:31:53Z</wsu:Expires>
  </wsu:Timestamp>
  <wsse:Security soap:mustUnderstand="1"
   xmlns:wsse="http://schemas.xmlsoap.org/ws/2002/07/secext">
    <xenc:ReferenceList
    xmlns:xenc="http://www.w3.org/2001/04/xmlenc#">
      <xenc:DataReference URI="#EncryptedContent-e492f789-995d-
      4c8a-b367-4ebdedb2ba89" />
    </xenc:ReferenceList>
  </wsse:Security>
 </soap:Header>
 <soap:Body>
  <xenc:EncryptedData Id="EncryptedContent-e492f789-995d-4c8a-
  b367-4ebdedb2ba89"
  Type="http://www.w3.org/2001/04/xmlenc#Content"
  xmlns:xenc="http://www.w3.org/2001/04/xmlenc#">
   <xenc:EncryptionMethod
    Algorithm="http://www.w3.org/2001/04/xmlenc#tripledes-cbc"
    />
   <KeyInfo xmlns="http://www.w3.org/2000/09/xmldsig#">
     <KeyName>AddEncrypt</KeyName>
   </KeyInfo>
   <xenc:CipherData>
   <xenc:CipherValue>DqLDgPHOa/P7MFqK9/rtkUDQsPo2TD
    /AAqZFzHkhCc/CK809lt3ONBnhlXMUcGrVUAjDCnU8k
    /62eeKhp/BGcr9ZXLByjm89</xenc:CipherValue>
   </xenc:CipherData>
  </xenc:EncryptedData>
 </soap:Body>
</soap:Envelope>
```

This is pretty exciting. As you can tell by looking at the SOAP message, the entire SOAP message is not encrypted, just the SOAP body itself. This is very important and one of the powers behind the WSE and WS-Security. The reason that you don't want to encrypt the entire SOAP message is that you are gong to want to leave parts of the SOAP message unencrypted so that others, such as intermediaries, can look at the pieces in the SOAP header that they are going to need in order to properly route SOAP messages to their appropriate destinations. As you can tell, the <path> and <Timestamp> nodes are legible, which means SOAP intermediaries can act on them.

A CLOSER LOOK AT THE SOAP HEADER

Within the SOAP message, there are a couple of places where encryption informa-tion is in place. The first place we will take a look at the encryption capabilities of this message is in the SOAP header. In addition to the `<path>` and `<Timestamp>` nodes, there is a `<Security>` node. You have been working with this node in the last few chapters; this node in the SOAP header handles all the message credentials, digital signing, and encryption of the SOAP messages. This time, though, there is only information contained within the `<Security>` node that deals with the encryption process. Following is a look of the child elements of this node.

<REFERENCELIST> The `<ReferenceList>` node contains one or more `<DataReference>` nodes.

<DATAREFERENCE> The `<DataReference>` node provides a reference to the part of the SOAP message that is encrypted. This node contains a single attribute, URI:

```
<xenc:DataReference
 URI="#EncryptedContent-e492f789-995d-4c8a-b367-4ebdedb2ba89" />
```

Notice that the value of the URI attribute of the `<DataReference>` child node is an identifier. This identifier is seen once again in the SOAP message. You will find this unique identifier contained as the value of the Id attribute contained within the opening SOAP body:

```
<soap:Body>
     <xenc:EncryptedData Id="EncryptedContent-e492f789-995d-4c8a-
     b367-4ebdedb2ba89"
     Type="http://www.w3.org/2001/04/xmlenc#Content"
     xmlns:xenc="http://www.w3.org/2001/04/xmlenc#">
```

A CLOSER LOOK AT THE SOAP BODY

In addition to the SOAP header containing information about the encryption applied to the message, there is plenty of action in the SOAP body as this is the part of the message that is actually getting encrypted. Let's take a close look at each of the pieces of the encrypted SOAP body to understand how this works.

<ENCRYPTEDDATA> The `<EncryptedData>` node is the replacement for the entire contents of the SOAP body. Not only were the parameter values that were sent into the XML Web service encrypted, but so were all the elements that were within the SOAP body. Therefore, you will notice that contained within the SOAP body, there isn't an `<a>` or `<b>` element from the simple Add WebMethod. Also, as mentioned, the `<EncryptedData>` node contains the ID of the unique identifier, which acts as a reference for which part of the SOAP message is encrypted.

<ENCRYPTEDMETHOD>   The `<EncryptedMethod>` node describes the method that was used to encrypt the SOAP message payload:

```
<xenc:EncryptionMethod
 Algorithm="http://www.w3.org/2001/04/xmlenc#tripledes-cbc" />
```

The method format used in the encryption process is defined within the only attribute, `Algorithm`. This attribute contains a value that specifies that the encryption method applied to this SOAP message is Triple DES encryption.

<KEYINFO>   With the `<KeyInfo>` node, you can uniquely identify the keys that were used in the encryption process. Receivers of an encrypted SOAP message can use the `<KeyInfo>` node to recover the key based upon a name or unique identifier.

<CIPHERDATA>   The `<CipherData>` node simply contains a `<CipherValue>` node.

<CIPHERVALUE>   The `<CipherValue>` node contains the value of data that was encrypted.

Building an XML Web service provider that accepts an encrypted SOAP message

Building an XML Web service provider that accepts encrypted SOAP messages is quite similar to the steps that you took in building the consumer application that sends out an encrypted SOAP message.

Since the example you are working with here uses a shared secret, both the XML Web service consumer applications and the XML Web service provider need to store a copy of the secret for reference when encrypting or decrypting the SOAP message.

MAKING CHANGES TO THE WEB.CONFIG FILE

There are many places to store shared secrets, but similar to the XML Web service consumer application that was just built, you will now build your XML Web service provider in the same manner and store the shared secret in the `web.config` file.

Therefore, in order to get at this shared secret, you need to add the code in Listing 5-6 to your application's `web.config` file.

Listing 5-6: Storing the XML Web service provider's shared secret in the web.config file

```
<?xml version="1.0" encoding="utf-8" ?>
<configuration>

  <appSettings>
    <add key="symmetricKey"
     value="BAA62349A24A77796116785784F54B149" />
```

Continued

Listing 5-6 *(Continued)*

```
    </appSettings>

    <system.web>
        <!-- The rest of the web.config file -->
    </system.web>
</configuration>
```

In addition to storing the shared secret directly in the `web.config` file, you also need to make additional changes to the `web.config` file in order for your application to work with the decryption process.

Also outside of the `<system.web>` nodes, but still contained within the `<configuration>` nodes of the `web.config` file, you have to add the code in Listing 5-7 to the file.

Listing 5-7: Storing information about the decryption process in the web.config file of the XML Web service provider application

```
<microsoft.web.services>
    <security>
        <decryptionKeyProvider
         type="WebService1.DecryptionKeyProvider, WebService1" />
    </security>
</microsoft.web.services>
```

In working with this style of encryption, you have to create a class that will retrieve the shared secret key. This setting in the `web.config` file specifies the class that retrieves the key.

In the example shown in Listing 5-7, the class that retrieves the key for decryption is called `DecryptionKeyProvider` and it is part of the `WebService1` namespace. You will soon see a full listing for this class and will then see how it relates to this setting in the configuration file.

CREATING AN XML WEB SERVICE PROVIDER THAT ACCEPTS ENCRYPTED SOAP MESSAGES

Now that you have the same secret stored somewhere locally within the application, it is time to build the XML Web service provider so that it can accept and interpret the encrypted SOAP body of the SOAP messages that it receives.

The XML Web service provider that you are creating here doesn't do much since we are working to show the power of encrypting SOAP messages and not too concerned about creating any fancy XML Web services to do this with. The XML Web service that you need contains a single WebMethod called `Add` that adds the two parameters that are passed to it and returns this new value back to the XML Web service consumer. Most of the code in this example is used to retrieve the shared secret key that will be used to decrypt the SOAP message. Listing 5-8 shows the entire XML Web service.

Listing 5-8: The XML Web service provider that accepts encrypted SOAP messages

[VB]

```
Imports System.Configuration
Imports Microsoft.Web.Services
Imports Microsoft.Web.Services.Security
Imports System.Security.Cryptography
Imports System.Security.Cryptography.Xml

<WebService(Namespace:="http://www.wiley.com")> _
Public Class Calculator
    Inherits System.Web.Services.WebService


    <WebMethod()> Public Function Add(ByVal a As Integer, ByVal b _
            As Integer) As Integer
        Return (a + b)
    End Function

End Class

Public Class DecryptionKeyProvider
    Implements IDecryptionKeyProvider

    Public Function GetDecryptionKey(ByVal algorithmUri As String, _
            ByVal keyInfo As KeyInfo) As DecryptionKey Implements _
            IDecryptionKeyProvider.GetDecryptionKey

        Dim clause As KeyInfoClause
        For Each clause In keyInfo
            If TypeOf clause Is KeyInfoName Then
                Dim myClause As KeyInfoName = clause
                If myClause.Value = "AddEncrypt" Then
                    Dim keyData As String = _
                        ConfigurationSettings.AppSettings("symmetricKey")

                    If keyData Is Nothing Then
                        Throw New ApplicationException("Symmetric key " & _
                            "not found in configuration.")
                    End If

                    Dim keyBytes As Byte() = _
```

Continued

Listing 5-8 *(Continued)*

```
                    Convert.FromBase64String(keyData)

                Return New SymmetricDecryptionKey _
                    (TripleDES.Create(), keyBytes)
            End If
        Else

            Throw New ApplicationException("Key name not supported.")

        End If

        Return Nothing

    Next
    End Function

End Class
```

[C#]

```csharp
using System;
using System.Collections;
using System.ComponentModel;
using System.Configuration;
using System.Data;
using System.Diagnostics;
using System.Web;
using System.Web.Services;
using System.Xml;
using System.Security.Cryptography;
using System.Security.Cryptography.Xml;
using Microsoft.Web.Services;
using Microsoft.Web.Services.Security;

namespace WebService1
{
  [WebService(Namespace="http://www.wiley.com")]
   public class Calculator : System.Web.Services.WebService
   {
      public Calculator()
      {
         InitializeComponent();
```

```
        }

    [WebMethod]
     public int Add(int a, int b)
     {
        return (a+b);
     }
}

public class DecryptionKeyProvider : IDecryptionKeyProvider
{
    public DecryptionKey GetDecryptionKey(string algorithmUri,
       KeyInfo keyInfo)
    {
       foreach ( KeyInfoClause clause in keyInfo )
       {
          if ( clause is KeyInfoName )
          {
             if ( ((KeyInfoName)clause).Value == "AddEncrypt")
             {
                string keyData =
                ConfigurationSettings.AppSettings["symmetricKey"];

                if ( keyData == null )
                   throw new ApplicationException("Symmetric key not
                      found in configuration.");

                byte[] keyBytes = Convert.FromBase64String(keyData);

                return new SymmetricDecryptionKey
                   (TripleDES.Create(),keyBytes);
             }
             else
             {
                throw new ApplicationException("Key name not
                   supported.");
             }
          }
       }

    return null;

    }

  }
}
```

This application is quite similar to the code that you saw in the XML Web service consumer application earlier in the chapter. Let's take a quick look through the code of this small application to understand how it will decrypt the encrypted SOAP messages that it receives.

The first step as in all .NET applications is to make the proper references to the namespaces that you will be using in the application. In this example, you need to make reference to an additional five namespaces:

```
using System.Configuration;
using Microsoft.Web.Services;
using Microsoft.Web.Services.Security;
using System.Security.Cryptography;
using System.Security.Cryptography.Xml;
```

For the same reasons that you imported the `System.Configuration` namespace into the XML Web service consumer application earlier, you will need to import this namespace into the XML Web service provider application in order to get access to the shared secret key value stored in the `web.config` file. In addition to the WSE namespaces that deal with security, you also need to import the `System.Security.Cryptography` and `System.Security.Cryptography.Xml` namespaces in order to work with encrypted values.

The XML Web service's WebMethod itself is rather simple and not much different than if you weren't dealing with encrypted SOAP messages. Contained within a class called `Calculator` there is only a single WebMethod called `Add`:

```
[WebMethod]
 public int Add(int a, int b)
 {
    return (a+b);
 }
```

For the `Calculator` class itself, this is all that needs to be done. There isn't much there because all the work is being done in this XML Web service is being done in the only other class on this page – the `DecryptionKeyProvider` class.

The sole purpose of the `DecryptionKeyProvider` class is to provide the key value of the shared secret that will be used by the WSE to decrypt the SOAP messages. Remember that the WSE knows where to get the shared secret because it is described in the `web.config` file.

The class that you build that will end up providing the decryption key needs to implement `IDecryptionKeyProvider` as the class `DecryptionKeyProvider` does:

```
public class DecryptionKeyProvider : IDecryptionKeyProvider
 {
 }
```

This class, `DecryptionKeyProvider`, only contains a single method. This method, `GetDecryptionKey`, takes a couple of parameters and returns an instance of the `DecryptionKey` object, which decrypts the SOAP message that is being processed by the WSE.

Then using the `KeyInfo` object, you can identify the keys that were used in the encryption process by the XML Web service consumer. Checks are made to ensure that the `KeyInfoName` is the same as what was specified on the consumer end. If they are the same, the key for decryption is retrieved from the `web.config` file:

```
foreach ( KeyInfoClause clause in keyInfo )
{
   if ( clause is KeyInfoName )
   {
      if ( ((KeyInfoName)clause).Value == "AddEncrypt")
      {
         string keyData =
            ConfigurationSettings.AppSettings["symmetricKey"];
      }
   }
}
```

Once you have the key value that was used in the encryption of the SOAP message, you then convert the shared secret that is of type `String` to a byte array and return an instance of this decryption key that is encrypted using Triple DES encryption:

```
byte[] keyBytes = Convert.FromBase64String(keyData);

return new SymmetricDecryptionKey(TripleDES.Create(),keyBytes);
```

Once this method is called by the WSE, the decryption key is passed back to the WSE where the message is decrypted.

LOOKING AT WHAT THE XML WEB SERVICE PROVIDER SENDS BACK TO THE CONSUMER

You saw the encrypted message that was sent from the XML Web service consumer to the XML Web service provider and how it was encrypted. The XML Web service that was built here simply decrypted the SOAP message that it received. Listing 5-9 shows you what was returned from the WebMethod call.

Listing 5-9: The SOAP response

```
<soap:Envelope
 xmlns:soap="http://schemas.xmlsoap.org/soap/envelope/"
 xmlns:xsi="http://www.w3.org/2001/XMLSchema-instance"
```

Continued

Listing 5-9 *(Continued)*

```
 xmlns:xsd="http://www.w3.org/2001/XMLSchema">
    <soap:Header>
      <wsu:Timestamp
       xmlns:wsu="http://schemas.xmlsoap.org/ws/2002/07/utility">
        <wsu:Created wsu:Id="Id-2cc6e24d-ab9a-4dfa-a977-
         29664587f6f6">2002-11-06T03:26:53Z</wsu:Created>
        <wsu:Expires wsu:Id="Id-7144fdb3-06ff-4d12-94a7-
         21eaaeb2dfdc">2002-11-06T03:31:53Z</wsu:Expires>
      </wsu:Timestamp>
    </soap:Header>
    <soap:Body>
      <AddResponse xmlns="http://www.wiley.com">
        <AddResult>86</AddResult>
      </AddResponse>
    </soap:Body>
</soap:Envelope>
```

Looking at this SOAP response, you will notice that there is nothing encrypted here in this message. It is a normal SOAP response. Just the fact that the message was returned means that the XML Web service, along with the WSE, was able to understand the encrypted SOAP message that it received. The message was received encrypted and after decrypting the message using the shared secret, the XML Web service (with the help of the WSE) returned a simple response to the consumer.

XML Web Services that Decrypt and Encrypt SOAP Messages

Encryption is a powerful tool, whether you are the consumer or the provider. In the example in this chapter, the XML Web service consuming application sent off a SOAP request that had the SOAP body of the message encrypted. This encrypted message was then retrieved by the XML Web service provider. Once retrieved, the encrypted SOAP message was decrypted and a simple SOAP response was sent back to the consumer.

In most cases this won't be the only thing that you will want to do with this ability to encrypt and decrypt SOAP messages. It is great that the SOAP request could be encrypted, but the ability to encrypt is not meant only for the XML Web service consumer. It can also be used by the XML Web service provider or by both the consumer and the provider.

By encrypting both the SOAP request and the SOAP response, you are ensuring a higher degree of security for your XML Web service traffic. For this same example, let's look at the portions of the code in both the consumer and the provider that you will have to change in order to allow you to encrypt both the SOAP request and the SOAP response. Just remember that encrypting both the request and the response means that you also have to decrypt them both.

XML Web service consumer changes

In order to allow your XML Web service consumer application to both encrypt and decrypt SOAP messages that it sends and receives, you need to make some changes to your application so that is has some of the same pieces that the XML Web service provider application has.

First, you have to make the appropriate changes to the `web.config` file using the same code that was shown in Listing 5-7. This will point to a class within your application that takes care of the decryption of the SOAP messages that come back to the consumer application. For instance, Listing 5-10 shows how this might change for your ASP.NET application.

Listing 5-10: Storing information about the decryption process in the web.config file of the XML Web service consumer application

```
<microsoft.web.services>
   <security>
    <decryptionKeyProvider
     type="WebApplication1.DecryptionKeyProvider, WebApplication1"
/>
   </security>
</microsoft.web.services>
```

Once that is in place, you need to add a `DecryptionKeyProvider` class to your ASP.NET application. This class, the same as the `DecryptionKeyProvider` class in the XML Web service provider application, will need to implement `IDecryptionKeyProvider`. This class is exactly the same as the `DecryptionKeyProvider` class that is the XML Web service provider application from Listing 5-8. Once those two items are in place, your XML Web service consumer application is not only ready to send encrypted messages, but it is also ready to receive encrypted message so that these messages can be decrypted and read.

XML Web service provider changes

For security reasons, you'll want your XML Web services to send SOAP responses to consumers encrypted. You are not always going to want the contents of the SOAP responses out there for the world or enterprise to read, and if there is any sensitivity to the data that is being sent, you are going to want to look at encrypting this information using the WSE.

For the `Add()` WebMethod that was shown in this chapter, if you want this WebMethod to not only receive encrypted SOAP messages, but to send encrypted SOAP message as well, then have to make some minor changes to the application.

The shared secret that you were using for decrypting SOAP messages that were received by the WebMethod is already in place in the web.config file. For encrypting SOAP responses, you are going to use the same shared secret key from the web.config file.

You need to make some changes within the WebService class itself. This is the only place in the XML Web service that you are going to have to make changes.

The first change that you have to make in the WebService class is to add a GetEncryptionKey method to the class for the WebMethod to access. In addition to this you have to make some changes to the actual WebMethod itself. Listing 5-11 shows how this might work.

Listing 5-11: Encrypting a SOAP response from an XML Web service's WebMethod

[VB]

```vb
<WebService(Namespace:="http://www.wiley.com")> _
Public Class Calculator
    Inherits System.Web.Services.WebService


    <WebMethod()> Public Function Add(ByVal a As Integer, ByVal b _
            As Integer) As Integer
        Dim responseContext As SoapContext = _
            HttpSoapContext.ResponseContext

        Dim key As EncryptionKey = GetEncryptionKey()

        responseContext.Security.Elements.Add(New EncryptedData(key))

        Return (a + b)
    End Function

    Private Function GetEncryptionKey() As EncryptionKey
        Dim baseKey As String = _
            ConfigurationSettings.AppSettings("symmetricKey")

        If baseKey Is Nothing Then
          Throw New ApplicationException("Symmetric key not " & _
              "found in configuration.")
        End If

        Dim keyBytes As Byte() = Convert.FromBase64String(baseKey)
        Dim key As SymmetricEncryptionKey = New _
```

```
                SymmetricEncryptionKey(TripleDES.Create(), keyBytes)

        Dim keyName As KeyInfoName = New KeyInfoName()
        keyName.Value = "AddEncrypt"
        key.KeyInfo.AddClause(keyName)

        Return key
    End Function

End Class
```

[C#]

```
[WebService(Namespace="http://www.wiley.com")]
 public class Calculator : System.Web.Services.WebService
 {
    public Calculator()
    {
       InitializeComponent();
    }

    [WebMethod]
     public int Add(int a, int b)
     {
        SoapContext responseContext =
           HttpSoapContext.ResponseContext;

        EncryptionKey key = GetEncryptionKey();

        responseContext.Security.Elements.Add(new
           EncryptedData(key));

        return (a+b);
     }

    private EncryptionKey GetEncryptionKey()
    {

       string keyData =
          ConfigurationSettings.AppSettings["symmetricKey"];

       if (keyData == null)
```

Continued

Listing 5-11 *(Continued)*

```
        {
            throw new ApplicationException("Symmetric key not found
                in configuration.");
        }

        byte[] keyBytes = Convert.FromBase64String(keyData);
        SymmetricEncryptionKey key = new
            SymmetricEncryptionKey(TripleDES.Create(), keyBytes);

        KeyInfoName keyName = new KeyInfoName();
        keyName.Value  = "AddEncrypt";
        key.KeyInfo.AddClause(keyName);

        return key;
    }
}
```

The big change to the class itself is that it now contains a method, GetEncryptionKey, which returns the encryption key that will be used in the encryption of the SOAP response.

The other big change in the XML Web service provider is that an instance of the SoapContext object called responseContext is created to deal with the SOAP response from the Web service. Remember that you are going to *encrypt* the SOAP response by working with the object responseContext:

```
SoapContext responseContext = HttpSoapContext.ResponseContext;
```

Once this object is created, the next step is to get the key to encrypt the SOAP response. This value is stored as an EncryptionKey object called key:

```
EncyptionKey key = GetEncryptionKey();
```

Before returning the SOAP response to the consumer, you need to simply add the encryption to the SOAP message:

```
responseContext.Security.Elements.Add(new EncryptedData(key));
```

After this is complete, you can then simply return the value of a+b to the end consumer of the WebMethod. This method will be encrypted just as the SOAP request was encrypted. The encrypted message that was sent from the WebMethod is shown in Listing 5-12.

Listing 5-12: The SOAP response encrypted

```
<soap:Envelope
 xmlns:soap="http://schemas.xmlsoap.org/soap/envelope/"
 xmlns:xsi="http://www.w3.org/2001/XMLSchema-instance"
 xmlns:xsd="http://www.w3.org/2001/XMLSchema">
    <soap:Header>
      <wsu:Timestamp
       xmlns:wsu="http://schemas.xmlsoap.org/ws/2002/07/utility">
        <wsu:Created wsu:Id="Id-a9e29d4b-9660-4a6a-a325-
          93c7025a2569">2002-11-10T04:37:55Z</wsu:Created>
        <wsu:Expires wsu:Id="Id-fdedf67e-4209-4325-85a0-
          cd432ec6ee19">2002-11-10T04:42:55Z</wsu:Expires>
      </wsu:Timestamp>
      <wsse:Security soap:mustUnderstand="1"
       xmlns:wsse="http://schemas.xmlsoap.org/ws/2002/07/secext">
        <xenc:ReferenceList
         xmlns:xenc="http://www.w3.org/2001/04/xmlenc#">
          <xenc:DataReference URI="#EncryptedContent-62470e28-1bad-
            4904-af63-4368d6b8f52d" />
        </xenc:ReferenceList>
      </wsse:Security>
    </soap:Header>
    <soap:Body>
      <xenc:EncryptedData Id="EncryptedContent-62470e28-1bad-4904-
       af63-4368d6b8f52d"
       Type="http://www.w3.org/2001/04/xmlenc#Content"
       xmlns:xenc="http://www.w3.org/2001/04/xmlenc#">
        <xenc:EncryptionMethod
         Algorithm="http://www.w3.org/2001/04/xmlenc#tripledes-cbc"
         />
        <KeyInfo xmlns="http://www.w3.org/2000/09/xmldsig#">
          <KeyName>AddEncrypt</KeyName>
        </KeyInfo>
        <xenc:CipherData>
        <xenc:CipherValue>QJuOiMjtFG3MZfSa72tgPSaiOze3ZDcSzBUE/
          DHg/eOG1/1GxYx85fKIUaKdv6xaud/b3LI8V/8EIgQjaOeV/
          4BKOhBKYLCQ7qdwqMRNyK+LyiWkb1gsW/KcDzGhvU7o
        </xenc:CipherValue>
        </xenc:CipherData>
      </xenc:EncryptedData>
    </soap:Body>
</soap:Envelope>
```

As you can tell, this is much the same as the encrypted SOAP request that was received by the Web service.

Now that you know how to encrypt SOAP messages from either the consumer or the provider application, you need to analyze the data being sent and received and decide whether the extra security needs to be applied to these requests and responses.

You, as a builder of XML Web services, are the one that can enforce whether the SOAP requests and the responses are encrypted. You can easily build your WebMethods so that they do not return a value if the SOAP body of the SOAP requests are not encrypted.

Other Ways of Storing Shared Secrets

There are of course other ways of storing this shared secret than storing it in the web.config file. You might find it better to store it inline, within SQL Server or any other database. You also may want to use the shared secret mechanism as a way to force others to register with you before they can use the XML Web service that you have developed. In any case, you should explore the alternatives.

Storing shared secrets inline

One option is to store shared secrets that you are going to use for encryption *inline*, meaning directly in the code of your application. Be forewarned that this isn't the most secure way of storing secrets, but it is an option.

If you are going to take this approach, you can do it either in the XML Web service consumer application or within the XML Web service itself. Listing 5-13 shows the GetEncryptionKey method from the consumer application.

Listing 5-13: Storing the shared secret inline within the GetEncryptionKey() method

[VB]

```
Private Function GetEncryptionKey() As EncryptionKey
   Dim keyData As String = "0C854B823582F7F8F4E16F5E8B154916"

   Dim keyBytes As Byte() = Convert.FromBase64String(keyData)

   Dim key As SymmetricEncryptionKey = New _
      SymmetricEncryptionKey(TripleDES.Create(), keyBytes)

   Dim keyName As KeyInfoName = New KeyInfoName()
   keyName.Value = "AddEncrypt"
```

```
    key.KeyInfo.AddClause(keyName)

    Return key
End Function
```

[C#]

```csharp
private EncryptionKey GetEncryptionKey()
{
    string keyData = "0C854B823582F7F8F4E16F5E8B154916";

    byte[] keyBytes = Convert.FromBase64String(keyData);

    SymmetricEncryptionKey key = new
        SymmetricEncryptionKey( TripleDES.Create(), keyBytes );

    KeyInfoName keyName = new KeyInfoName();
    keyName.Value  = "AddEncrypt";
    key.KeyInfo.AddClause(keyName);

    return key;
}
```

This being private-key encryption or symmetric encryption, the XML Web service will also have to get this key in some manner and it is not required that the key be stored in the same way. The only requirement is that the same key needs to be used. It just needs to be stored in such a way that it is retrievable at the time that it is needed.

If you are going to store this private key inline within the XML Web service, you need to construct your GetDecryptionKey method as shown in Listing 5-14.

Listing 5-14: Storing the shared secret inline within the GetDecryptionKey() method

[VB]

```vb
Public Function GetDecryptionKey(ByVal algorithmUri As String, _
            ByVal keyInfo As KeyInfo) As DecryptionKey Implements _
            IDecryptionKeyProvider.GetDecryptionKey

    Dim clause As KeyInfoClause
    For Each clause In keyInfo
        If TypeOf clause Is KeyInfoName Then
            Dim myClause As KeyInfoName = clause
```

Continued

Listing 5-14 *(Continued)*

```
        If myClause.Value = "AddEncrypt" Then
            Dim keyData As String =
                "0C854B823582F7F8F4E16F5E8B154916"

            Dim keyBytes As Byte() = _
                Convert.FromBase64String(keyData)

            Return New SymmetricDecryptionKey _
                (TripleDES.Create(), keyBytes)
            End If
        Else

            Throw New ApplicationException("Key name not supported.")

        End If

        Return Nothing

    Next
End Function
```

[C#]

```
public DecryptionKey GetDecryptionKey(string algorithmUri,
    KeyInfo keyInfo)
{
    foreach ( KeyInfoClause clause in keyInfo)
    {
        if ( clause is KeyInfoName )
        {
            if (((KeyInfoName)clause).Value == "AddEncrypt")
            {
                string keyData = "0C854B823582F7F8F4E16F5E8B154916";

                byte[] keyBytes = Convert.FromBase64String(keyData);
                SymmetricDecryptionKey key = new SymmetricDecryptionKey(
                    TripleDES.Create(), keyBytes );

                return key;
            }
            else
            {
                throw new ApplicationException("Key name not
                    supported.");
```

```
        }
      }
    }
      return null;
}
```

There are many different options on how to store a shared secret. Next, we'll take a look at an example that shows you how to use SQL Server to store your private keys. This is one of the best places that you can store these shared secrets.

Storing shared secrets in SQL Server

From all the available options of where you are able to store your "shared secrets," storing them in SQL Server will be one of they most secure methods that you can employ. Of course, there is a lot you can do to lock down SQL Server as well as work to make it as secure as possible from a network standpoint, but this section will just show you how to work with stored private keys that might be housed within this database.

Similar to the approaches mentioned earlier of storing these private keys inline or within the web.config file, you can employ these methods from within the client application or within the XML Web service. Listing 5-15 shows you how to change the GetEncryptionKey() method on the client in order for your client application to grab the private key from SQL Server.

Listing 5-15: Storing the shared secret within SQL Server

[VB]

```
Private Function GetEncryptionKey() As EncryptionKey
   Dim connStr As String = "Data Source=localhost; Initial
      Catalog=WSE; User id=sa"
   Dim conn As New SqlConnection(connStr)
   conn.Open()

   Dim cmd As New SqlCommand("Select Pkey From WSE_Key", conn)

   Dim myDataReader As SqlDataReader
   myDataReader = _
      cmd.ExecuteReader(CommandBehavior.SingleResult)

   If myDataReader.Read() Then
      Dim keyData As String = myDataReader(0).ToString()

      Dim keyBytes As Byte() = Convert.FromBase64String(keyData)
```

Continued

Listing 5-15 *(Continued)*

```vbnet
        Dim key As SymmetricEncryptionKey = New _
            SymmetricEncryptionKey(TripleDES.Create(), keyBytes)

        Dim keyName As KeyInfoName = New KeyInfoName()
        keyName.Value = "AddEncrypt"
        key.KeyInfo.AddClause(keyName)

        Return key
    Else
        Throw New Exception("Private Key is not present in " & _
            "system.")
    End If

    conn.Close()

End Function
```

[C#]

```csharp
private EncryptionKey GetEncryptionKey()
{
    string connStr = "Data Source=localhost; Initial
        Catalog=WSE; User id=sa";
    SqlConnection conn = new SqlConnection(connStr);
    conn.Open();

    SqlCommand cmd = new SqlCommand("Select Pkey From
        WSE_Key", conn);

    SqlDataReader myDataReader;
    myDataReader =
        cmd.ExecuteReader(CommandBehavior.SingleResult);

    if (myDataReader.Read())
    {
        string keyData = myDataReader[0].ToString();

        byte[] keyBytes = Convert.FromBase64String(keyData);

        SymmetricEncryptionKey key = new
            SymmetricEncryptionKey( TripleDES.Create(), keyBytes );

        KeyInfoName keyName = new KeyInfoName();
```

```
      keyName.Value  = "AddEncrypt";
      key.KeyInfo.AddClause(keyName);

      return key;
  }
  else
  {
     throw new Exception("Private key is not present in
        system.");
  }

  conn.Close();
}
```

Then since we are dealing with private key encryption, the XML Web service provider will also need to have a copy of the private key that was used to do the encryption. If the XML Web service provider want to also provide the decryption key from SQL Server it would do so in the following manner as shown here in Listing 5-16.

Listing 5-16: Storing the shared secret within SQL Server for decrypting the SOAP message

[VB]

```
Public Function GetDecryptionKey(ByVal algorithmUri As String, _
        ByVal keyInfo As KeyInfo) As DecryptionKey Implements _
        IDecryptionKeyProvider.GetDecryptionKey

  Dim clause As KeyInfoClause
  For Each clause In keyInfo
    If TypeOf clause Is KeyInfoName Then
       Dim myClause As KeyInfoName = clause
       If myClause.Value = "AddEncrypt" Then

          Dim connStr As String = "Data Source=localhost; Initial
             Catalog=WSE; User id=sa"
          Dim conn As New SqlConnection(connStr)
          conn.Open()

          Dim cmd As New SqlCommand("Select Pkey From WSE_Key", _
             conn)

          Dim myDataReader As SqlDataReader
          myDataReader = _
```

Continued

Listing 5-16 *(Continued)*

```
              cmd.ExecuteReader(CommandBehavior.SingleResult)

        If myDataReader.Read() Then
            Dim keyData As String = myDataReader(0).ToString()

            Dim keyBytes As Byte() = _
                Convert.FromBase64String(keyData)

            Return New SymmetricDecryptionKey _
                (TripleDES.Create(), keyBytes)
        End If

        conn.Close()
    Else

        Throw New ApplicationException("Key name not supported.")

    End If

    Return Nothing

    Next
End Function
```

[C#]

```
public DecryptionKey GetDecryptionKey(string algorithmUri,
    KeyInfo keyInfo)
{
    foreach ( KeyInfoClause clause in keyInfo)
    {
        if ( clause is KeyInfoName )
        {
            if (((KeyInfoName)clause).Value == "AddEncrypt")
            {
                string connStr = "Data Source=localhost; Initial
                    Catalog=WSE; User id=sa";
                SqlConnection conn = new SqlConnection(connStr);
                conn.Open();

                SqlCommand cmd = new SqlCommand("Select Pkey From
                    WSE_Key", conn);

                SqlDataReader myDataReader;
```

```
        myDataReader =
           cmd.ExecuteReader(CommandBehavior.SingleResult);

        if (myDataReader.Read())
        {
           string keyData = myDataReader[0].ToString();

           byte[] keyBytes = Convert.FromBase64String(keyData);
           SymmetricDecryptionKey key = new
              SymmetricDecryptionKey(TripleDES.Create(),
              keyBytes );

           return key;
        }

        conn.close();

     }
     else
     {
        throw new ApplicationException("Key name not
           supported.");
     }
   }
  }
  return null;
}
```

As mentioned earlier, there are so many different ways in which you can store these shared secrets. In the end, you will employ the method that works best for the security and performance models of your application and the demands of your integrators.

Encrypting SOAP Messages Using an X.509 Certificate

So far in this chapter, you have been looking at how to encrypt either the SOAP request or the SOAP response using symmetric encryption, otherwise known as private-key encryption. As you learned, this is because the keys used to encrypt and decrypt the SOAP request or the SOAP response are known only by the XML Web service consumer and the XML Web service provider.

You can also use another type of encryption to encrypt and decrypt your SOAP messages, known as asymmetric or public-key encryption.

Just as you can use X.509 certificates to apply credentials to your SOAP messages, you can also use them for encrypting your SOAP messages. The first part of this chapter used a string key to encrypt the SOAP message; now we will take a look at how to use X.509 certificates to apply encryption.

You will notice that building an XML Web service consumer using certificates is quite similar to that of building an XML Web service consumer that uses private-key encryption. Listing 5-17 shows you an example of an XML Web service consumer that encrypts SOAP requests from the consumer. This ASP.NET page is the same as the page that was used earlier in this chapter, but it includes a drop-down list that allows you to choose a certificate that you will use for the encryption.

Listing 5-17: The ASP.NET page

```
<%@ Page language="c#" Codebehind="Add.aspx.cs"
 AutoEventWireup="false" Inherits="WebService1.Add" %>
<!DOCTYPE HTML PUBLIC "-//W3C//DTD HTML 4.0 Transitional//EN" >
<HTML>
    <HEAD>
        <title>Add with Certificates</title>
    </HEAD>
    <body>
    <form id="Add" method="post" runat="server">
        <P>
        <asp:DropDownList id="DropDownList1"
            runat="server"></asp:DropDownList></P>
        <P>
        <asp:TextBox id="TextBox1" runat="server"></asp:TextBox></P>
        <P>
        <asp:TextBox id="TextBox2" runat="server"></asp:TextBox></P>
        <P>
        <asp:Button id="Button1" runat="server"
         Text="Add"></asp:Button></P>
        <P>
        <asp:Label id="Label1" runat="server"></asp:Label></P>
    </form>
    </body>
</HTML>
```

Remember that even though you are allowed to select whatever certificate you want from the drop-down list, you need to choose the certificate that the XML Web service will have the private key for so that the SOAP message can be decrypted.

Listing 5-18 shows the code-behind for this simple ASP.NET page.

Listing 5-18: The code-behind for the ASP.NET page that encrypts a SOAP request

[VB]

```vb
Imports Microsoft.Web.Services
Imports Microsoft.Web.Services.Security
Imports Microsoft.Web.Services.Security.Cryptography
Imports Microsoft.Web.Services.Security.Cryptography.X509

Public Class WSE_Consumer
    Inherits System.Web.UI.Page
    Protected WithEvents Button1 As System.Web.UI.WebControls.Button
    Protected WithEvents DropDownList1 As
        System.Web.UI.WebControls.DropDownList
    Protected WithEvents TextBox1 As
        System.Web.UI.WebControls.TextBox
    Protected WithEvents TextBox2 As
        System.Web.UI.WebControls.TextBox
    Protected WithEvents Label1 As System.Web.UI.WebControls.Label

Private Sub Page_Load(ByVal sender As System.Object, ByVal e As
        System.EventArgs) Handles MyBase.Load
        Dim myCertStore As X509CertificateStore
        myCertStore = X509CertificateStore.
            CurrentUserStore(X509CertificateStore.MyStore)

        myCertStore.OpenRead()

        Dim Cert As X509Certificate
        For Each Cert In myCertStore.Certificates
            DropDownList1.Items.Add(Cert.GetName())
        Next
    End Sub

Private Sub Button1_Click(ByVal sender As System.Object, ByVal e
        As System.EventArgs) Handles Button1.Click
        Dim ws As New localhost.Calculator()

        Dim myCertStore As X509CertificateStore
        myCertStore = X509CertificateStore.
            CurrentUserStore(X509CertificateStore.MyStore)
        myCertStore.OpenRead()

        Dim myCert As X509Certificate
```

Continued

Listing 5-18 *(Continued)*

```
        myCert = myCertStore.
          Certificates(DropDownList1.SelectedIndex)

        If (myCert.SupportsDataEncryption And _
            myCert.PrivateKeyAvailable) Then
          Dim myCertToken as X509SecurityToken = New _
            X509SecurityToken(myCert)

          ws.RequestSoapContext.Security.Elements.Add(New _
            EncryptedData(myCertToken))
          Label1.Text = ws.Add(TextBox1.Text.ToString(), _
            TextBox2.Text.ToString())
      End Sub
End Class
```

`[C#]`

```
using System;
using System.Collections;
using System.ComponentModel;
using System.Data;
using System.Drawing;
using System.Web;
using System.Web.SessionState;
using System.Web.UI;
using System.Web.UI.WebControls;
using System.Web.UI.HtmlControls;
using Microsoft.Web.Services;
using Microsoft.Web.Services.Security;
using Microsoft.Web.Services.Security.Cryptography;
using Microsoft.Web.Services.Security.Cryptography.X509;

namespace WebApplication1
{
  public class WSE_Consumer : System.Web.UI.Page
  {
    protected System.Web.UI.WebControls.DropDownList DropDownList1;
    protected System.Web.UI.WebControls.TextBox TextBox1;
    protected System.Web.UI.WebControls.TextBox TextBox2;
    protected System.Web.UI.WebControls.Button Button1;
    protected System.Web.UI.WebControls.Label Label1;

    private void Page_Load(object sender, System.EventArgs e)
    {
```

```
        X509CertificateStore myCertStore;
        myCertStore = X509CertificateStore.
        CurrentUserStore(X509CertificateStore.MyStore);

        myCertStore.OpenRead();

        foreach (X509Certificate Cert in myCertStore.Certificates)
        {
            DropDownList1.Items.Add(Cert.GetName());
        }
    }

    private void Button1_Click(object sender, System.EventArgs e)
    {
        localhost.Calculator ws = new localhost.Calculator();

        X509CertificateStore myCertStore;
        myCertStore = X509CertificateStore.
            CurrentUserStore(X509CertificateStore.MyStore);
        myCertStore.OpenRead();

        X509Certificate myCert;
        myCert = (X509Certificate)myCertStore.
            Certificates[DropDownList1.SelectedIndex];

        if (myCert.SupportsDataEncryption &&
            myCert.PrivateKeyAvailable)
        {
            X509SecurityToken myCertToken = new
                X509SecurityToken(myCert);

            ws.RequestSoapContext.Security.Elements.Add(new
                EncryptedData(myCertToken));

            Label1.Text = ws.Add(int.Parse(TextBox1.Text),
             int.Parse(TextBox2.Text)).ToString();
        }
    }
}
}
```

This ability to use certificates is not much different than using certificates in applying credentials or applying a digital signature to your SOAP messages. The code line that is different involves shaping the RequestSoapContext, as shown here:

```
ws.RequestSoapContext.Security.Elements.Add(New _
    EncryptedData(myCertToken))
```

The other difference is that, before you work with the SOAP request, the SupportsDataEncryption property checks to ensure that the certificate supports data encryption):

```
If (myCert.SupportsDataEncryption And _
    myCert.PrivateKeyAvailable) Then
```

Now the your consumer is ready to encrypt the SOAP message, you need to make your XML Web service ready for decrypting the SOAP message using the private key of the certificate. You do this simply by storing the certificate that the SOAP message was encrypted in the local machine's certificate store.

Encrypting and Decrypting Custom SOAP Header Elements

Just as it is possible to digitally sign any custom SOAP header extensions, it is also possible to encrypt these custom extensions.

Because you can pack the SOAP header with your own custom constructions, you invariably will want to encrypt this construction along with the SOAP body of the SOAP request or SOAP response.

It is actually quite an easy task to encrypt any custom constructions that you might have in your SOAP headers using the WSE. The following sections look at how you might accomplish this.

The XML Web service provider

The first step is to create a custom construction within the XML Web service provider that will be a required part of every SOAP header of all the SOAP requests that the XML Web service receives. To make it simple, use the same class that you created in the last chapter where you needed to digitally sign your custom SOAP header constructions. Therefore, in building your XML Web service, you need to make sure that you have made the appropriate changes to the web.config file and that your file makes the proper namespace imports as shown in Listing 4-9 (from the last chapter).

The most important namespaces are Microsoft.Web.Services and Microsoft. Web.Services.Security. They allow you to decrypt the SOAP requests that you receive. The next namespaces that you need to pay attention to are the System. Web.Services.Protocols namespace, in order to create a class that inherits from the SoapHeader class, and the System.Xml.Serialization namespace so that you can apply an XmlAttribute to one of the fields within the class you will create.

After you have made the proper namespace imports into your file, you then need to create a class that inherits from the `SoapHeader` class. Listing 5-19 shows you an example of how this class should be constructed. Please note that this is the same class that was presented in Listing 4-10 in the last chapter.

Listing 5-19: The class that extends the SOAP header

[VB]

```vb
Public Class PersonalInformation
    Inherits SoapHeader

    <XmlAttribute("Id", _
    Namespace:="http://schemas.xmlsoap.org/ws/2002/07/utility")> _
    Public Id As String

    Public Name As String
    Public EmailAddress As String
End Class
```

[C#]

```csharp
public class PersonalInformation: SoapHeader
 {
[XmlAttribute("Id",
Namespace="http://schemas.xmlsoap.org/ws/2002/07/utility")]
public string Id;

  public string Name;
  public string EmailAddress;
 }
```

Remember that the `Id` field should always be present in this custom construction because it will be used as an attribute of your custom element that will be placed within the SOAP header. The consumer will have to assign a value to this `Id` field so that the WSE can find the element and all of its child elements and apply encryption to these items. You will see this shortly.

The next step is to create a WebMethod that will work with your custom class. For this, you will still have a WebMethod that does a simple add calculation, but at the same time, it will require that each SOAP request assign a value to the `EmailAddress` field of the custom class that you created. You will find an example of this in Listing 5-20.

Listing 5-20: The WSE_Encrypt.asmx Web service

[VB]

```vb
<WebService(Namespace:="http://www.wiley.com")> _
Public Class WSE_Encrypt
    Inherits System.Web.Services.WebService

    Public PersonalInformation As PersonalInformation

<WebMethod(), SoapHeader("PersonalInformation")> _
    Public Function Add(ByVal a As Integer, ByVal b _
            As Integer) As Integer

        PersonalInformation.MustUnderstand = True

        Dim EmailRegex As Regex = _
            New Regex("([\w-]+@([\w-]+\.)+[\w-]+)")
        Dim M As Match = _
            EmailRegex.Match(PersonalInformation.EmailAddress)

        If M.Success Then
            PersonalInformation.DidUnderstand = True
        Else
            PersonalInformation.DidUnderstand = False
        End If

        Return (a+b)
    End Function
End Class
```

[C#]

```csharp
[WebService(Namespace="http://www.wiley.com")]
 public class WSE_Encrypt: System.Web.Services.WebService
 {
  public PersonalInformation PersonalInformation;

  [WebMethod]
  [SoapHeader("PersonalInformation")]
  public int Add(int a, int b)
  {
   PersonalInformation.MustUnderstand = true;

   Regex EmailRegex = new Regex("([\w-]+@([\w-]+\.)+[\w-]+)");
```

```
    Match M = EmailRegex.Match(PersonalInformation.EmailAddress);

    If (M.Success)
    {
        PersonalInformation.DidUnderstand = true;
    }
    else
    {
        PersonalInformation.DidUnderstand = false;
    }

    return (a+b);
    }
}
```

Now your XML Web service file should contain two classes: the custom class that you built that inherits from the `SoapHeader` class, and the Web service itself. Once these two classes are in place, you need to create a class that implements `IDecryptionKeyProvider` (review Listing 5-8). Also remember to register this class as needed in the `web.config` file so that the SOAP requests can be properly decrypted.

Now that you have your XML Web service all ready to accept decrypted SOAP requests, you can construct the client application that will be your XML Web service consumer.

The XML Web service consumer

Once the XML Web service is in place, you can go ahead and build the client application that will not only encrypt the SOAP body of the SOAP request, but will also have the custom `<PersonalInformation>` section as required. The payload of this element will be encrypted as well along with the SOAP body.

The first step is to make the necessary changes to the `web.config` file as you did earlier in this chapter from Listing 5-2. Also remember to make the proper Web reference to the XML Web service that you are trying to consume and change the proxy class so that it inherits from `Microsoft.Web.Services.WebServices ClientProtocol`.

The next step is to create an `.aspx` page that is the same as the one specified in Listing 5-1. This page has two textboxes, a Button control, and a Label control. The idea is that the user will enter a number into each of the textboxes and click the button, thereby invoking the XML Web service and displaying the result from the XML Web service call in the Label control at the bottom of the page.

Now that you have the `web.config` file and the proxy class all in place, you can build the code-behind for the `.aspx` page. There will be basically two functions within the code-behind for this page. One is the button-click event and the other is a function that gets the encryption key that will be used in the encryption process.

Since we already have developed the encryption retrieval function in this chapter, you can use the same GetEncryptionKey function that is used in Listing 5-4.

For the button-click event, use the code that is shown in Listing 5-21.

Listing 5-21: The Button1_Click event that will encrypt the SOAP body
and parts of the SOAP header

[VB]

```
Private Sub Button1_Click(ByVal sender As System.Object, _
    ByVal e As System.EventArgs) Handles Button1.Click

        Dim ws As New localhost.WSE_Encrypt()
        Dim wsHeader As New localhost.PersonalInformation()

        wsHeader.Name = "Bill Evjen"
        wsHeader.EmailAddress = "evjen@yahoo.com"
        wsHeader.Id = "Id:05d2518d-d6db-481f-846d-2e8872b6e56d"

        ws.PersonalInfoValue = wsHeader

        Dim key As EncryptionKey = GetEncryptionKey()
        Dim encData1 As EncryptedData = New EncryptedData(key)
        Dim encData2 As EncryptedData = New EncryptedData(key, _
            "#Id:05d2518d-d6db-481f-846d-2e8872b6e56d")

        ws.RequestSoapContext.Security.Elements.Add(encData1)
        ws.RequestSoapContext.Security.Elements.Add(encData2)

        Label1.Text = ws.Add(TextBox1.Text.ToString(), _
            TextBox2.Text.ToString())
End Sub
```

[C#]

```
private void Button1_Click(object sender, System.EventArgs e)
{
    localhost.WSE_Encrypt ws = new localhost.WSE_Encrypt();
    localhost.PersonalInformation wsHeader = new
        localhost.PersonalInformation();

    wsHeader.Name = "Bill Evjen";
    wsHeader.EmailAddress = "evjen@yahoo.com";
    wsHeader.Id = "Id:05d2518d-d6db-481f-846d-2e8872b6e56d";
```

```
    ws.PersonalInfoValue = wsHeader;

    EncryptionKey key = GetEncryptionKey();
    EncryptedData encData1 = new EncryptedData(key);
    EncryptedData encData2 = new EncryptedData(key,
        "#Id:05d2518d-d6db-481f-846d-2e8872b6e56d");

    ws.RequestSoapContext.Security.Elements.Add(encData1);
    ws.RequestSoapContext.Security.Elements.Add(encData2);

    Label1.Text = ws.Add(int.Parse(TextBox1.Text),
        int.Parse(TextBox2.Text)).ToString();
}
```

Now let's examine the code for this event. First, an instance of the WebMethod is created. An instantiation of the custom class that is required by the XML Web service provider is also created:

```
Dim ws As New localhost.WSE_Encrypt()
Dim wsHeader As New localhost.PersonalInformation()
```

After this, you simply populate the fields of the PersonalInformation object. The two most important fields to pay attention to here are the EmailAddress field and the Id field. The PersonalInformation object is a required part of every SOAP header, and the value of EmailAddress is validated against a regular expression and therefore has to be a valid construction. It is also important to give the Id field a unique identifier so that the WSE can find the serialized PersonalInformation object within the SOAP header and apply the encryption to it using the encryption key for the GetEncryptionKey method. The value of the Id field needs to be of type xsd:Id. After these fields are populated, you can assign them as a value that you will be passing along with your SOAP request:

```
wsHeader.Name = "Bill Evjen"
wsHeader.EmailAddress = "evjen@yahoo.com"
wsHeader.Id = "Id:05d2518d-d6db-481f-846d-2e8872b6e56d"

ws.PersonalInfoValue = wsHeader
```

After this is all set, you need to create an instance of the EncryptionKey class. This class holds the cryptographic key that encrypts the data of the SOAP body and the PersonalInformation object that will be held in the SOAP header. The value assigned to this instance of the EncryptionKey class contains the value that is retrieved from the GetEncryptionKey method call:

```
Dim key As EncryptionKey = GetEncryptionKey()
```

Once the encryption key is in place, you then have to specify all the pieces of the SOAP message that you need to encrypt using this key. These pieces of the SOAP message are referred to as *encrypted data objects*. In the previous example, the first instance of the `EncryptedData` object simply encrypts the entire SOAP body as was done earlier in this chapter. The second instance of the `EncryptedData` object, `encData2`, is more interesting. This instance not only uses the key that will be used in the encryption process, but there is also a reference made to the unique `Id` that was used for the instance of the `PersonalInformation` object that is being placed in the SOAP header. Please note that the `Id` is preceded by a number sign (#). With this reference, the WSE can look through the SOAP request that is being constructed and encrypt the section of the message that contains that specific `Id`:

```
Dim encData1 As EncryptedData = New EncryptedData(key)
Dim encData2 As EncryptedData = New EncryptedData(key, _
   "#Id:05d2518d-d6db-481f-846d-2e8872b6e56d")
```

Now that the encryption key has been retrieved and the pieces of the SOAP request that you want encrypted have been targeted, you can assign the following references to the outgoing SOAP request that the WSE is constructing:

```
ws.RequestSoapContext.Security.Elements.Add(encData1)
ws.RequestSoapContext.Security.Elements.Add(encData2)
```

After these references are made, you can simply invoke the XML Web service and the result will be displayed in the ASP.NET page's Label control.

Next, take a look at the SOAP message that the client application sent to the XML Web service.

Looking at the SOAP request

The client application populated the `PersonalInformation` object and made this a part of the SOAP message by placing this object within the SOAP header of the SOAP request. Then using the same encryption key, the client application used the WSE to encrypt two parts of the SOAP request message. The first part was the serialized instance of the `PersonalInformation` object that resides within the SOAP header and the second encrypted section of the SOAP message was the SOAP body itself.

Listing 5-22 shows the entire SOAP request that was sent from the client application. The two encrypted sections of the message are shown in bold.

Listing 5-22: The encrypted SOAP request

```
<soap:Envelope
xmlns:soap="http://schemas.xmlsoap.org/soap/envelope/"
 xmlns:xsi="http://www.w3.org/2001/XMLSchema-instance"
 xmlns:xsd="http://www.w3.org/2001/XMLSchema">
```

```
<soap:Header>
  <PersonalInformation
   d3p1:Id="Id:05d2518d-d6db-481f-846d-2e8872b6e56d"
   xmlns:d3p1="http://schemas.xmlsoap.org/ws/2002/07/utility"
   xmlns="http://www.wiley.com">
    <xenc:EncryptedData
     Id="EncryptedContent-2c328da0-9265-4b15-973a-bbed816b50be"
     Type="http://www.w3.org/2001/04/xmlenc#Content"
     xmlns:xenc="http://www.w3.org/2001/04/xmlenc#">
      <xenc:EncryptionMethod
       Algorithm="http://www.w3.org/2001/04/xmlenc#tripledes-cbc"
       />
      <KeyInfo xmlns="http://www.w3.org/2000/09/xmldsig#">
        <KeyName>AddEncrypt</KeyName>
      </KeyInfo>
      <xenc:CipherData>
        <xenc:CipherValue>
         LgV3ZfQk8ge+E23i39LtrjIIfKrz02+xnJ6HbYe894P1dAkXDRiHu
         4n+OlRjhUv+dv2VIpBviCiqHKD6gq2f7bNPQqiMmuW+9p33
         FVK/OOGfA2Rwb14+ZPzsUcl/ttPg1vcuabeRNN1WMhx+Nc6
         9MIpE8Ilq6HKxklyrzrrPpaxToBOcje/9zw==
        </xenc:CipherValue>
      </xenc:CipherData>
    </xenc:EncryptedData>
  </PersonalInformation>
  <wsrp:path
   soap:actor="http://schemas.xmlsoap.org/soap/actor/next"
   soap:mustUnderstand="1"
   xmlns:wsrp="http://schemas.xmlsoap.org/rp">
    <wsrp:action>http://www.wiley.com/Add</wsrp:action>
    <wsrp:to>http://localhost/WSE1/WSE_Encrypt.asmx</wsrp:to>
    <wsrp:id>uuid:6d6f97a6-cda3-4a15-aa22-9c038b33a8ab</wsrp:id>
  </wsrp:path>
  <wsu:Timestamp
   xmlns:wsu="http://schemas.xmlsoap.org/ws/2002/07/utility">
    <wsu:Created>2002-12-03T21:39:45Z</wsu:Created>
    <wsu:Expires>2002-12-03T21:44:45Z</wsu:Expires>
  </wsu:Timestamp>
  <wsse:Security soap:mustUnderstand="1"
   xmlns:wsse="http://schemas.xmlsoap.org/ws/2002/07/secext">
    <xenc:ReferenceList
     xmlns:xenc="http://www.w3.org/2001/04/xmlenc#">
```

Continued

Listing 5-22 *(Continued)*

```
                <xenc:DataReference
                URI="#EncryptedContent-2c328da0-9265-4b15-973a-
                bbed816b50be" />
            </xenc:ReferenceList>
            <xenc:ReferenceList
              xmlns:xenc="http://www.w3.org/2001/04/xmlenc#">
                <xenc:DataReference URI="#EncryptedContent-6896d0e2-3ba2-
                418a-bca6-51a6454495dd" />
            </xenc:ReferenceList>
        </wsse:Security>
    </soap:Header>
<soap:Body
        xmlns:wsu="http://schemas.xmlsoap.org/ws/2002/07/utility"
        wsu:Id="Id-01535791-6526-4f15-bad1-c4c4145b039d">
        <xenc:EncryptedData
        Id="EncryptedContent-6896d0e2-3ba2-418a-bca6-51a6454495dd"
        Type="http://www.w3.org/2001/04/xmlenc#Content"
        xmlns:xenc="http://www.w3.org/2001/04/xmlenc#">
            <xenc:EncryptionMethod
            Algorithm="http://www.w3.org/2001/04/xmlenc#tripledes-cbc"
/>
            <KeyInfo xmlns="http://www.w3.org/2000/09/xmldsig#">
                <KeyName>AddEncrypt</KeyName>
            </KeyInfo>
            <xenc:CipherData>
                <xenc:CipherValue>
                UgurquUuqjlYQ+IKzTIJo7w63We3HxeUa7MHIV
                xbx8dNKtcPk1S2ziFT/+mwiGdXAbcKQsAQCApM
                mPMYNFPfz1D5cmAzrV5g</xenc:CipherValue>
            </xenc:CipherData>
        </xenc:EncryptedData>
    </soap:Body>
</soap:Envelope>
```

You will notice after looking at the two encrypted sections of the SOAP request that the information that describes the encryption key used to encrypt the section is defined within the `<KeyInfo>` element. Both encrypted sections of the message are using the same key as defined by the `<KeyName>` element. In this case, they are using an encryption key with the key name of AddEncrypt.

The next section looks at how to again encrypt two sections of your SOAP messages, but this time using separate encryption keys.

Using Two Encryption Keys

Now that you have seen how to encrypt your custom SOAP header constructions along with the SOAP body of the message, let's now take a look at another possible scenario. Suppose that you not only want to encrypt this custom SOAP header construction along with the SOAP body, but you also want to use a different encryption key for the SOAP header portion than you use for the SOAP body portion of the SOAP request. This is possible with the WSE.

For this example, continue to use the same application used in Listings 5-19, 5-20, and 5-21. You are going to have to make some additional changes to both the XML Web service and the client application that is going to be sending the SOAP request. Let's first take a look at the changes to the client application that sends the SOAP request to the XML Web service.

The XML Web service consumer

The XML Web service consumer, or client application, is going to only have to make a few changes from the application that was just built in this chapter in order to work with multiple keys in encrypting multiple parts of the SOAP request.

The first step in building a client application that will do this is to have multiple keys in place for encrypting the SOAP request. You have been storing the keys so far in the web.config file. Therefore, you need to add another key to the web.config file so that the GetEncryptionKey method can retrieve these keys for encrypting the SOAP request. Note that you also have to make sure that the XML Web service itself will be using both of these keys to decrypt the SOAP request that it receives.

Listing 5-23 shows the addition to the web.config file.

Listing 5-23: Storing two shared secrets in the web.config file

```
<?xml version="1.0" encoding="utf-8" ?>
<configuration>

   <appSettings>
      <add key="symmetricKey1"
       value="BAA62349A24A7796116785784F54B149" />
      <add key="symmetricKey2"
       value="520DB84E9F7F9808510EFE2710B8ABCD" />
   </appSettings>

   <system.web>
      <!-- The rest of the web.config file -->
   </system.web>
</configuration>
```

Notice that there are now two encryption key values stored within the web.config file, symmetricKey1 and symmetricKey2. You will be using both of these keys later to encrypt SOAP requests that you will be sending. You will notice that the keys are quite different, and because you are working with symmetric encryption here, both the client application that performs the encryption and the XML Web service that performs the decryption have to know *both* of these shared secrets in order for this to work properly.

After you have both encryption key values stored within the web.config file, you need to change the GetEncryptionKey method that was presented in Listing 5-4 so that it can work with getting two encryption key values depending on the parameter provided. The revised GetEncryptionKey method is shown in Listing 5-24.

Listing 5-24: The revised GetEncryptionKey() method

[VB]

```
Private Function GetEncryptionKey(ByVal encKeyName As String) _
        As EncryptionKey
   Dim baseKey As String
   If encKeyName = "AddEncrypt" Then
      baseKey = ConfigurationSettings.AppSettings("symmetricKey1")
   ElseIf encKeyName = "AddCustomHeader" Then
      baseKey = ConfigurationSettings.AppSettings("symmetricKey2")
   Else
      Throw New ApplicationException("Symmetric key not " & _
         "found in configuration.")
   End If

   Dim keyBytes As Byte() = Convert.FromBase64String(baseKey)
   Dim key As SymmetricEncryptionKey = New _
      SymmetricEncryptionKey(TripleDES.Create(), keyBytes)

   Dim keyName As KeyInfoName = New KeyInfoName()
   keyName.Value = encKeyName
   key.KeyInfo.AddClause(keyName)

   Return key
End Function
```

[C#]

```
private EncryptionKey GetEncryptionKey(string encKeyName)
{
   string baseKey;
```

```
    if (encKeyName == "AddEncrypt")
    {
        baseKey = ConfigurationSettings.AppSettings["symmetricKey1"];
    }
    else if (encKeyName == "AddCustomHeader")
    {
        baseKey = ConfigurationSettings.AppSettings["symmetricKey2"];
    }
    else
    {
        throw new ApplicationException("Symmetric key not found in
            configuration.");
    }

    byte[] keyBytes = Convert.FromBase64String(baseKey);
    SymmetricEncryptionKey key = new
        SymmetricEncryptionKey(TripleDES.Create(), keyBytes);

    KeyInfoName keyName = new KeyInfoName();
    keyName.Value  = encKeyName;
    key.KeyInfo.AddClause(keyName);

    return key;
}
```

With this revised GetEncryptionKey method, depending on the name of the
encryption key that is being used to encrypt a portion of the SOAP message, that
name is passed into the method as a parameter and the appropriate key value is
retrieved from the web.config file.

Before the key is returned to the caller, a KeyInfoName instance is created and
the value provided is the name that is provided as the parameter. This allows the
XML Web service provider to look at each of the encryptions and differentiate the
encoded sections based on this name that is used so that it can decrypt that particular portion of the SOAP message with the appropriate encryption key.

The user of this application enters a number into each of the textboxes that
appear on the .aspx page and once the button on the page is clicked, the XML Web
service is invoked in order to provide the add calculation that will then be displayed
in the Label control. The button-click event in the code-behind for this .aspx page
will encrypt two sections of the SOAP request, with each section using its own
encryption key. Listing 5-25 shows the code that you need to use for the
Button1_Click event in order to accomplish this. This event will use the
GetEncryptionKey method that you just revised from Listing 5-24.

Listing 5-25: The button-click event that will invoke the XML Web service

[VB]

```vb
Private Sub Button1_Click(ByVal sender As System.Object, _
   ByVal e As System.EventArgs) Handles Button1.Click

   Dim ws As New localhost1.WSE_Encrypt()
   Dim wsHeader As New localhost1.PersonalInfo()

   wsHeader.Name = "Bill Evjen"
   wsHeader.EmailAddress = "evjen@yahoo.com"
   wsHeader.Id = "Id:05d2518d-d6db-481f-846d-2e8872b6e56d"

   ws.PersonalInfoValue = wsHeader

   Dim key1 As EncryptionKey = GetEncryptionKey("AddEncrypt")
   ws.RequestSoapContext.Security.Elements.Add(New _
      EncryptedData(key1))

   Dim key2 As EncryptionKey = GetEncryptionKey("AddCustomHeader")
   Dim encData As EncryptedData = New EncryptedData(key2, _
      "#Id:05d2518d-d6db-481f-846d-2e8872b6e56d")
   ws.RequestSoapContext.Security.Elements.Add(encData)

   Label1.Text = ws.Add(TextBox1.Text.ToString(), _
      TextBox2.Text.ToString())
End Sub
```

[C#]

```csharp
private void Button1_Click(object sender, System.EventArgs e)
{
   localhost.WSE_Encrypt ws = new localhost.WSE_Encrypt();
   localhost.PersonalInformation wsHeader = new
      localhost.PersonalInformation();

   wsHeader.Name = "Bill Evjen";
   wsHeader.EmailAddress = "evjen@yahoo.com";
   wsHeader.Id = "Id:05d2518d-d6db-481f-846d-2e8872b6e56d";

   ws.PersonalInfoValue = wsHeader;

   EncryptionKey key1 = GetEncryptionKey("AddEncrypt")
   ws.RequestSoapContext.Security.Elements.Add(new
```

```
            EncryptedData(key1));

    EncryptionKey key2 = GetEncryptionKey("AddCustomHeader");
    EncryptedData encData = new EncryptedData(key2,
        "#Id:05d2518d-d6db-481f-846d-2e8872b6e56d");
    ws.RequestSoapContext.Security.Elements.Add(encData);

    Label1.Text = ws.Add(int.Parse(TextBox1.Text),
        int.Parse(TextBox2.Text)).ToString();
}
```

This simple little method does some great things – all made possible with the WSE. The first thing that is accomplished is that the `PersonalInformation` object is instantiated, populated with data and assigned to the instance of the WebMethod. This was shown and discussed earlier in this chapter, so there is no need to go over it again.

Now that the SOAP body is going to be encrypted in the SOAP request, the next step is to make sure that the serialized `PersonalInformation` object that will reside in the SOAP header of the SOAP request will also be encrypted, but with an altogether different encryption key.

In this case, you need to create another instance of the `EncryptionKey` object (`key2`) and populate it with another encryption key value. This value is retrieved by the `GetEncryptionKey` method for the `AddCustomHeader` key. Once you have this value from the `GetEncryptionKey` method, you need to create an instance of the `EncryptedData` class. This class is a pointer to the specific piece of the SOAP message that you are going to work on. In this case, you are interested in encrypting the portion of the SOAP message that the `EncryptedData` object refers to. For this example, you are using the `key2` object and referring to the portion of the SOAP message that has an `Id` attribute value that is equal to the `xsd:Id` type unique identifier that you are supplying. Once the `EncryptedData` object, `encData`, is populated, you can assign it to the SOAP request that is going to be sent by the WSE:

```
Dim key2 As EncryptionKey = GetEncryptionKey("AddCustomHeader")
Dim encData As EncryptedData = New EncryptedData(key2, _
    "#Id:05d2518d-d6db-481f-846d-2e8872b6e56d")
ws.RequestSoapContext.Security.Elements.Add(encData)
```

Once this is all in place, you can simply invoke the XML Web service's `Add` WebMethod. Now let's take a look at the changes that need to be made to the XML Web service itself.

The XML Web service provider

The XML Web service itself has to be able to look for multiple encryption keys and to decide what key to use when it is decrypting a specific piece of the SOAP message. Since you are storing the encryption key values in the `web.config` file for this example, the first step you will need to do is to put another encryption key value within the web.config file the same as you did in Listing 5-23 for the client application. Remember that the client application and the XML Web service need to use the same encryption key values so that the XML Web service can decrypt the SOAP requests that it receives.

The WebMethod of the XML Web service, Add, is not going to change from what is shown in Listing 5-20, but the class that implements IDecryptionKeyProvider will have to change so that it will be able to work with two keys as opposed to one. So in order to create a class that will work with multiple encryption keys, take a look at Listing 5-26. This is the code that you should use for the DecryptionKeyProvider class.

Listing 5-26: The DecryptionKeyProvider class that works with two encryption key values

[VB]

```vb
Public Class DecryptionKeyProvider
    Implements IDecryptionKeyProvider

    Public Function GetDecryptionKey(ByVal algorithmUri As String, _
            ByVal keyInfo As KeyInfo) As DecryptionKey Implements _

            IDecryptionKeyProvider.GetDecryptionKey

        Dim clause As KeyInfoClause
        For Each clause In keyInfo
            If TypeOf clause Is KeyInfoName Then
                Dim keyData As String

                Dim myClause As KeyInfoName = clause
                If myClause.Value = "AddEncrypt" Then
                    keyData = _

ConfigurationSettings.AppSettings("symmetricKey1")
                ElseIf myClause.Value = "AddCustomHeader" Then
                    keyData = _

ConfigurationSettings.AppSettings("symmetricKey2")
                Else
                    Throw New _
                        ApplicationException("Key name not
supported.")
                End If

                If keyData Is Nothing Then
```

```vbnet
                    Throw New ApplicationException("Symmetric key " & _

                        "not found in configuration.")
                End If

                Dim keyBytes As Byte() = _
                    Convert.FromBase64String(keyData)

                Return New SymmetricDecryptionKey _
                    (TripleDES.Create(), keyBytes)
            End If

            Return Nothing

        Next
    End Function

End Class
```

[C#]

```csharp
public class DecryptionKeyProvider : IDecryptionKeyProvider
{
    public DecryptionKey GetDecryptionKey(string algorithmUri,
        KeyInfo keyInfo)
    {
        foreach ( KeyInfoClause clause in keyInfo )
        {
            if ( clause is KeyInfoName )
            {
                if ( ((KeyInfoName)clause).Value == "AddEncrypt")
                {
                    string keyData =

ConfigurationSettings.AppSettings["symmetricKey1"];
                }
                else if ( ((KeyInfoName)clause).Value ==
"AddCustomHeader")
                {
                    string keyData =

ConfigurationSettings.AppSettings["symmetricKey2"];
                }
```

Continued

Listing 5-26 *(Continued)*

```
        else
        {
            throw new ApplicationException("Key name not
                supported.");
        }

        if ( keyData == null )
            throw new ApplicationException("Symmetric key not
                found in configuration.");

        byte[] keyBytes = Convert.FromBase64String(keyData);

        return new SymmetricDecryptionKey
            (TripleDES.Create(),keyBytes);
    }
}

    return null;

    }
}
```

Notice that the code in the DecryptionKeyProvider class iterates through all the instances of the KeyInfo properties of the EncryptionKey objects that it receives in the message. This is so that the DecryptionKeyProvider class can recover the values needed to decrypt the encrypted section of the SOAP message based on the KeyInfo property's name. In the previous code example, the KeyInfo names that are retrieved are run through a conditional statement and if the KeyInfo name value is either AddEncrypt or AddCustomHeader, a symmetric key is retrieved from the web.config file for the XML Web service application. If the KeyInfo name value is not either of these, an exception is thrown that an appropriate key value wasn't used. Once retrieved, this class then returns the appropriate key to the WSE for decrypting the encrypted data.

Examining the SOAP request

Now let's take a look at the SOAP request that was sent from the client application to the XML Web service. The two encrypted sections of the SOAP request are shown in bold in Listing 5-27.

Listing 5-27: The encrypted SOAP request

```
<soap:Envelope
xmlns:soap="http://schemas.xmlsoap.org/soap/envelope/"
 xmlns:xsi="http://www.w3.org/2001/XMLSchema-instance"
```

```
    xmlns:xsd="http://www.w3.org/2001/XMLSchema">
      <soap:Header>
        <PersonalInformation
        d3p1:Id="Id:05d2518d-d6db-481f-846d-2e8872b6e56d"
        xmlns:d3p1="http://schemas.xmlsoap.org/ws/2002/07/utility"
        xmlns="http://www.wiley.com">
          <xenc:EncryptedData Id="EncryptedContent-4981d738-c1b3-40b6-
          8d6c-81162afc514f"
          Type="http://www.w3.org/2001/04/xmlenc#Content"
          xmlns:xenc="http://www.w3.org/2001/04/xmlenc#">
            <xenc:EncryptionMethod
             Algorithm="http://www.w3.org/2001/04/xmlenc#tripledes-cbc"
            />
            <KeyInfo xmlns="http://www.w3.org/2000/09/xmldsig#">
              <KeyName>AddCustomHeader</KeyName>
            </KeyInfo>
            <xenc:CipherData>
               <xenc:CipherValue>
                 LLS3AL3FsWOrptt9Vv6qw+4BvYZIn8CR7GJT1zwaN
                 HuHzauOZlnRnSZ/LkAvMRA7Q6jNMLWYmjeuJ5OuyU
                 GQdU+vBuE8NeWrTazVpDy6VHPQ2HvBsOZmZ2csGWe
                 JPgRO+5bNemNHRm/zF8t7VMvgv4D6ARfWnRXSrXuL
                 Vr1Z1QY4/n7COy/hAw==</xenc:CipherValue>
            </xenc:CipherData>
          </xenc:EncryptedData>
        </PersonalInformation>
        <wsrp:path
         soap:actor="http://schemas.xmlsoap.org/soap/actor/next"
         soap:mustUnderstand="1"
         xmlns:wsrp="http://schemas.xmlsoap.org/rp">
          <wsrp:action>http://www.wiley.com/Add</wsrp:action>
          <wsrp:to>http://localhost/WSE1/WSE_Encrypt.asmx</wsrp:to>
          <wsrp:id>uuid:1c1096ec-c3f2-4bab-a344-41f3ab32adb8</wsrp:id>
        </wsrp:path>
        <wsu:Timestamp
         xmlns:wsu="http://schemas.xmlsoap.org/ws/2002/07/utility">
          <wsu:Created>2002-12-05T02:24:26Z</wsu:Created>
          <wsu:Expires>2002-12-05T02:29:26Z</wsu:Expires>
        </wsu:Timestamp>
        <wsse:Security soap:mustUnderstand="1"
         xmlns:wsse="http://schemas.xmlsoap.org/ws/2002/07/secext">
          <xenc:ReferenceList
           xmlns:xenc="http://www.w3.org/2001/04/xmlenc#">
```

Continued

Listing 5-27 *(Continued)*

```
                <xenc:DataReference URI="#EncryptedContent-4981d738-c1b3-
                  40b6-8d6c-81162afc514f" />
              </xenc:ReferenceList>
              <xenc:ReferenceList
                xmlns:xenc="http://www.w3.org/2001/04/xmlenc#">
                <xenc:DataReference URI="#EncryptedContent-f0dd4e3f-df2c-
                  4e37-a695-05099b08ce15" />
              </xenc:ReferenceList>
            </wsse:Security>
          </soap:Header>
          <soap:Body
            xmlns:wsu="http://schemas.xmlsoap.org/ws/2002/07/utility"
            wsu:Id="Id-2a0af39a-52c3-456c-ba8b-aa8423568fbc">
            <xenc:EncryptedData Id="EncryptedContent-f0dd4e3f-df2c-4e37-
              a695-05099b08ce15"
              Type="http://www.w3.org/2001/04/xmlenc#Content"
              xmlns:xenc="http://www.w3.org/2001/04/xmlenc#">
              <xenc:EncryptionMethod
                Algorithm="http://www.w3.org/2001/04/xmlenc#tripledes-cbc" />
              <KeyInfo xmlns="http://www.w3.org/2000/09/xmldsig#">
                <KeyName>AddEncrypt</KeyName>
              </KeyInfo>
              <xenc:CipherData>
                 <xenc:CipherValue>
                  hzCLLhMkxvoLhEarSRJFIANOoOgqKYw7povAkXYFfH8hA8O
                  ++E7qyC/L9CC7i3toYl1mcQM7WMu8SHuT9+Agnym4/WCKhva+
                 </xenc:CipherValue>
              </xenc:CipherData>
            </xenc:EncryptedData>
          </soap:Body>
        </soap:Envelope>
```

After looking at the encrypted SOAP request that was sent from the client application to the XML Web service, you will notice that there are two sections of the SOAP request that are encoded. You can also see that there are two separate keys used to encrypt these separate sections of the SOAP message based on the fact that the <KeyName> elements have different values. These are the elements that the XML Web service is looking for in deciding what key to use to decrypt that particular section of the SOAP message. Remember that the actual keys to decrypt the SOAP messages are not sent only with the SOAP request, but instead, a reference to the key is used in the encryption process by using the key name.

Summary

Encryption is one of the more important things you can do to your SOAP messages as they are sent between the consumer and the provider. In many cases you are sending sensitive data back and forth and if you don't want this sensitive data to be exposed to the rest of the world, then you will need to apply what you have learned in this chapter.

You can encrypt SOAP messages with either a shared secret, also called private-key encryption or symmetric encryption, or by using public-key encryption, also known as asymmetric encryption, where one key is private and one is public. These two keys are mathematically linked and can be used to encrypt and decrypt your SOAP messages. You can achieve asymmetric encryption by using X.509 certificates.

Chapter 6

Using the Three Aspects of WS-Security Together

IN THIS CHAPTER

- ◆ Setting up SQL Server to work with your SOAP messages
- ◆ Building the XML Web service
- ◆ Building the consumer application
- ◆ Compiling and running the application

YOU HAVE DONE quite a bit with the WS-Security specification so far in this section of the book. You used username/password combinations as well as X.509 certificates to apply credentials to your SOAP messages. In addition to this, you used WS-Security to digitally sign your SOAP messages as well as encrypt the SOAP body of the messages that you were sending. The ability to use WS-Security in your SOAP messages is indeed a powerful tool and the WSE doesn't make it too difficult to implement this specification into your .NET XML Web services.

When you are architecting your XML Web services and applications at large, you should take a look at each and every opportunity to use the proper security for what you are trying to accomplish. That's not to say that you need to apply each aspect of WS-Security to every XML Web service that you build. Instead, you need to consider each aspect and decide whether it is proper to use for the level of security that you need.

Although previous chapters reviewed individual pieces of the WS-Security pie, you can use these specifications together to give you the best possible security arrangement for your XML Web services. As an example, create an XML Web service that requires a username/password combination to access the Web service. You'll also need to send in your SOAP requests digitally signed as well as encrypted using a private key.

This is a very code-intensive chapter and is meant to review everything you learned about how the WSE implements the WS-Security specification. Also, as stated, you learn how to use the WS-Security implementation in a single application.

Setting Up SQL Server

For the purposes of encrypting the SOAP responses from the XML Web service, you need someplace to store the private key for applying symmetric encryption. One of the better places to store this key is within SQL Server as it is one of the most secure storage options.

So far in this book, you have seen how to use symmetric encryption using a single private key for encrypting the SOAP requests.

One of the first steps in creating this application is to set up SQL Server. Within the WSE database that you created earlier in the book, create a new table called WSE_Key. Place a single column called PrivateKey within this table. You can use the script in Listing 6-1 to create this table.

Listing 6-1: The SQL script for creating a table that will store the private key to use for encrypting SOAP responses from the XML Web service

```
if exists (select * from dbo.sysobjects where id =
object_id(N'[dbo].[WSE_Key]') and OBJECTPROPERTY(id,
N'IsUserTable') = 1)
drop table [dbo].[WSE_Key]
GO

CREATE TABLE [dbo].[WSE_Key] (
    [PrivateKey] [varchar] (32) COLLATE
    SQL_Latin1_General_CP1_CI_AS NOT NULL
    ) ON [PRIMARY]
GO
```

Place the following value with the PrivateKey column within the WSE_Key table:

```
PrivateKey
BAA62349A24A7796116785784F54B149
```

Now that you have a table in place, you are ready to create an XML Web service that will use this table. For the consumers to send a SOAP request to the XML Web service, they need to provide the appropriate usernames and passwords. The consumers also have to encrypt the SOAP body using the appropriate private key that is associated with this particular username and password.

 We will not go through in code how to get the users the appropriate key to use to encrypt the message, as there are a variety of means of how you will get your XML Web service consumers the appropriate key that they will use.

The next section takes a look at how to build the XML Web service provider.

Building the XML Web Service

The provider accepts SOAP messages from consumers who send in a SOAP request. This request is encrypted using the appropriate private key, and also provides credentials for authorization to invoke the XML Web service. In addition to encrypting and providing credentials, the consuming application also digitally signs the message. Therefore, you have to build the XML Web service to look for all three of these aspects from the consumer.

After the XML Web service processes a SOAP request that has credentials, is digitally signed, and is encrypted using a specific private key, the SOAP response from the XML Web service needs to be encrypted using the same key and returned to the consuming application. If the consuming application has the key used to encrypt the original SOAP request, the consumer can decrypt the SOAP response from the XML Web service.

To start this process, open Visual Studio .NET and create a new ASP.NET Web Service project called VB_Sec or CS_Sec.

Building the password provider class

The first step is to create a new class within your project. Name the class myPasswordProvider.vb or myPasswordProvider.cs. The code for this class is the same as previous password provider classes that have been used so far. You can find the code for this class in Listing 3-6. This class will allow you to fetch a password from SQL Server for an associated username that is provided with the UsernameToken object. Once the password is retrieved, this password is then compared to the password that is contained within the UsernameToken object.

Adding to the web.config file

You have to make changes to the web.config file for what you are trying to achieve with this XML Web service. One of the first additions you need to make to the web.config file is a <configSections> node that refers to the WSE DLL. Recall from earlier chapters that you do not have to place the <configSections> node within the web.config file if you have placed this within the machine.config or app.config file. The other section that needs to be placed within the web.config file is the <soapExtensionTypes> node. This will allow your XML Web services to have the WSE work with the SOAP requests and responses. This is all shown in Listing 6-2. Remember that the <add> node within the <soapExtensionTypes> and <section> nodes needs to be on a single line to avoid error. It is only shown in this fashion because of the book's size limitations.

Listing 6-2: Adding a reference to the WSE DLL in the web.config file

```
<configuration>

  <configSections>
    <section name="microsoft.web.services"
     type="Microsoft.Web.Services.Configuration.
    WebServicesConfiguration, Microsoft.Web.Services,
     Version=1.0.0.0, Culture=neutral,
     PublicKeyToken=31bf3856ad364e35" />
  </configSections>

  <system.web>
    <webServices>
      <soapExtensionTypes>
        <add type="Microsoft.Web.Services.WebServicesExtension,
         Microsoft.Web.Services, Version=1.0.0.0,
Culture=neutral,
         PublicKeyToken=31bf3856ad364e35" priority="1"
group="0"/>
      </soapExtensionTypes>
    </webServices>

    <!-- The rest of the web.config file -->

  </system.web>

</configuration>
```

Once these references are in place, you need to add some information to the web. config file. Outside of the `<system.web>` nodes, but within the `<configuration>` nodes, add the code as shown in Listing 6-3 to the web.config file.

Listing 6-3: Adding references and settings to the web.config file

```
<microsoft.web.services>
  <security>
    <passwordProvider type="VB_Sec.myPasswordProvider, VB_Sec" />
    <decryptionKeyProvider type="VB_Sec.DecryptionKeyProvider,
     VB_Sec" />
  </security>
</microsoft.web.services>
```

This `<security>` node points the WSE to the class that will take care of getting the password to verify credentials with the `<passwordProvider>` node. As you can tell from this example, it points to the myPasswordProvider class that was recently created.

The second reference within the `<security>` node points to the class that will take care of decrypting the SOAP request that the XML Web service receives. In this case, it is pointing to a class that you will create later called `DecryptionKeyProvider`.

With these items in place, your `web.config` file is ready.

Working with Service1.asmx

Within your ASP.NET Web Service project, you will have a single XML Web service in place called `Service1.asmx`. The `Service1` class, which is already constructed in the template of the page, contains three methods that you will build. One method will be the WebMethod itself. Because this example simply demonstrates the capabilities of the WSE, this will be a simple `Add` method again.

In addition to the `Add` WebMethod, you will create a method that returns an encryption key and a third method that returns the private key that is being stored in SQL Server.

Before you create any of the classes or methods for this page, you have to import the proper namespaces into the file. Listing 6-4 shows you the namespaces that you need to import.

Listing 6-4: Importing the proper namespaces into the file

[VB]

```
Imports System.Web.Services
Imports System.Web.Services.Protocols
Imports Microsoft.Web.Services
Imports Microsoft.Web.Services.Security
Imports System.Data
Imports System.Data.SqlClient
Imports System.Security.Cryptography
Imports System.Security.Cryptography.Xml
```

[C#]

```
using System.Web.Services;
using System.Web.Services.Protocols;
using Microsoft.Web.Services;
using Microsoft.Web.Services.Security;
using System.Data;
using System.Data.SqlClient;
using System.Security.Cryptography;
using System.Security.Cryptography.Xml;
```

The WSE namespaces are imported in order to work with the WSE's WS-Security implementation. The `System.Data` and `System.Data.SqlClient` namespaces are

imported in order to get the private key out of SQL Server, and finally, the cryptography namespaces are in place to encrypt the SOAP response that is sent from the
XML Web service. Once these are in place, you are ready to build the methods and
classes of the file.

GETPRIVATEKEY()

The `GetPrivateKey` method is constructed within the `Service1` class. The
`Service1` class is your Web service. The entire purpose of this class is to retrieve
the private key that will be used to encrypt and decrypt the SOAP messages that are
sent to and from the XML Web service. Listing 6-5 shows you the code for this
method.

Listing 6-5: The GetPrivateKey method

[VB]

```
Public Function GetPrivateKey() As String
Dim connStr As String = "Data Source=localhost; Initial" & _
        "Catalog=WSE; User id=sa"
    Dim conn As New SqlConnection(connStr)
    conn.Open()

Dim cmd As New SqlCommand("Select PrivateKey From WSE_Key", _
        conn)

    Dim myDataReader As SqlDataReader
    myDataReader = cmd.ExecuteReader(CommandBehavior.SingleResult)

    Dim keyData As String
    If myDataReader.Read() Then
        keyData = myDataReader(0).ToString()
    Else
        Throw New Exception("EncryptionKey is not present in" & _
            "system.")
    End If

    conn.Close()

    If keyData Is Nothing Then
        Throw New ApplicationException("Symmetric key not found" & _
            "in database.")
    End If

    Return keyData
End Function
```

[C#]

```csharp
private string GetPrivateKey()
{
    string connStr = "Data Source=localhost; Initial
        Catalog=WSE; User id=sa";
    SqlConnection conn = new SqlConnection(connStr);
    conn.Open();

    SqlCommand cmd = new SqlCommand("Select PrivateKey From
        WSE_Key", conn);

    SqlDataReader myDataReader;
    myDataReader =
        cmd.ExecuteReader(CommandBehavior.SingleResult);

    string keyData;
    if (myDataReader.Read())
    {
        keyData = myDataReader[0].ToString();
    }
    else
    {
        throw new Exception("EncryptionKey is not present in
            system.");
    }
    conn.Close();

    if (keyData == null)
    {
        throw new ApplicationException("Symmetric key not found
            in database.");
    }

    return keyData
}
```

As you can see, this method returns a simple string that contains the private key that will be used for the encryption-decryption process.

GETENCRYPTIONKEY()

This method is also contained within the Service1 class. The GetEncryptionKey method returns the encryption key that is of type EncryptionKey. This private method is shown in Listing 6-6.

Listing 6-6: The GetEncryptionKey method

[VB]

```vb
Private Function GetEncryptionKey() As EncryptionKey
    Dim baseKey As String = GetPrivateKey()
    Dim keyBytes As Byte() = Convert.FromBase64String(baseKey)
Dim key As SymmetricEncryptionKey = New _
        SymmetricEncryptionKey(TripleDES.Create(), keyBytes)

    Dim keyName As KeyInfoName = New KeyInfoName()
    keyName.Value = "AddEncrypt"
    key.KeyInfo.AddClause(keyName)

Return key
End Function
```

[C#]

```csharp
private EncryptionKey GetEncryptionKey()
{
    string baseKey = GetPrivateKey()
    byte[] keyBytes = Convert.FromBase64String(keyData);
    SymmetricEncryptionKey key = new
      SymmetricEncryptionKey(TripleDES.Create(), keyBytes);

    KeyInfoName keyName = new KeyInfoName();
    keyName.Value  = "AddEncrypt";
    key.KeyInfo.AddClause(keyName);

    return key;
}
```

This method gets the string private key from SQL Server by using the GetPrivateKey() method. Once retrieved, it is converted to a byte array and then assigned as a value to an instance of an EncryptionKey object. This object is returned from the method.

ADD()

Probably the most important method in the Service1 class is the Add() WebMethod itself. This WebMethod brings everything together. The Add() WebMethod takes hold the SOAP request, checks the credentials sent in with it to make sure that they are valid, checks the digital signature, and then decrypts the SOAP body. Then this WebMethod performs the not-too-complicated addition and sends back the encrypted response. Listing 6-7 shows the code from this WebMethod.

Listing 6-7: The Add() WebMethod

[VB]

```
<WebMethod()> Public Function Add(ByVal a As Integer, ByVal b As _
        Integer) As Integer
    Dim requestContext As SoapContext = _
        HttpSoapContext.RequestContext()

    Dim userToken As UsernameToken
    Dim elem As Object
    Dim returnValue As String = ""

    If requestContext Is Nothing Then
        Throw New ApplicationException("Non-SOAP request.")
    End If

    For Each userToken In requestContext.Security.Tokens

        If userToken.PasswordOption = PasswordOption.SendHashed Then
            For Each elem In requestContext.Security.Elements
                If TypeOf elem Is _
                        Microsoft.Web.Services.Security.Signature Then
                    Dim clientSign As _
                        Microsoft.Web.Services.Security.Signature _
                        = CType(elem, _
                        Microsoft.Web.Services.Security.Signature)

                    If TypeOf clientSign.SecurityToken Is UsernameToken _
                        Then
                        Dim responseContext As SoapContext = _
                            HttpSoapContext.ResponseContext

                        Dim key As EncryptionKey = GetEncryptionKey()

                        responseContext.Security.Elements.Add(New _
                            EncryptedData(key))

                        returnValue = (a + b)
                    End If
                End If
            Next
        Else
            Throw New SoapException("You must provide a hashed
```

Continued

Listing 6-7 *(Continued)*

```
                password.", SoapException.ClientFaultCode)
        End If

    Next
    Return returnValue
End Function
```

[C#]

```csharp
[WebMethod]
 public int Add(int a, int b)
 {
    SoapContext requestContext =
       HttpSoapContext.RequestContext;

    UsernameToken userToken;
    object elem;
    string returnValue = "";


    if (requestContext == null)
    {
       throw new ApplicationException("Non-SOAP request.");
    }

    foreach (UsernameToken userToken in
       requestContext.Security.Tokens)
    {
       if (userToken.PasswordOption == PasswordOption.SendHashed)
       {
          foreach (Object elem in
             requestContext.Security.Elements)
          {
             if (elem is Signature)
             {
                Signature clientSign = (Signature)elem;

                if (clientSign.SecurityToken is UsernameToken)
                   EncryptionKey key = GetEncryptionKey();

                   responseContext.Security.Elements.Add(new
                      EncryptedData(key));
```

```
                    returnvalue = (a+b);

                }
            }
        }
    }
    else
    {
        throw new SoapException("You must provide a hashed
            password.", SoapException.ClientFaultCode);
    }
}
return returnValue;
}
```

This WebMethod has a higher level of security than was possible before the WSE came along. Each of the `UsernameToken` objects included with the SOAP request are checked to make sure that the password is hashed. It also ensures that the SOAP request was digitally signed.

Because it is specified in the `web.config` file, the `DecryptionKeyProvider` class (discussed next) will take care of decrypting the SOAP body of the SOAP request. Then before the result of the `Add` method call is returned to the consumer, it is encrypted.

THE DECRYPTIONKEYPROVIDER CLASS

The `DecryptionKeyProvider` class is in place to decrypt the SOAP requests. The WSE finds this class from the reference to the class within the `web.config` file. Both the consumer and provider applications will have to have this class and reference in place if encryption and decryption is enabled for both the SOAP requests and SOAP responses. Listing 6-8 shows the code for the `DecryptionKeyProvider` class. The reference that is made in the `web.config` file has already been shown in Listing 6-3.

Listing 6-8: The DecryptionKeyProvider class

[VB]

```
Public Class DecryptionKeyProvider
    Implements IDecryptionKeyProvider

    Public Function GetDecryptionKey(ByVal algorithmUri As String,
        ByVal keyInfo As KeyInfo) As DecryptionKey Implements
        IDecryptionKeyProvider.GetDecryptionKey

        Dim clause As KeyInfoClause
```

Continued

Listing 6-8 *(Continued)*

```vb
        For Each clause In keyInfo
            If TypeOf clause Is KeyInfoName Then
                Dim myClause As KeyInfoName = clause
                If myClause.Value = "AddEncrypt" Then
                    Dim GetKey As New VB_Sec.Service1()
                    Dim keyData As String
                    keyData = GetKey.GetPrivateKey()

                    Dim keyBytes As Byte() = _
                        Convert.FromBase64String(keyData)

                    Return New _
                        SymmetricDecryptionKey(TripleDES.Create(), _
                        keyBytes)
                End If
            Else
                Throw New ApplicationException("Key name not _
                    supported.")
            End If

            Return Nothing
        Next
    End Function

End Class
```

[C#]

```csharp
public class DecryptionKeyProvider : IDecryptionKeyProvider
  {
      public DecryptionKey GetDecryptionKey(string algorithmUri,
          KeyInfo keyInfo)
      {
          foreach ( KeyInfoClause clause in keyInfo )
          {
              if ( clause is KeyInfoName )
              {
                  if ( ((KeyInfoName)clause).Value == "AddEncrypt")
                  {
                      CS_Sec.Service1 GetKey = new CS_Sec.Service1();
                      string keyData;
                      keyData = GetKey.GetPrivateKey();
```

```
            byte[] keyBytes = Convert.FromBase64String(keyData);

            return new SymmetricDecryptionKey
              (TripleDES.Create(),keyBytes);
          }
          else
          {
            throw new ApplicationException("Key name not
                supported.");
          }
        }
      }
    return null;
    }
}
```

As already stated, this class takes care of decrypting the SOAP messages that are received by the WSE. The WSE finds the class from the reference that is made to it in the `web.config` file.

The `DecryptionKeyProvider` class needs to implement `IDecryptionKeyProvider`. The `KeyInfo` property of the encryption key that is sent in is checked to make sure that the encryption key that is being used is the one that you want. This is referenced by the name `AddEncrypt`.

Once it is determined that this is the encryption key that you are looking for, the private key is called. In this case, it is retrieved from the `GetPrivateKey()` method. When this private key is retrieved, it is then passed to the WSE.

Now with all of this in place, you are ready to build an application that will work with this XML Web service. The application will make requests that provide appropriate credentials, as well as send digitally signed and encrypted SOAP requests. Let's get on with building the consumer application.

Building the Consumer Application

Now there is an XML Web service in place. As a potential consumer of this XML Web service, you need to understand how to consume this application. Figure 6-1 shows you what the ASP.NET Web interface to the XML Web service looks like if called up in an application.

The `Add()` method shows that the parameters, a and b, are both of type `integer` and are required in order to consume this XML Web service. This Web interface to the `Add()` method also shows that in return you will be receiving an `integer` that is the result of the calculation that the `Add()` method performs.

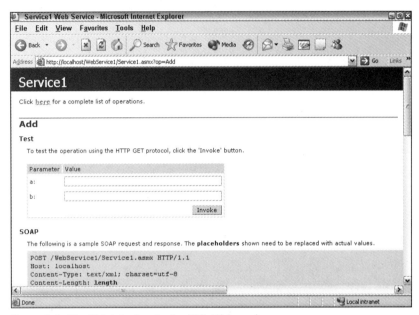

Figure 6-1: The Web interface to the XML Web service

The problem with this is that there is nothing stated that says that you need to provide credentials in a specific format, that the message is digitally signed, or that the SOAP request and the SOAP response are encrypted. This is a problem and you as the builder of the XML Web service need to relay to your consumers the need for these items and how their SOAP requests need to be constructed in order to interact with your XML Web service.

You also need to relay to the consumers what kind of SOAP response they should expect from your XML Web service. In this case, they receive a SOAP response that is encrypted with a private key. Consumers also need to know that the SOAP response is encrypted with a specific private key that they need to have access to.

Let's get started in building the application that will consume the XML Web service that you built earlier in this chapter. Start a new ASP.NET Web Application project called VB_Consumer or CS_Consumer depending on the language you're using.

Remember that the consumer of this application is not required to be an ASP.NET application; you could just as easily do this in a Windows Form application.

Adding to the web.config file

For the consumer application, you need to make some additions to the web.config file in order to work with the WSE in understanding and constructing SOAP requests and responses that abide by the GXA specifications. This is similar to what you did with the XML Web service provider application earlier in this chapter.

One of the first additions to the web.config file involves making the appropriate reference to the WSE DLL, as shown in Listing 6-2.

The next addition involves making a reference to the class that provides the decryption key for the encrypted SOAP responses that are being retrieved from the XML Web service. This addition is shown in Listing 6-9.

Listing 6-9: Adding references and settings within the web.config file

```
<microsoft.web.services>
  <security>
    <decryptionKeyProvider
      type="VB_Consumer.DecryptionKeyProvider, VB_Consumer" />
  </security>
</microsoft.web.services>
```

 If you are interested in seeing a record of the SOAP requests and responses that are traded between the consuming application and the XML Web service, take a look at Appendix A. It discusses different ways that you can work with the tracing of these SOAP messages. You have to make to the web.config file for this to occur.

The next change is that instead of storing the private key within SQL Server, the consuming application will store this key directly in the web.config file. You can see an example of this in Listing 5-2 (in Chapter 5).

Now that you are done making changes to the web.config file, it is time to build the ASP.NET page and the DecryptionKeyProvider class.

Building the myAdd.aspx page

Within your ASP.NET application, create a new Web Form called myAdd.aspx. This page will allow the users to enter in their credentials in order to invoke the XML Web service. There will also be a set of textboxes that will allow the users to enter the numbers that they want to send to the Add() WebMethod. The result that is sent back from the XML Web service is then presented in the Label control at the bottom of the page. Listing 6-10 shows the code for the .aspx page.

Listing 6-10: Code for the .aspx page

```
<%@ Page Language="vb" AutoEventWireup="false"
 Codebehind="myAdd.aspx.vb" Inherits="VB_Consumer.myAdd" %>
<!DOCTYPE HTML PUBLIC "-//W3C//DTD HTML 4.0 Transitional//EN">
<HTML>
```

Continued

Listing 6-10 *(Continued)*

```
    <HEAD>
       <title>myAdd</title>
    </HEAD>
    <body>
       <form id="Form1" method="post" runat="server">
          <P>
          <asp:Panel id="Panel1" runat="server" Font-Size="X-Small"
           Font-Names="Verdana" BackColor="#FFC080"
           BorderColor="Black" BorderStyle="Solid"
           BorderWidth="1px"> Username
          <asp:TextBox id="TextBox1"
           runat="server"></asp:TextBox>
            Password
          <asp:TextBox id="TextBox2" runat="server"
           TextMode="Password"></asp:TextBox>
             
          </asp:Panel></P>
          <P><FONT face="Verdana" size="2"><U>Calculator ADD<BR>
          </U>Value of a :
          <asp:TextBox id="TextBox3"
           runat="server"></asp:TextBox><BR>
          Value of b :
          <asp:TextBox id="TextBox4"
           runat="server"></asp:TextBox></FONT></P>
          <P>
          <asp:Button id="Button1" runat="server"
           Text="Add"></asp:Button></P>
          <P><FONT face="Verdana" size="2">Result :
          <asp:Label id="Label1" runat="server">0</asp:Label></P>
          </FONT>
       </form>
    </body>
</HTML>
```

With this code in place, your ASP.NET page should appear as shown in Figure 6-2.

Now that you have the base of the ASP.NET page in place, you are ready to start building the rest of the application. The next step is to make the appropriate references to the XML Web service that you want to consume.

Creating the proxy class

To make a reference to the XML Web service that you are trying to consume, within Visual Studio .NET right-click on your project and select **Add Web Reference.**

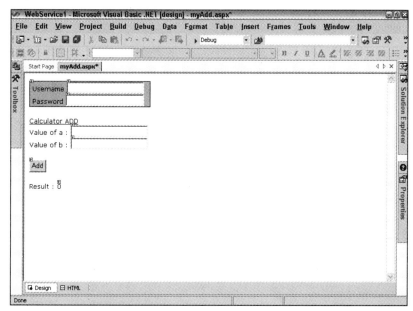

Figure 6-2: The ASP.NET page

Within the Add Reference dialog box, make the appropriate references to the XML Web service. You do this by typing the URL of the Web service in the address box. In your case, it is `http://localhost/vb_sec/service1.asmx`. Once the reference is made, find the proxy class within your project. To find this class, expand the Web Reference that was made (it will be called `localhost`). Make sure that the **Show All Files** button has been clicked. After expanding the tree of the Web reference `localhost`, you will find a class called `Reference.vb` or `Reference.cs`. This is the proxy class.

Open this class and change from where this class inherits. You need to do this in order to get this proxy class to interact with the WSE. This process is shown in Listing 6-11. Recompile the application after making these changes.

Listing 6-11: Changing the class from which the proxy inherits

`[VB]`

```
Namespace localhost

    '<remarks/>
    <System.Diagnostics.DebuggerStepThroughAttribute(), _
     System.ComponentModel.DesignerCategoryAttribute("code"), _
    System.Web.Services.
```

Continued

Listing 6-11 *(Continued)*

```
        WebServiceBindingAttribute(Name:="Service1Soap", _
[Namespace]:="http://www.wiley.com/")>  _
    Public Class Service1
        Inherits Microsoft.Web.Services.WebServicesClientProtocol
```

[C#]

```
/// <remarks/>
[System.Diagnostics.DebuggerStepThroughAttribute()]
[System.ComponentModel.DesignerCategoryAttribute("code")]
[System.Web.Services.WebServiceBindingAttribute(Name="Service1Soap",
 Namespace="http://www.wiley.com")]
public class Service1 :
Microsoft.Web.Services.WebServicesClientProtocol
```

Now that you have the proxy class ready and in place, you can start to build the code-behind for the ASP.NET page that will consume the Add() WebMethod.

Building the code-behind page

Within the code-behind page, you will have two classes. The myAdd class takes care of all the actions that occur on the page and finds the encryption key that will be used to encrypt the SOAP request before it is sent on its way.

The second class, DecryptionKeyProvider, finds the private key in order to decrypt the encrypted SOAP responses that come from the XML Web service. Once these two classes are in place, you can run the application and consume the Add() WebMethod.

Before you build any of these methods, you need to make sure that the code-behind for your ASP.NET page imports the namespaces shown in Listing 6-12.

Listing 6-12: Importing the proper namespaces into the file

[VB]

```
Imports Microsoft.Web.Services
Imports Microsoft.Web.Services.Security
Imports System.Configuration
Imports System.Security.Cryptography
Imports System.Security.Cryptography.Xml
```

[C#]

```
using Microsoft.Web.Services;
using Microsoft.Web.Services.Security;
```

```
using System.Configuration;
using System.Security.Cryptography;
using System.Security.Cryptography.Xml
```

The WSE namespaces are imported in order to work with the WSE's implementation of the WS-Security specification. The namespace `System.Configuration` is imported so that you can get at the private key value that is stored within the `web.config` file. The last two cryptography namespaces are imported so that you can work with the Triple DES encryption capabilities that you are using to encrypt the SOAP request.

Let's now take a look at the `DecryptionKeyProvider` class that needs to be included on this page.

THE DECRYPTIONKEYPROVIDER CLASS

This class is almost exactly the same as the `DecryptionKeyProvider` class that was built for the XML Web service in Listing 6-8. The main difference is that instead of using a method that retrieves the private key for the decryption process from SQL Server, you will construct this consumer application by building the `DecryptionKeyProvider` class so that it retrieves this key from the `web.config` file. Listing 6-13 shows you the differences (highlighted in bold) in this class when compared to the `DecryptionKeyProvider` class contained within the XML Web service application.

Listing 6-13: The DecryptionKeyProvider class for the consuming application

[VB]

```
Public Class DecryptionKeyProvider
    Implements IDecryptionKeyProvider

    Public Function GetDecryptionKey(ByVal algorithmUri As String,
        ByVal keyInfo As KeyInfo) As DecryptionKey Implements
        IDecryptionKeyProvider.GetDecryptionKey

        Dim clause As KeyInfoClause
        For Each clause In keyInfo
            If TypeOf clause Is KeyInfoName Then
                Dim myClause As KeyInfoName = clause
                If myClause.Value = "AddEncrypt" Then
                    Dim keyData As String = _
                    ConfigurationSettings.AppSettings("symmetricKey")

                    If keyData Is Nothing Then
                        Throw New ApplicationException("Symmetric" & _
                            "key not found in configuration.")
```

Continued

Listing 6-13 *(Continued)*

```vb
                        End If

                        Dim keyBytes As Byte() =
                            Convert.FromBase64String(keyData)

                        Return New
                            SymmetricDecryptionKey(TripleDES.Create(),
                            keyBytes)
                    End If
                Else
                    Throw New ApplicationException("Key name not
                        supported.")
                End If

                Return Nothing
            Next
        End Function

End Class
```

[C#]

```csharp
public class DecryptionKeyProvider : IDecryptionKeyProvider
  {
      public DecryptionKey GetDecryptionKey(string algorithmUri,
         KeyInfo keyInfo)
      {
          foreach ( KeyInfoClause clause in keyInfo )
          {
              if ( clause is KeyInfoName )
              {
                  if ( ((KeyInfoName)clause).Value == "AddEncrypt")
                  {
                      string keyData =
                          ConfigurationSettings.AppSettings["symmetricKey"];

                      if ( keyData == null )
                          throw new ApplicationException("Symmetric key not
                              found in configuration.");

                      byte[] keyBytes = Convert.FromBase64String(keyData);

                      return new SymmetricDecryptionKey
```

```
            (TripleDES.Create(),keyBytes);
        }
        else
        {
            throw new ApplicationException("Key name not
                supported.");
        }
    }
}
return null;
}
}
```

Now that you have the `web.config` file completed as well as the `DecryptionKeyProvider` class in place within the code-behind page for `myAdd.aspx`, you are ready to complete the `myAdd` class that is also contained within this code-behind page.

BUILDING THE MYADD CLASS

The `myAdd` class contained within the ASP.NET page's code-behind contains two important events. The first event is a simple method that retrieves the private key that will be used to encrypt the SOAP request before it is sent to the XML Web service. The second method is a button-click event that will instantiate the XML Web service. Listing 6-14 shows the method that retrieves the private key from the `web.config` file.

Listing 6-14: The GetEncryptionKey method

[VB]

```
Private Function GetEncryptionKey() As EncryptionKey
    Dim baseKey As String = _
        ConfigurationSettings.AppSettings("symmetricKey")

    If baseKey Is Nothing Then
        Throw New ApplicationException("Symmetric key not found" & _
            "in configuration.")
    End If

    Dim keyBytes As Byte() = Convert.FromBase64String(baseKey)
    Dim key As SymmetricEncryptionKey = New _
        SymmetricEncryptionKey(TripleDES.Create(), keyBytes)

    Dim keyName As KeyInfoName = New KeyInfoName()
```

Continued

Listing 6-14 *(Continued)*

```
    keyName.Value = "AddEncrypt"
    key.KeyInfo.AddClause(keyName)

    Return key
End Function
```

[C#]

```
private EncryptionKey GetEncryptionKey()
{

    string baseKey =
        ConfigurationSettings.AppSettings["symmetricKey"];

    if (baseKey == null)
    {
        throw new ApplicationException("Symmetric key not found
            in configuration.");
    }

    byte[] keyBytes = Convert.FromBase64String(baseKey);
    SymmetricEncryptionKey key = new
        SymmetricEncryptionKey(TripleDES.Create(), keyBytes);

    KeyInfoName keyName = new KeyInfoName();
    keyName.Value  = "AddEncrypt";
    key.KeyInfo.AddClause(keyName);

    return key;
}
```

The big difference between this GetEncryptionKey method and the one that is present in the XML Web service is that the GetEncryptionKey method in the consuming application retrieves the private key from the web.config file instead of from SQL Server.

The last method that you need to add to the myAdd class is a method that is called when the Add button is clicked on the ASP.NET page. The code for this method is shown in Listing 6-15.

Listing 6-15: The Button1_Click method that is contained within the myAdd class

[VB]

```
Private Sub Button1_Click(ByVal sender As System.Object, ByVal _
        e As System.EventArgs) Handles Button1.Click
```

```vb
Dim ws As New localhost.Service1()
Dim userToken As UsernameToken
userToken = New UsernameToken(TextBox1.Text.ToString(), _
    TextBox2.Text.ToString(), PasswordOption.SendHashed)
Dim key As EncryptionKey = GetEncryptionKey()

ws.RequestSoapContext.Security.Tokens.Add(userToken)
ws.RequestSoapContext.Security.Elements.Add(New _
    Microsoft.Web.Services.Security.Signature(userToken))
ws.RequestSoapContext.Security.Elements.Add(New _
    EncryptedData(key))

Label1.Text = ws.Add(TextBox3.Text, TextBox4.Text)
End Sub
```

[C#]

```csharp
private void Button1_Click(object sender, System.EventArgs e)
{
    localhost.Service1 ws = new localhost.Service1();
    UsernameToken userToken;
    userToken = new UsernameToken(TextBox1.Text.ToString(),
        TextBox2.Text.ToString(), PasswordOption.SendHashed);

    EncryptionKey key = GetEncryptionKey();

    ws.RequestSoapContext.Security.Tokens.Add(userToken);
    ws.RequestSoapContext.Security.Elements.Add(new
        Microsoft.Web.Services.Security.Signature(userToken));
    ws.RequestSoapContext.Security.Elements.Add(new
        EncryptedData(key));

    Label1.Text = ws.Add(int.Parse(TextBox1.Text),
        int.Parse(TextBox2.Text)).ToString();
}
```

There isn't much code here since much of the work is being done in other methods or classes within the application. However, when the Add button on the ASP.NET page is clicked, the proxy class is instantiated. A UsernameToken object is created with the username and password that the users entered into some of the textboxes on the ASP.NET page. The password included with the UsernameToken object is hashed, because this is a requirement to consume the XML Web service.

After this, the private key is retrieved from the web.config file using the GetEncryptionKey method. Then the UsernameToken object is added to the SOAP header of the SOAP request message that is being constructed. Once this is complete, the SOAP request is digitally signed and encrypted before the Add() method of the XML Web service is instantiated.

It is important to point out that in order to use the encryption and digital signature technologies together, you have to fully qualify the Signature class to digitally sign the SOAP request. The reason for this is because the System.Security.Cryptography.Xml namespace is imported. This namespace also contains a Signature class and there is therefore a similar name conflict. For this reason, you need to fully qualify each use of the Signature class.

Compiling and Running the Application

Now everything is in place, and you can simply compile and run the application. Figure 6-3 shows you what the page will look like when you have successfully run the application. Remember that you have to use valid login credentials to instantiate the XML Web service or you will receive an error.

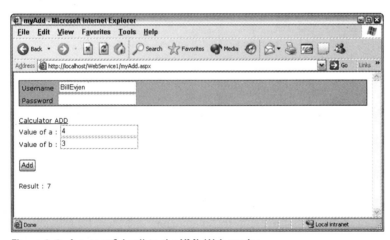

Figure 6-3: A successful call to the XML Web service

Listing 6-16 looks at the SOAP request that was actually sent from the ASP.NET application to the XML Web service.

Listing 6-16: The SOAP request

```
<soap:Envelope
 xmlns:soap="http://schemas.xmlsoap.org/soap/envelope/"
 xmlns:xsi="http://www.w3.org/2001/XMLSchema-instance"
 xmlns:xsd="http://www.w3.org/2001/XMLSchema">
    <soap:Header>
      <wsrp:path
        soap:actor="http://schemas.xmlsoap.org/soap/actor/next"
        soap:mustUnderstand="1"
        xmlns:wsrp="http://schemas.xmlsoap.org/rp">
        <wsrp:action
          xmlns:wsu="http://schemas.xmlsoap.org/ws/2002/07/utility"
          wsu:Id="Id-12246b4f-d561-44e5-9064-93cb62c72e2a">
          http://www.wiley.com/Add</wsrp:action>
        <wsrp:to
          xmlns:wsu="http://schemas.xmlsoap.org/ws/2002/07/utility"
          wsu:Id="Id-02a4f8e4-1a5e-4faa-9085-42d1aa811f02">
          http://localhost/vb_sec/service1.asmx</wsrp:to>
        <wsrp:id
          xmlns:wsu="http://schemas.xmlsoap.org/ws/2002/07/utility"
          wsu:Id="Id-6d91b8b1-b6c6-4d90-8b09-8e769bc35fab">
          uuid:e2911ec8-4138-4da8-a50e-23f240fbfe98</wsrp:id>
      </wsrp:path>
      <wsu:Timestamp
        xmlns:wsu="http://schemas.xmlsoap.org/ws/2002/07/utility">
        <wsu:Created wsu:Id="Id-e52ad5ff-214b-4e14-9841-
          83069338f24a">2002-11-16T18:45:37Z</wsu:Created>
        <wsu:Expires wsu:Id="Id-9d25d001-ade3-4ded-bd12-
          8535498e439c">2002-11-16T18:50:37Z</wsu:Expires>
      </wsu:Timestamp>
      <wsse:Security soap:mustUnderstand="1"
        xmlns:wsse="http://schemas.xmlsoap.org/ws/2002/07/secext">
        <wsse:UsernameToken Id="SecurityToken-af60a5d6-127e-4eab-
          bc6e-7a40b0c1adbe">
          <wsse:Username>BillEvjen</wsse:Username>
          <wsse:Password Type="wsse:PasswordDigest">
           ihIfxVLadJrtaXesOP3htcThBxA=</wsse:Password>
          <wsse:Nonce>cFvkv39rHdMlJ4LIVEkzqA==</wsse:Nonce>
          <wsu:Created
          xmlns:wsu="http://schemas.xmlsoap.org/ws/2002/07/utility">
          2002-11-16T18:45:37Z</wsu:Created>
        </wsse:UsernameToken>
        <xenc:ReferenceList
```

Continued

Listing 6-16 *(Continued)*

```
            xmlns:xenc="http://www.w3.org/2001/04/xmlenc#">
             <xenc:DataReference URI="#EncryptedContent-c765b497-a48b-
             4993-9c03-79ef4dba3f51" />
           </xenc:ReferenceList>
           <Signature xmlns="http://www.w3.org/2000/09/xmldsig#">
             <SignedInfo>
               <CanonicalizationMethod
               Algorithm="http://www.w3.org/2001/10/xml-exc-c14n#" />
               <SignatureMethod
               Algorithm="http://www.w3.org/2000/09/xmldsig#hmac-sha1"
               />
               <Reference URI="#Id-909c26dd-b5bc-4146-a0d9-
               c799b0a99979">
                 <Transforms>
                   <Transform Algorithm="http://www.w3.org/2001/10/xml-
                   exc-c14n#" />
                 </Transforms>
                 <DigestMethod
                 Algorithm="http://www.w3.org/2000/09/xmldsig#sha1" />
                 <DigestValue>puDlgib2Y5LOdfW3iMZADGJMElM=</DigestValue>
               </Reference>
             </SignedInfo>
           <SignatureValue>q2LuON3pslAx/c63+FKZdD5uwU4=</SignatureValue>
             <KeyInfo>
               <wsse:SecurityTokenReference>
                 <wsse:Reference URI="#SecurityToken-af60a5d6-127e-
                 4eab-bc6e-7a40b0c1adbe" />
               </wsse:SecurityTokenReference>
             </KeyInfo>
           </Signature>
         </wsse:Security>
       </soap:Header>
  <soap:Body
       xmlns:wsu="http://schemas.xmlsoap.org/ws/2002/07/utility"
       wsu:Id="Id-909c26dd-b5bc-4146-a0d9-c799b0a99979">
         <xenc:EncryptedData Id="EncryptedContent-c765b497-a48b-4993-
         9c03-79ef4dba3f51"
         Type="http://www.w3.org/2001/04/xmlenc#Content"
         xmlns:xenc="http://www.w3.org/2001/04/xmlenc#">
           <xenc:EncryptionMethod
           Algorithm="http://www.w3.org/2001/04/xmlenc#tripledes-cbc"
           />
           <KeyInfo xmlns="http://www.w3.org/2000/09/xmldsig#">
             <KeyName>AddEncrypt</KeyName>
```

```
        </KeyInfo>
        <xenc:CipherData>
          <xenc:CipherValue>bSxcfCmk7uy+LyEULe25rwlH5
          TCpbwvXkq3CX3/+UK/MbzYHUrSBr9PYtTWRxhvqH9a1YTuutP6Kt
          /zAvIUE64DfOcBBH6kk</xenc:CipherValue>
        </xenc:CipherData>
      </xenc:EncryptedData>
    </soap:Body>
</soap:Envelope>
```

 Note that many of the `<Reference>` elements from the SOAP request were removed for space reasons.

As you know, this SOAP request from the ASP.NET application is doing a lot. It contains information about the path, timestamp, signature, credentials, and encryption of the message.

The XML Web service received this message and created the SOAP response that is shown in Listing 6-17.

Listing 6-17: The SOAP response

```
<soap:Envelope
 xmlns:soap="http://schemas.xmlsoap.org/soap/envelope/"
 xmlns:xsi="http://www.w3.org/2001/XMLSchema-instance"
 xmlns:xsd="http://www.w3.org/2001/XMLSchema">
    <soap:Header>
      <wsu:Timestamp
       xmlns:wsu="http://schemas.xmlsoap.org/ws/2002/07/utility">
        <wsu:Created wsu:Id="Id-f50cdef3-51c0-4c12-a213-
        688ea3293e4c">2002-11-16T18:45:37Z</wsu:Created>
        <wsu:Expires wsu:Id="Id-0cd3ccaa-253b-4ec0-97fc-
        f1334eb13079">2002-11-16T18:50:37Z</wsu:Expires>
      </wsu:Timestamp>
      <wsse:Security soap:mustUnderstand="1"
       xmlns:wsse="http://schemas.xmlsoap.org/ws/2002/07/secext">
        <xenc:ReferenceList
         xmlns:xenc="http://www.w3.org/2001/04/xmlenc#">
          <xenc:DataReference URI="#EncryptedContent-2ad10449-b38f-
          47a1-89f7-2a58f6453451" />
        </xenc:ReferenceList>
      </wsse:Security>
```

Continued

Listing 6-17 *(Continued)*

```
    </soap:Header>
    <soap:Body>
      <xenc:EncryptedData Id="EncryptedContent-2ad10449-b38f-47a1-
      89f7-2a58f6453451"
      Type="http://www.w3.org/2001/04/xmlenc#Content"
      xmlns:xenc="http://www.w3.org/2001/04/xmlenc#">
        <xenc:EncryptionMethod
         Algorithm="http://www.w3.org/2001/04/xmlenc#tripledes-cbc"
        />
        <KeyInfo xmlns="http://www.w3.org/2000/09/xmldsig#">
          <KeyName>AddEncrypt</KeyName>
        </KeyInfo>
        <xenc:CipherData>
          <xenc:CipherValue>
          xNkti9U2aUu7u6liitthk5gGALQv294zO9NPxO+OE6S3J50U+
          wfWzSKJyVox6HXSq3LPqAyQB/AChv5XCEsuI4ixxA6Xkf1DH/Cg+
          KEJ/cAUuI6GKQdVF/1PkmCpl6tk</xenc:CipherValue>
        </xenc:CipherData>
      </xenc:EncryptedData>
    </soap:Body>
</soap:Envelope>
```

As you can see from Listing 6-17, the SOAP response is encrypted. It therefore has to be decrypted by the ASP.NET application in order to retrieve the value that the XML Web service returned. Included with the encryption is the KeyInfo for this particular encryption. You will notice that you used the same name as you did for the encrypted SOAP message that was sent from the consuming application to the XML Web service, although it could have just as easily been a new name for the encryption key. It is up to you to decide how you construct this.

Summary

Remember that it is possible to "roll your own" security in the XML Web services that you build. In all these cases, you can build your own classes that work with SOAP headers or SOAP extensions to apply credential verification, digital signing, or encryption. What the WSE does instead of this approach is to apply these capabilities according to specifications that have been thus far supported by a wide section of the IT industry.

By abiding by the WS-Security specification, you ensure that your XML Web services are interoperable and compatible with the consumers that want to invoke your service – regardless of the platform on which the consuming application resides. The specification is the common language in this multi-lingual world and that is why it is so important to use.

Chapter 7

Routing SOAP Messages

IN THIS CHAPTER

- ◆ Understanding the advantages of routing SOAP messages
- ◆ Building a SOAP router
- ◆ Building consuming applications that work with SOAP routers

THE ROUTING OF INFORMATION is an important part of any network topology. Before the WSE, .NET developers were primarily limited to developing XML Web services that operated point-to-point.

This means that a consuming application sends a SOAP request directly to an XML Web service, which then processes the SOAP message and sends a SOAP response in return to the consuming application. *Point-to-point* is quite adequate in most situations.

The WSE allows developers to create XML Web services that are capable of routing SOAP messages (shown in Figure 7-1). This means messages are able to travel to a SOAP router or intermediary that will redirect the SOAP message to an appropriate endpoint.

In the scenario in Figure 7-1, a consuming application sends a SOAP request to a SOAP router, which then routes the SOAP message to an XML Web service. The SOAP router decides on the appropriate endpoint based upon settings contained within an XML-based configuration file. The appropriate XML Web service then receives the SOAP message and processes it before sending a response back on the same path that the request came in on. Therefore, a SOAP request is then sent from the XML Web service back to the SOAP router, where the router takes the SOAP message and sends it back to the original requestor.

Advantages of Routing SOAP Messages

With all of the XML Web services that you might have built so far on the .NET platform, most of them, if not all of them thus far, have been point-to-point Web services. Because of this, you might be wondering what the advantages would be for routing SOAP messages through a SOAP intermediary. One of the main advantages to routing SOAP messages through a SOAP router is that it gives you more power over the consumption of your XML Web services. You will see this power as you work through this chapter. For example, if you have a SOAP router that sits between the consumer and XML Web service you have the power of redirection. There will be times when you are working with XML Web services that are mission critical and need to have as close to 100% uptime as is possible. This can be achieved a lot easier by using a SOAP router.

In this situation, you would create another instance of your XML Web service and re-route all SOAP requests to the second instance while you repair or upgrade the first instance of the XML Web service. Once the first instance is upgraded or repaired, you can reconfigure the SOAP router to route SOAP requests back to the original XML Web service. Doing this re-routing process using the WSE makes it much easier to take your servers offline for this kind of work.

Another advantage to routing SOAP requests using the WSE is that you can have multiple XML Web services throughout your enterprise and re-route SOAP requests completely based upon the naming structure of the Web service. Not only does the WSE give you control over routing SOAP messages based on a full name specification of the XML Web service that the consuming application is requesting, but you also can also add some wildcard name declarations into the mix of routing scenarios. For instance, you can specify that every SOAP request that comes in for an XML Web service that starts with the letter "A" should be routed to some specific endpoint and every SOAP request that comes in for an XML Web service that starts with the letter "B" should go to some other endpoint.

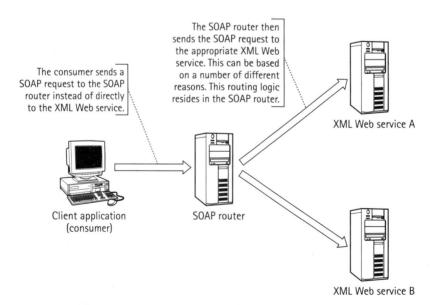

Figure 7-1: SOAP messages being routed to a SOAP endpoint

In the end, by using the WSE to route SOAP requests, you end up with considerably more control over your environment.

This chapter takes a look at how to construct a routing scenario on your computer. First, you will build the XML Web service that will serve as the final endpoint, and then construct the SOAP router that will route all incoming requests to this final endpoint. Finally, you will build the consuming application that will be constructed to send all SOAP requests to the desired endpoint via the SOAP router.

Building the Web Service Endpoint

When routing SOAP messages, you want to have an XML Web service to route SOAP messages to. The great thing about the construction of XML Web services that you are going to route SOAP messages to is that you don't have to do much to the XML Web service in order to get it to interact properly with routed SOAP messages. You have to make some additions to your web.config file in order for your XML Web service to allow consumers to consume the Web service using routing. Listing 7-1 shows you the changes that you have to make in order for routed SOAP messages to be understood by the XML Web service that you are going to build.

Listing 7-1: The XML Web service's web.config file

```xml
<?xml version="1.0" encoding="utf-8" ?>
<configuration>

  <configSections>
    <section name="microsoft.web.services"
    type="Microsoft.Web.Services.
    Configuration.WebServicesConfiguration,
    Microsoft.Web.Services, Version=1.0.0.0, Culture=neutral,
    PublicKeyToken=31bf3856ad364e35" />
  </configSections>

<system.web>

<webServices>
    <soapExtensionTypes>
      <add type="Microsoft.Web.Services.WebServicesExtension,
      Microsoft.Web.Services,Version=1.0.0.0,
      Culture=neutral,PublicKeyToken=31bf3856ad364e35"
      priority="1" group="0"/>
      </soapExtensionTypes>
```

Continued

Listing 7-1 *(Continued)*

```
    </webServices>

  </system.web>

</configuration>
```

The reason that you need to include this when you are working with version 1.0 of the .NET Framework is that by default, the .NET Framework 1.0 makes it a requirement that SOAP headers need to be understood by the XML Web service. This is covered in more detail when you look at the SOAP request and the response that are generated when the consumer calls the XML Web service later in the chapter.

Therefore, for the purposes of this demonstration of SOAP routing using the WSE, build a simple XML Web service that simply adds two numbers together. If you are using Visual Studio .NET, you need to create a new ASP.NET Web Service project called AddWS. Once created, this project will contain a single XML Web service file called Service1.asmx.

Use the code from Listing 7-2 for this simple XML Web service.

Listing 7-2: A simple XML Web service

[VB]

```
Imports System.Web.Services

<WebService(Namespace:="http://www.wiley.com")> _
Public Class Service1
    Inherits System.Web.Services.WebService

<WebMethod()> Public Function Add(ByVal a As Integer, _
        ByVal b As Integer) As Integer
        Return (a + b)
    End Function
End Class
```

[C#]

```
using System;
using System.Collections;
using System.ComponentModel;
using System.Data;
using System.Diagnostics;
using System.Web;
using System.Web.Services;

namespace AddWS
```

```
{
    public class Service1 : System.Web.Services.WebService
    {
        [WebMethod]
        public int Add(int a, int b)
        {
            return (a+b);
        }
    }
}
```

As mentioned earlier, you don't have to do anything to this XML Web service itself. You only have to make the necessary changes to the web.config file. There is no need to make any references to the WSE in the code. Your XML Web service should now be ready to consume.

Building the SOAP Router – The web.config File

Now comes the fun part. In order for SOAP requests to be routed through a SOAP router that you control, you need to create a virtual directory that will contain the configuration files that will end up performing the SOAP routing.

Within Visual Studio .NET, create an ASP.NET Web Application project called Router. This will create the virtual directory for you and will make it easy for you to create these needed configuration files including the base of the web.config file that you will need for your SOAP router.

To get this new application to act as a SOAP router, you first need to make some additions to the web.config file, as shown in Listing 7-3.

Listing 7-3: The SOAP router's web.config file in order to turn your application into a SOAP router

```
<?xml version="1.0" encoding="utf-8" ?>
<configuration>

    <configSections>
        <section name="microsoft.web.services"
        type="Microsoft.Web.Services.Configuration.
        WebServicesConfiguration, Microsoft.Web.Services,
        Version=1.0.0.0, Culture=neutral,
        PublicKeyToken=31bf3856ad364e35" />
```

Continued

Listing 7-3 *(Continued)*

```
    </configSections>

    <system.web>

        <httpHandlers>
            <add verb="*" path="Service1.asmx"
            type="Microsoft.Web.Services.Routing.RoutingHandler,
            Microsoft.Web.Services, Version=1.0.0.0,
            Culture=neutral, PublicKeyToken=31bf3856ad364e35" />
        </httpHandlers>

        <!-- The rest of the web.config file -->

    </system.web>

</configuration>
```

For readability purposes, the code of the `type` attribute for both the `<add>` and `<section>` elements in the `web.config` example in Listing 7-3 appears in multiple lines of code. In the actual file, the value of this attribute must be on a single, unbroken line.

Adding <configSections>

The first item that you need to add to the `web.config` file is a reference to the WSE by using the `<configSections>` element, as illustrated in Chapter 3. It does not need to be present if this element is present in either the `machine.config` or `app.config` files.

Adding <httpHandlers>

The second element is something new. Within the `web.config` file, you need to create an HTTP handler for a SOAP request that might be received by the application.

The `<add>` element contains a number of important attributes. You need to modify these attributes to get the router to perform in the desired manner.

VERB

The `verb` attribute within the `<add>` element specifies the type of SOAP request that this handler will take care of. The possible values that the `verb` accepts include `GET`, `POST`, and `PUT`. If you include more than one of these HTTP verbs, you separate them by commas. For instance, if you were only going to route SOAP requests that came to the SOAP router using HTTP POST and PUT , you would specify the `verb` attribute as such:

```
verb="POST,PUT"
```

The other option is to apply this handler to any type of SOAP request that the SOAP router might receive. You would apply a wildcard to the value of the `verb` attribute to make this happen:

```
verb="*"
```

PATH

The `path` attribute is the most important attribute in the `<add>` element. This element allows you to specify which SOAP requests the routing handler should take of, because the handler does not have to route every SOAP request that the SOAP router receives.

In the example you are working with, you are using the following value for the `path` attribute:

```
path="Service1.asmx"
```

This means that every request that comes in for the file `Service1.asmx` to the SOAP router will be passed by this handler to the WSE first. Using the `path` attribute, you can also include regular application files within your project and are not limited to simply using the application as a SOAP router.

So this means that if you made a request to `http://localhost/router/service1.asmx`, that request would be intercepted by the WSE and routed to an endpoint that will be later specified in a different configuration file. This second configuration file is discussed shortly.

If you then made a request for any other file within the application, such as `Service2.asmx` or `myWebPage.aspx`, you will find that because of the settings in the `web.config` file, the handler will not intercept these requests.

You can alter the value of the `path` attribute within the `<add>` element so that there is blanket coverage over all the SOAP requests that this particular handler will intercept. For instance, by using a wildcard, you can specify that you want every request for an XML Web service to be routed to your specified endpoint:

```
path="*.asmx"
```

The value `*.asmx`, indicates that every request made to the SOAP router for an XML Web service will be routed to an endpoint that you specify. So, for instance, it doesn't matter if the request is for `Service1.asmx` or `StLouisRams.asmx`; the request will be intercepted and forwarded to another endpoint that will process the SOAP message or even route it elsewhere.

It is also possible to use this wildcard character with a combination of characters to even further specify which requests the SOAP router should handle. Here's an example:

```
path="A*.asmx"
```

Using this combination of characters with a wildcard will mean that every request that comes in that starts with the letter A will be intercepted by the WSE and routed to the appropriate endpoint. Whether the request is for `Apple.asmx` or `Abracadabra.asmx`, the handler will take care of routing it to its specified endpoint. If the request is for `Opensaysame.asmx` though, it will not be handled by the SOAP router and will be processed by a file with that name contained within the application or an exception will be thrown if no endpoint is found at all.

TYPE

The `type` attribute is a specification of the strongly-typed assembly that will take care of routing the SOAP messages. The value of the `type` attribute must be specified on a single line.

Using multiple <httpHandlers> elements

You are not limited to just one `<httpHandlers>` element, so you can place as many of these qualifications within the `web.config` file that you deem necessary. For instance, if you were going to handle all requests for `Service1.asmx` as well as for any requests that start with the word `myWebService`, you construct your `<httpHandlers>` element as shown in Listing 7-4.

Listing 7-4: The SOAP router's web.config file that contains multiple <httpHandlers> elements to handle multiple requests

```xml
<?xml version="1.0" encoding="utf-8" ?>
<configuration>

<system.web>

    <httpHandlers>
      <add verb="*" path="Service1.asmx"
       type="Microsoft.Web.Services.Routing.RoutingHandler,
       Microsoft.Web.Services, Version=1.0.0.0, Culture=neutral,
       PublicKeyToken=31bf3856ad364e35" />
    </httpHandlers>

    <httpHandlers>
      <add verb="*" path="myWebService*.asmx"
       type="Microsoft.Web.Services.Routing.RoutingHandler,
```

```
        Microsoft.Web.Services, Version=1.0.0.0, Culture=neutral,
        PublicKeyToken=31bf3856ad364e35" />
    </httpHandlers>

    <!-- The rest of the web.config file -->

</system.web>

</configuration>
```

With this kind of construction, this SOAP router will handle all requests for Service1.asmx as well as any requests for XML Web services that start with the word myWebService. For instance, a request for myWebService11.asmx would be routed to the appropriate endpoint, whereas a request for Service2.asmx would not be. It would instead be handled by the application where the SOAP router resides if there is a file by that name residing there. If there isn't a file within the application by that particular name, then an exception will be thrown instead.

For this example, stick with having a single <httpHandlers> element that points to Service1.asmx, as shown in Listing 7-3.

Additional changes to the web.config file

The last item that you need to add to the web.config file is a specification of where the WSE will find the file that will show the path that the routed SOAP requests will need to take as based upon what is specified by the <httpHandlers> elements. This specification is simple and shown in Listing 7-5.

Listing 7-5: The SOAP router's web.config file that contains a reference to the file that specifies the routing scenario

```
<?xml version="1.0" encoding="utf-8" ?>
<configuration>

    <microsoft.web.services>
        <referral>
            <cache name="referralCache1.config" />
        </referral>
    </microsoft.web.services>

    <system.web>

        <!-- The rest of the web.config file -->

    </system.web>

</configuration>
```

The file that contains the SOAP routing directives is called a *referral cache*. The file is not required to be of the .config type, but it is highly recommended. By using the .config extension, you are guaranteed a higher level of security because this extension is locked down by IIS and is not browser-accessible.

It is also important to think about how you are going to name your routing files. You will find it a best practice to stick to some kind of nomenclature when naming these types of files. The reason for this is that once the WSE uses this file for routing SOAP messages, the file is then locked down and not changeable. Therefore, if your SOAP router's referral cache file was called referralCache1.config, it would be impossible to open up this file, make a change to the routing structure, and have the WSE automatically change its routing paths. Instead, you have to create a new file, maybe called referralCache2.config, and then make the appropriate changes to the web.config file. Then once you are ready to return to using referralCache1.config, you can make that change to the web.config file.

Now that you have specified which file specifies the routing and which SOAP requests you will route, you are ready to create the file that specifies where to route these SOAP messages.

Building the SOAP Router – The referralCache1.config File

The referralCache1.config file allows you to specify the routing of any SOAP messages that are intercepted by the handlers specified in the web.config file. As stated, it is not required that the file be of type .config, but it is recommended because you will find this to be more secure than using .xml, .txt, or something else that would be easily accessible using a browser.

The contents of this file are specified by the WS-Referral specification, as developed by Microsoft and IBM. Listing 7-6 shows the referralCache1.config file that will be used in your router application.

Listing 7-6: The SOAP router's referralCache1.config file that specifies the route the SOAP messages will take

```
<?xml version="1.0" ?>
<r:referrals
 xmlns:r="http://schemas.xmlsoap.org/ws/2001/10/referral">
  <r:ref>
    <r:for>
      <r:exact>http://localhost/Router/Service1.asmx</r:exact>
    </r:for>
    <r:if />
    <r:go>
      <r:via>http://localhost/AddWS/Service1.asmx</r:via>
```

```
    </r:go>
    <r:refId>uuid:fa469956-0057-4e77-962a-81c5e192f2ae</r:refId>
  </r:ref>
</r:referrals>
```

The `referralCache1.config` file contains some important information about how the SOAP message is routed to the appropriate endpoint. You will notice right away that like the `web.config` file, this is an XML-based file. Let's take a look at the structure of this file.

<referrals>

The `<referrals>` element specifies the schema that this file is being associated with.

<ref>

The `<ref>` element specifies where a SOAP request should be routed based on the request that is being received. It is possible to have more than one `<ref>` element contained within your `<referrals>` element, but there must be at least one `<ref>` element present.

<for>

There can only be one `<for>` element contained within the `<ref>` element. This element specifies the incoming request that is being received by the SOAP router.

<exact>

The `<exact>` element specifies the exact URL that is used by the incoming SOAP request. For this example, any request that comes in for `http://localhost/Router/Service1.asmx` is routed as specified in the `<go>` element (described shortly). It is important to realize that there isn't an actual file at this location, but this is the URL that the consuming application will use when sending the SOAP request.

The value that is presented within the `<exact>` element in this example is case-sensitive. When using the WSE, make sure that all values given with the `<exact>` and `<prefix>` elements are case-sensitive (even though the WS-Referral specification states that these elements can contain values that are case-insensitive!).

<go>

There can only be one `<go>` element contained within a `<ref>` element. This element specifies where the SOAP requests are rerouted.

<via>

The `<via>` element specifies the location of where the SOAP requests are routed if there is a match with the `<for>` element in the file. Unlike the `<exact>` element that is a child element of the `<for>` element, there isn't a requirement that the value contained within the `<via>` element be case-sensitive. As stated in the WS-Referral specification, the value contained within the `<via>` element can be case-insensitive and that is the case as well when using the WSE.

<refId>

The `<refId>` element allows you to give your routing instructions unique identifiers. The value that is used within this element can be anything you choose, but it is recommended that you use some type of unique GUID.

What happens when the SOAP router is initiated

When the SOAP router receives a request, the `web.config` file decides whether the request should be handled by the WSE as defined by the `<httpHandlers>` element. If it falls into the rules that are defined within the `web.config` file and is indeed handled by the WSE for routing, then the WSE takes a look at the contents of the routing file specified from the `<cache>` element within the `web.config` file.

In this case, the `referralCache1.config` file is examined for where to route the SOAP requests that are sent to the SOAP router. If the request is sent to the exact URL of `http://localhost/Router/Service1.asmx`, then the SOAP request is routed to the value that is specified within the `<via>` element in the same file. Then the SOAP router makes this request on behalf of the consuming application that sent the SOAP request and a SOAP response is returned. The SOAP router then returns this SOAP response directly to the consuming application that made the original request.

 After you have made a single SOAP request that has been processed by the SOAP router, the configuration file `referralCache1.config` becomes locked; you are unable to make any changes to the file. If you want to make changes to how SOAP requests are routed, you have to create a new routing file and point to this file from within the `web.config` file.

Routing beyond exact locations

Going back to the `web.config` file, as you saw earlier in the chapter, it is possible to construct the `<httpHandlers>` element so that it intercepts all SOAP requests that fit into a wildcard schema that you defined.

```
path="*.asmx"
```

For instance, this example allows for routing to occur for every request for an `.asmx` file. If you have something like this in your file, each request for an XML Web service is being intercepted and the URL is being examined by the WSE using the routing file that you have created. If your `web.config` file is set up with this wildcard, you are going to have some problems due to the fact that in the routing file, you have specified an exact structure that needs to be used by the consumer with the `<exact>` element.

If you look back at the routing file that you created in Listing 7-6, you will see that you specified an exact URL:

```
<r:exact>http://localhost/Router/Service1.asmx</r:exact>
```

This structure means that the URL that is used in the SOAP request needs to be *exactly* this — `http://localhost/Router/Service1.asmx`. If the request is for something else, the handler will pass on the SOAP request to the WSE, but it will soon find that there is no place to route the SOAP request to.

In these cases, you use the `<prefix>` element instead. The `<prefix>` element allows you to get away from specifying exact URLs; you can specify URL prefixes that will be part of the URL of the SOAP request.

For instance, if in the `web.config` file, you are specifying that you are going to route all requests for XML Web services (using `"*.asmx"` as the value of the `path` attribute), then you can use the following `<prefix>` element instead of the `<exact>` element in the routing file:

```
<r:prefix>http://localhost/Router/</r:prefix>
```

From this example, you can see that the value of the `<prefix>` element is simply `http://localhost/Router/`. As stated, when the WSE uses this value to make a comparison of the URL that the SOAP request is using, there will only be a comparison made to the beginning of the URL, or the prefix of the URL. If there is a match, then the SOAP request is routed regardless of what appears beyond the prefix.

Therefore, the SOAP request could be using `http://locahost/Router/Service1.asmx` or `http://localhost/Router/StLouisRams.asmx` and both requests will be routed to the value that is stated in the `<go>` element. Remember that the `<prefix>` element, like that of the `<exact>` element, is case-sensitive and you will then need to have the URL in the proper case in order to avoid receiving an error when your SOAP messages are interpreted by the SOAP router.

Routing to multiple destinations

As stated earlier, you can have more than one `<ref>` element contained within your routing configuration file, which enables you to specify multiple routing scenarios.

For instance, you might accept all SOAP requests for any `.asmx` files because this is what is specified in the `web.config` file by using the attribute `path="*.asmx"`. Although for this example, imagine that even though you are intercepting all SOAP requests for XML Web services for routing, you want to funnel all requests to a `WebService1.asmx` except when there is a SOAP request made for `WebService2.asmx`. If there is SOAP request for `WebService2.asmx`, then you want to route that particular request to an entirely different XML Web service than where you are going to route every other SOAP request.

Listing 7-7 shows a routing configuration file that would take care of these types of multiple routing scenarios.

Listing 7-7: A routing configuration file that contains multiple routing scenarios

```
<?xml version="1.0" ?>
<r:referrals
 xmlns:r="http://schemas.xmlsoap.org/ws/2001/10/referral">
  <r:ref>
    <r:for>
      <r:prefix>http://localhost/Router/</r:prefix>
    </r:for>
    <r:if />
    <r:go>
      <r:via>http://localhost/AddWS/WebService1.asmx</r:via>
    </r:go>
    <r:refId>uuid:fa469956-0057-4e77-962a-81c5e192f2ae</r:refId>
  </r:ref>
  <r:ref>
    <r:for>
      <r:exact>http://localhost/Router/WebService2.asmx</r:exact>
    </r:for>
    <r:if />
    <r:go>
      <r:via>http://localhost/AddWS/WebService2.asmx</r:via>
    </r:go>
    <r:refId>uuid:fa469956-0057-4e77-962a-81c5e192f2ae</r:refId>
  </r:ref>
</r:referrals>
```

From this routing configuration file, you can see that for any request that comes in for any XML Web service that has a URL prefix of `http://localhost/Router/`, that it will be handled by the SOAP router. Then if the SOAP request is for `WebService2.asmx`, then this will be routed to a different XML Web service than any other request made. This is because there is also a definition in place for just a WebService2.asmx SOAP request by using the <exact> element.

So in the end, with this structure, SOAP requests through this SOAP router will be handled as shown in Table 7-1.

TABLE 7-1 THE ROUTING CONFIGURATION FILE'S HANDLING OF SOAP REQUESTS

SOAP Requests Made	Routing Action
WebService1.asmx	Routed to WebService1.asmx
StLouisRams.asmx	Routed to WebService1.asmx
WS1.asmx	Routed to WebService1.asmx
WebService2.asmx	Routed to WebService2.asmx

By constructing your routing configuration files appropriately, you can build routing structures that will answer every type of SOAP request that might be intercepted by the SOAP router.

Building the Consumer

As the XML Web service provider, in this situation, you're going to want all SOAP requests that come for your XML Web service to be run through the SOAP router that you have created and in which requests are defined in the routing configuration file that is shown in Listing 7-6.

As stated earlier, there are a number of benefits in routing SOAP requests to the appropriate endpoints as opposed to allowing consumers to work with XML Web services directly. One of the main reasons that you will find it easier to use a SOAP router is the ability to take down your XML Web services for maintenance or updating without the consumer seeing any downtime.

In this case, you have a simple XML Web service in place at http://localhost/AddWS/Service1.asmx. Instead of having the prospective consumer of this XML Web service consume it directly, you are going to have them work through the SOAP router that you have created at http://localhost/Router/.

Now construct an ASP.NET application that will work directly with the SOAP router to invoke the Web service built earlier in the chapter. Create an ASP.NET Web Application project called RouterConsume. The first step in working with a SOAP router from a client perspective is creating a proxy class that will work with the SOAP router instead of one that works directly with the XML Web service.

Unfortunately, if you make a Web reference to the SOAP router as you would do to the XML Web service, Visual Studio .NET will not create the appropriate proxy class because there is no actual .wsdl file on the SOAP router that will allow Visual Studio .NET to construct this proxy class.

Therefore, if you are using Visual Studio .NET, you need to make a reference to the actual XML Web service as you normally do as if you weren't working with SOAP routing at all. So, for this example, you have to right-click on the project name within the Solution Explorer and select Add Web Reference. Then you need to make a reference to http://localhost/AddWS/Service1.asmx.

After you have added this reference to your project, Visual Studio .NET creates a proxy class for you that will work with this XML Web service. However, you don't to want to work directly with the XML Web service. Instead, you want to work with the SOAP router that will, in turn, work with the XML Web service on your behalf. Therefore, you need to make some changes to the proxy class that was created for you by Visual Studio .NET in order to get your client application communicating with the SOAP router that you created earlier in this chapter.

You can find the proxy class by clicking the Show All Files button in the Solution Explorer and navigating down the tree to RouterConsume → Web References → localhost → Reference.map → Reference.[vb or cs]. Open the Reference class file because this is the proxy class that is going to need to be changed in order to work with the SOAP router.

Because your SOAP header will contain WS-Routing information, you need to make it so that the proxy class inherits from Microsoft.Web.Service. WebServicesClientProtocol instead of from System.Web.Services.Protocols. SoapHttpClientProtocol. This will allow the WSE to intercept the outgoing SOAP requests and place the appropriate information into the SOAP header so that the SOAP router can act upon the SOAP message.

Once you have made this change, look for the code in the proxy class shown in Listing 7-8.

Listing 7-8: The piece of code to look for in the proxy class

[VB]

```
Public Sub New()
   MyBase.New
   Me.Url = "http://localhost/addws/service1.asmx"
End Sub
```

[C#]

```
public Service1() {
   this.Url = "http://localhost/addws/service1.asmx";
}
```

When you find this section of code within the proxy class, you need to change the `Url` property's value from the reference to the XML Web service to a URL that points to the SOAP router. Listing 7-9 shows you how to do this.

Listing 7-9: Changes made to the Url property in the proxy class

[VB]

```
Public Sub New()
   MyBase.New
   Me.Url = "http://localhost/Router/Service1.asmx"
End Sub
```

[C#]

```
public Service1() {
   this.Url = "http://localhost/Router/Service1.asmx";
}
```

In this case, the value of the `Url` property was changed to `http://localhost/Router/Service1.asmx`. It is now pointing to the SOAP router instead of the XML Web service itself.

The absolute URL that you provide as the value to the `Url` property is case-sensitive.

After you make these changes to the proxy class, you need to recompile the class by choosing Build → Build Solution in Visual Studio .NET.

The ASP.NET page, `WebForm1.aspx`, is a simple ASP.NET page that contains two textboxes, a Button control, and a Label Control. Again, as in other chapters, the user enters an integer into each of the textboxes and clicks the button. The XML Web service will then display the returned result in the Label control. You don't need to do anything different to the ASP.NET page to work with the SOAP router. Listing 7-10 shows the code-behind for the ASP.NET page.

Listing 7-10: The code-behind for the ASP.NET page that will send a SOAP request to the SOAP router

[VB]

```
Public Class WebForm1
  Inherits System.Web.UI.Page
```

Continued

Listing 7-10 *(Continued)*

```
Protected WithEvents TextBox1 As System.Web.UI.WebControls.TextBox
Protected WithEvents TextBox2 As System.Web.UI.WebControls.TextBox
Protected WithEvents Button1 As System.Web.UI.WebControls.Button
Protected WithEvents Label1 As System.Web.UI.WebControls.Label

  Private Sub Button1_Click(ByVal sender As System.Object, _
     ByVal e As System.EventArgs) Handles Button1.Click

       Dim ws As New localhost.Service1()

       Label1.Text = ws.Add(TextBox1.Text.ToString(), _
          TextBox2.Text.ToString())
    End Sub

End Class
```

[C#]

```
using System;
using System.Collections;
using System.ComponentModel;
using System.Data;
using System.Drawing;
using System.Web;
using System.Web.SessionState;
using System.Web.UI;
using System.Web.UI.WebControls;
using System.Web.UI.HtmlControls;

namespace WebApplication1
{
    public class WebForm1 : System.Web.UI.Page
    {
        protected System.Web.UI.WebControls.TextBox TextBox1;
        protected System.Web.UI.WebControls.TextBox TextBox2;
        protected System.Web.UI.WebControls.Button Button1;
        protected System.Web.UI.WebControls.Label Label1;

        private void Button1_Click(object sender, System.EventArgs e)
        {
          localhost.Service1 ws = new localhost.Service1();

           Label1.Text = ws.Add(int.Parse(TextBox1.Text),
```

```
            int.Parse(TextBox2.Text)).ToString();
        }
    }
}
```

The difference is that the ASP.NET application will send the SOAP request not to the XML Web service, but instead will send it directly to the SOAP router.

Listing 7-11 shows the SOAP request that is sent from the client application to the SOAP router. This WS-Routing information is shown in bold.

Listing 7-11: The SOAP request sent from the client application to the SOAP router

```
<soap:Envelope
 xmlns:soap="http://schemas.xmlsoap.org/soap/envelope/"
 xmlns:xsi="http://www.w3.org/2001/XMLSchema-instance"
 xmlns:xsd="http://www.w3.org/2001/XMLSchema">
    <soap:Header>
      <wsrp:path
       soap:actor="http://schemas.xmlsoap.org/soap/actor/next"
       soap:mustUnderstand="1"
       xmlns:wsrp="http://schemas.xmlsoap.org/rp">
        <wsrp:action>http://www.wiley.com/Add</wsrp:action>
        <wsrp:to>http://localhost/Router/Service1.asmx</wsrp:to>
        <wsrp:id>uuid:2e862cf6-82c1-4025-9173-bb2025dc1f24</wsrp:id>
      </wsrp:path>
      <wsu:Timestamp
       xmlns:wsu="http://schemas.xmlsoap.org/ws/2002/07/utility">
        <wsu:Created>2002-12-12T02:40:38Z</wsu:Created>
        <wsu:Expires>2002-12-12T02:45:38Z</wsu:Expires>
      </wsu:Timestamp>
    </soap:Header>
    <soap:Body>
      <Add xmlns="http://www.wiley.com/">
        <a>11</a>
        <b>6</b>
      </Add>
    </soap:Body>
</soap:Envelope>
```

The first point to notice about the WS-Routing information is that there is a mustUnderstand attribute with a value of 1 within the <path> element. A value of 1 also means *true*. Therefore the SOAP router is required to understand the contents of the SOAP header. The SOAP router will only understand the SOAP header information if it understands WS-Routing. Recall that you did set up the SOAP router with the WSE, so you can be assured that it will understand the contents of the SOAP header contained with this SOAP request.

The first child node within the `<path>` element is the `<action>` element. This is a required element that indicates the intent of the message. So, in this case, the `<action>` element's value is the namespace that is declared by the XML Web service followed by the name of the WebMethod that is being invoked.

The next child node is the `<to>` element, which is the receiver of the SOAP request. In this case, it is the SOAP router that was created earlier in the chapter. The SOAP router takes care of forwarding the SOAP message to the actual XML Web service.

The last child node is the `<id>` element. This element provides a unique identifier for the SOAP message.

The rest of the SOAP request is what you would expect from a WSE constructed SOAP request. Listing 7-12 shows the SOAP message sent from the SOAP router to the XML Web service.

Listing 7-12: The SOAP message sent from the SOAP router to the XML Web service

```
<soap:Envelope
 xmlns:soap="http://schemas.xmlsoap.org/soap/envelope/"
 xmlns:xsi="http://www.w3.org/2001/XMLSchema-instance"
 xmlns:xsd="http://www.w3.org/2001/XMLSchema">
    <soap:Header>
      <wsu:Timestamp
       xmlns:wsu="http://schemas.xmlsoap.org/ws/2002/07/utility">
        <wsu:Created>2002-12-12T02:40:38Z</wsu:Created>
        <wsu:Expires>2002-12-12T02:45:38Z</wsu:Expires>
        <wsu:Received Actor="http://localhost/Router/Service1.asmx"
        Delay="1012">2002-12-12T02:40:39Z</wsu:Received>
      </wsu:Timestamp>
      <wsrp:path
       soap:actor="http://schemas.xmlsoap.org/soap/actor/next"
       soap:mustUnderstand="1"
       xmlns:wsrp="http://schemas.xmlsoap.org/rp">
        <wsrp:action>http://www.wiley.com/Add</wsrp:action>
        <wsrp:to>http://localhost/Router/Service1.asmx</wsrp:to>
        <wsrp:fwd>
          <wsrp:via>http://localhost/AddWS/service1.asmx</wsrp:via>
        </wsrp:fwd>
        <wsrp:id>uuid:2e862cf6-82c1-4025-9173-bb2025dc1f24</wsrp:id>
      </wsrp:path>
    </soap:Header>
    <soap:Body>
      <Add xmlns="http://www.wiley.com/">
        <a>11</a>
        <b>6</b>
```

```
    </Add>
   </soap:Body>
</soap:Envelope>
```

Once the SOAP router receives the SOAP request from the client application, the WSE takes hold of it and makes a few additions to the SOAP header. The first addition that is made is to the `<Timestamp>` element. The SOAP router makes a registration of when the SOAP request was received from the client application. This time is registered in within the `<Received>` child node. The `Delay` attribute of the `<Received>` element specifies the amount of time that has elapsed from when the SOAP request was sent by the client application to the time that the SOAP request was received by the SOAP router. This time, which is the numerical value, is represented as milliseconds.

The second addition to the SOAP header of the SOAP request that is received is to the `<Path>` element. The `<fwd>` child node contains a `<via>` element. The value of the `<via>` element is the path to where the SOAP message is being sent from the SOAP router. This path is retrieved from the routing configuration file within the SOAP router application.

After these changes are made to the SOAP message, this message is sent to the final endpoint—the XML Web service. The XML Web service then takes this message, processes it, and sends back a simple SOAP response. This SOAP response from the XML Web service is shown in Listing 7-13.

Listing 7-13: The SOAP response from the XML Web service to the SOAP router

```
<soap:Envelope
 xmlns:soap="http://schemas.xmlsoap.org/soap/envelope/"
 xmlns:xsi="http://www.w3.org/2001/XMLSchema-instance"
 xmlns:xsd="http://www.w3.org/2001/XMLSchema">
    <soap:Header>
      <wsu:Timestamp
       xmlns:wsu="http://schemas.xmlsoap.org/ws/2002/07/utility">
        <wsu:Created>2002-12-12T02:40:40Z</wsu:Created>
        <wsu:Expires>2002-12-12T02:45:40Z</wsu:Expires>
      </wsu:Timestamp>
    </soap:Header>
    <soap:Body>
      <AddResponse xmlns="http://www.wiley.com/">
        <AddResult>17</AddResult>
      </AddResponse>
    </soap:Body>
</soap:Envelope>
```

The SOAP response is what you would expect. Note in Listings 7-12 and 7-13 that the mustUnderstand attribute was set to a true value of 1. This means that the

receiver of that SOAP message must understand the SOAP header information, otherwise the receiving application throws an exception. Therefore, with this attribute
set to *true*, the final XML Web service that receives this SOAP message that contains this SOAP header also needs to understand the contents of the SOAP header.
That is why at the beginning of this chapter, when you were building the XML Web
service, you built the XML Web service so that it works with the WSE. You did this
by making the proper WSE registrations within the `web.config` file.

The ideal situation would be to route your SOAP messages to any endpoint,
whether or not that XML Web service understood the information that was contained in the SOAP header. Unfortunately, this isn't possible if you are working
with the .NET Framework 1.0, which at the time of this writing is the only version
of the .NET Framework that the WSE works on.

It is possible to use the WSE to set the `mustUnderstand` attribute to false within
the code of your application, as shown here in Visual Basic .NET:

```
ws.RequestSoapContext.Path.MustUnderstand = False
```

What this does is that instead of setting the `mustUnderstand` to 0 (which means
false), the WSE completely removes the `mustUnderstand` attribute from the SOAP
request. This unfortunately is a problem if you are working with the .NET
Framework version 1.0, because this version of the framework requires that all
XML Web services *must* understand the SOAP headers of all SOAP requests.

This changes with version 1.1 of the .NET Framework, in which the default setting will be that XML Web services do *not* need to understand the SOAP header
information. If you are going to want your XML Web services to be forced to
understand all the SOAP headers of the SOAP messages that it receives, then you
will have to explicitly set this in the code of your XML Web service.

With this kind of structure, again, if you are working with the .NET Framework
version 1.0, all your XML Web services must work with and understand the SOAP
headers. This means that you always have to set the appropriate values within the
`web.config` file so that your XML Web services will work with the WSE.

With that said, let's now take a look at the SOAP message that is sent from the
SOAP router back to the origin of the first message – the client application. This is
shown in Listing 7-14.

Listing 7-14: The SOAP message sent from the SOAP router to the client application

```
<soap:Envelope
 xmlns:soap="http://schemas.xmlsoap.org/soap/envelope/"
 xmlns:xsi="http://www.w3.org/2001/XMLSchema-instance"
 xmlns:xsd="http://www.w3.org/2001/XMLSchema">
    <soap:Header>
      <wsu:Timestamp
       xmlns:wsu="http://schemas.xmlsoap.org/ws/2002/07/utility">
        <wsu:Created>2002-12-12T02:40:40Z</wsu:Created>
        <wsu:Expires>2002-12-12T02:45:40Z</wsu:Expires>
```

```
    <wsu:Received Actor="http://localhost/Router/Service1.asmx"
     Delay="22">2002-12-12T02:40:40Z</wsu:Received>
   </wsu:Timestamp>
  </soap:Header>
  <soap:Body>
   <AddResponse xmlns="http://www.wiley.com/">
    <AddResult>17</AddResult>
   </AddResponse>
  </soap:Body>
</soap:Envelope>
```

As you can see from this example, the SOAP router simply adds information to the `<Timestamp>` element within the SOAP header. As it did when it received the SOAP request from the client application, the SOAP router adds to the `<Timestamp>` element a child element that specifies when it received the SOAP message from the XML Web service. The value assigned to the `<Received>` element is the time that the SOAP message was received, and the `Delay` attribute is used to show the time in milliseconds from when the message was sent from the XML Web service to the SOAP router.

In the end, the client application receives the SOAP response that was sent from the XML Web service through the SOAP router. The client application can then work with the SOAP response just as if it were received from the XML Web service itself. As the owner of the router, you can control how consumers use the XML Web services that they might be working with. You are able to make changes to the routing configuration file and point the SOAP messages to new XML Web services. The consumer will not know the difference. When done right, this can be a powerful tool.

Summary

As you have seen from this chapter, SOAP routing can be powerful if used correctly. It should be noted that at present only Microsoft is supporting WS-Routing and WS-Referral; therefore, you can only use these routing scenarios with applications running on the Microsoft platform.

Even though you are limited in this fashion, SOAP routing is still powerful and full of benefits. When you need to have significant uptime for your XML Web services or if you have to turn off an XML Web service for any reason, you should look at SOAP routing as a solution to providing the best possible service to the consumers of your services.

Chapter 8

Understanding WS-Attachments and DIME

IN THIS CHAPTER

◆ Working with attachments before and after the arrival of WS-Attachments and DIME

◆ Looking closely at DIME processing

◆ Modifying the construction of DIME records

◆ Comparing serialization to DIME encapsulation

THE POINT OF WEB SERVICES is to expose data and application logic to others using a common language that will make it easy for others to consume. That is the power of Web services, because this model and the specifications that are in place do make it easy. Not all the data that you want to expose is ASCII-based data, but instead can be in different forms such as images, documents, or even a collection of documents or files. How do you include these items in any XML Web services that you build?

This is an important inclusion to many applications and there are a couple of ways to do it. This chapter looks at how to include these items without the WSE, and then covers how the WSE performs these operations. It also looks at how the WSE does this differently, and takes a close look at the technologies that makes it all happen. The following section looks at how to send images with your SOAP messages without using the WSE first as this would be a good way to compare to two formats.

Sending Attachments Before the Advent of WS-Attachments and DIME

As mentioned, the emphasis on Web services is how to pass textual data, formulated into XML, from the XML Web service to consuming endpoints.

This type of data, pressed into XML, is easily understood by receiving applications. But how do you put an image into XML format? Invariably, you will want to use this great means of passing information to send other items such as Word documents, PDF files, and images.

Before WS-Attachments and DIME came onto the scene, it was possible to accomplish these tasks by converting the images and other objects to text format. Once converted, the binary text of the images was encased in the SOAP envelope and then passed from the XML Web service's WebMethod.

For an example of this, look at a simple XML Web service that returns an image from a specified file path (see Listing 8-1). You might need to make a reference to the System.Drawing DLL within the Solution Explorer for this to work.

Listing 8-1: The ImageSend.asmx Web Service

[VB]

```
Imports System.Web.Services
Imports System.Drawing
Imports System.IO

<WebService(Namespace:="http://www.wiley.com")> _
Public Class ImageSend
    Inherits System.Web.Services.WebService

    <WebMethod()> Public Function GetImage(ByVal FilePath _
        As String) As Byte()

        Dim myBitmap as Bitmap
        Dim myMemoryStream as MemoryStream

        myMemoryStream = New MemoryStream()

        Try
            myBitmap = New Bitmap(Filepath)
            myBitmap.Save(myMemoryStream, _
                System.Drawing.Imaging.ImageFormat.Jpeg)

            Return myMemoryStream.ToArray()
        Catch
            Return Nothing
        End Try
    End Function

End Class
```

[C#]

```
using System;
using System.Collections;
using System.ComponentModel;
```

```
using System.Data;
using System.Diagnostics;
using System.Web;
using System.Web.Services;
using System.Drawing;
using System.IO;

namespace WebService1
{
 public class ImageSend : System.Web.Services.WebService
 {
  [WebMethod]
  public Byte[] GetImage(string FilePath)
{
    Bitmap myBitmap;
    MemoryStream myMemoryStream;

    myMemoryStream = new MemoryStream();

    try
    {
       myBitmap = new Bitmap(FilePath);
       myBitmap.Save(myMemoryStream,
          System.Drawing.Imaging.ImageFormat.Jpeg);

       return myMemoryStream.ToArray();
    }
    catch
    {
       return null;
    }
   }
  }
}
```

This XML Web service returns a byte array and stuffs the image into this byte array using the `Bitmap` class that loads the image into a memory stream. Using the `Try` command, it first tries to serialize the image into a memory stream to the format of a JPEG image using the `System.Drawing` namespace. If the `try` is unsuccessful, it returns a `null` value. The other namespace to be imported into this XML Web service in order to gain access to the memory stream is the `System.IO` namespace.

When this XML Web service is invoked, there isn't an actual image in the SOAP envelope, as you will see, but a binary representation of the image. This is shown in Figure 8-1.

All in all, this is pretty simple and straightforward. This XML Web service can easily return an image without requiring much code. On the other end, the user must consume this XML Web service and display the image that is sent to it as a byte array. You'll see how to consume this type of XML Web service later in the chapter when we make comparisons between sending attachments in this manner and sending attachments using WS-Attachments and DIME. Now let's take a look at what happens when this XML Web service sends an image that has been serialized into a SOAP envelope.

Figure 8-1: A serialized image

As you can see from the XML that was returned from the XML Web service, it is rather verbose and there is a huge cost in serializing and deserializing this data. That is the problem with sending attachments in this manner. Being this verbose, this operation doesn't provide you with the best possible performance. Especially when you are dealing with images or documents that can be rather large in size, you will find that this means of exposing these objects can be difficult for your consumers.

In answer to this problem, the WS-Attachments specification was developed. The next section looks at how the WSE will answer this same problem in a different manner.

Understanding WS-Attachments and DIME

Right away, many people working with passing documents in the previous manner realized that this wasn't going to be the best way of exposing documents. WS-Attachments and DIME were developed to address the problems with the previous method.

WS-Attachments and DIME allow you to attach documents outside of the SOAP envelope instead of having to be serialized and placed inside of the SOAP body. Being outside of the SOAP envelope, these attachments therefore don't need to be serialized into XML. Here is a list of some of the objects that you might want to keep outside of the SOAP message itself by using WS-Attachments and DIME:

- Images (.jpg, .gif, and .bmp)

- Compressed documents (.zip)

- Microsoft Office documents (.doc, .xls, .ppt, and .mdb)

- Other document types (.pdf)

- XML files and fragments and related XML technologies (.xml, .xslt, and .xsd)

- Other SOAP messages

Consider the last two items specifically. This specification allows you to place XML and SOAP messages outside of the typical SOAP body. It is difficult at times to include your own XML inside of a standard SOAP body because your XML might be of a different encoding than that in the SOAP body. Also, just as you send emails with an attached email, you might also have applications that send SOAP messages along with their SOAP messages so that some entity can act upon its contents. For instance, you might be sending a collection of SOAP messages as attachments along with your SOAP message to another application as a batch collection for processing by the receiving application.

DIME is the key to it all, so it is important to understand the structure of DIME and understand how it performs this little piece of magic.

Looking at DIME

DIME, which stands for *Direct Internet Message Encapsulation,* is simply a specification that allows you to encapsulate binary data into a series of records. These records, like SOAP messages, contain a header and a body. Figure 8-2 shows a simple abstract structure of this collection of DIME records.

Figure 8-2: A series of DIME records

The great thing about building messages using these DIME records is that you are not limited to the number of DIME records that can be sent with your SOAP message. You are also not required to know the length of the DIME messages that you send — this is taken care of for you.

The other important item to notice from Figure 8-2 is that the first record is specified with a simple flag that designates the record as the first in the series of DIME records. There is also a flag on the last DIME record that designates it as the last in the series. One thing that is not reflected in Figure 8-2 is that there is no set length to the size the DIME records can be. Some records can be small and others can be large.

The following sections look at each of the main pieces of the DIME record and what this means for sending the binary items that you want to send outside of the typical SOAP message.

THE DIME HEADER

The DIME header contains a structured set of flags that allow the WSE to work with the DIME records in a quick and logical manner. Figure 8-3 shows the structure of the DIME header and body.

The first item in the DIME header is the DIME version specification that is being used in the DIME record. The DIME version specification in the DIME header uses five bits of the header. The next three items in the DIME header are DIME header flags.

The first flag, labeled MB in the diagram, is a designation of whether the DIME record is the first record of the series. The value of 1 means that the particular DIME record is the first DIME record of the series. A value of 0 means that it isn't the first record and is therefore either one of the following records or the last record in the series.

The second flag contained with the first row of the DIME header is labeled ME (meaning Message End) in the diagram. This is a flag to specify whether this particular DIME record is the last record in the series of DIME records. Just like the MB flag, a value of 1 means that this particular record is the last of the DIME record series and a value of 0 means that it is either the first DIME record or one of the DIME records in the middle of the series.

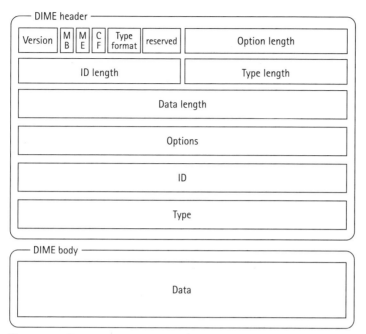

Figure 8-3: The DIME header and body

If there is only one DIME record in the series of DIME records, both the MB flag and the ME flag will contain a value of 1. This construction specifies that the DIME record is the first and last of the series.

The last flag contained within the DIME header is a *chunked data* flag designation. This flag specifies whether the data contained within the record is a part of a collection of data that is contained in one or more other DIME records within the series. The chunked record scenario is discussed in more detail later in this chapter.

Each of the flags consists of only one bit of information in the DIME header. Beyond the DIME version specification and the three flags, the next section in the DIME header is the Type Format section, which specifies the format and structure of the Type field. There are really two ways to specify the DIME record type. The first way is by absolute URI and the second is by MIME-media type. This section of the DIME header is only four bits in length. Table 8-1 shows you some example values of what each of these type format descriptions mean.

The next section is good idea of the developers of the DIME specification. This section is titled Reserved, meaning that for now, it does absolutely nothing and is held in reserve for potential future use. This reserved section of the DIME header consists of four bits.

TABLE 8-1 MOST COMMON TYPE FORMATS

Most Common Type Formats	Example
Absolute URI	http://schemas.xmlsoap.org/soap/envelope
MIME-media Type	image/JPEG

The last section of the first 32-bit row in the DIME header is the Options Length section. Since a section of the DIME header can consist of items that are of a variable length, the Options Length section and the next two sections (ID and Type Length) are there for the sole purpose of describing the length of these sections of the DIME record. For instance, the 16-bit Options Length section describes the length in bytes of the Options section of the DIME header. The 16-bit ID Length section describes in bytes the length of the ID section, and finally the Type Length section describes in bytes the length of the Type section. These sections and the sections that they describe are all contained within the DIME header.

The Data Length section describes the length of the data field contained within the DIME body. The Data Length field is 32 bits. While the other section-length sections of the DIME header have been only 16-bits long, they are describing sections of the DIME record that are only up to 64 bits in length. The Data Length section is larger due to the fact that it is describing a section of the DIME record that can be up to 4GB.

Everything described so far from the DIME header are of a fixed length. The next three items that are contained within the DIME header are of a variable length. The first of these variable length sections is the Options section.

The Options section contains optional information that might be used by the DIME parser. Since it can be of a variable length, its length is described in the Options Length section of the DIME header. The Options section allows for an extra 64 bits of extension to the DIME record.

The ID section is another section that can be of a variable length and therefore has its length specified in the ID Length section of the DIME header. The ID field provides a unique ID for the entire DIME record.

The last section within the DIME header is the Type section. The Type section is a 64-bit description of the encoding of the data that is contained in the Data section of the DIME record. The most common type descriptions are an absolute URI or a MIME-media type.

THE DIME BODY

The other section of the DIME record is the DIME body. It consists of the data payload. Since the size of the data payload can be of a variable length of up to 4GB, the size of the data that is contained within the Data section is defined by the Data Length section in the DIME header.

Chunked data

You might be looking at the DIME body size and wondering how you might send items within a DIME record that are longer than 4GB. You are not limited to 4GB because of the limitation of the DIME record. The DIME specification allows you to separate your attachments across multiple DIME records in a process known as *chunking*.

As you might remember, there are three flags contained at the beginning of the DIME record's header. One of the flags is a Chunked Data (CF) flag. If this flag is set (by a value of 1), this indicates that the DIME record is part of a series of DIME records in which the attachment is spread across.

When the DIME parser is processing a series of DIME records, the first record received that contains a CF flag is considered to be the first DIME record of the chunked data record collection.

The attachment can be broken into as many DIME records as you wish and you are not required to use the entire 4GB of the DIME record. For example, one of your DIME records might contain a Data section that is only 2GB, whereas the next might contain only 100KB of information. It is also important to note that your series of DIME records can contain as many chunked data collections as you want.

When the DIME parser reaches a DIME record in the series that does not have the CF flag set, the DIME parser considers this DIME record to be the last in the series of Chunked Data DIME records. Figure 8-4 shows you how the chunked data flags are set in a series of Chunked Data DIME records.

Figure 8-4: A series of DIME records with a series of Chunked Data records

Now that you know more about how your attachments are sent across wire using SOAP and DIME, you are ready to build a simple XML Web service that exposes a single image and a consuming application that will invoke the Web service and display the image.

Exposing a Single Image Using DIME

Now let's have a little fun and start sending DIME records to a client application. This is going to be quite different than the type of XML Web service that you built earlier in this chapter, because you pass the image that you are going to expose outside of the SOAP message itself but within a DIME record.

Let's start stepping through the creation of this XML Web service and create the XML Web service that will expose an image using DIME and WS-Attachments.

Creating the XML Web service provider

The XML Web service for this first application is a simple XML Web service. It contains a single WebMethod called `GetImage()` that simply exposes a specific image from the file server. For this application, create an ASP.NET Web Service project within Visual Studio .NET titled `MyGetImage`.

The first step in this process is to make the necessary changes to the `web.config` file so that it will work with the WSE and, in turn, be able to send items outside of the SOAP message in DIME records. You need to add a reference to the WSE DLL outside of the `<system.web>` elements if you have not already made this reference in the `machine.config` or the `app.config` files. This is shown in Listing 8-2. Remember that the value of `type` needs to be on a single line in the configuration file.

Listing 8-2: Adding a reference to the WSE in the web.config file

```
<configuration>

   <configSections>
      <section name="microsoft.web.services"
       type="Microsoft.Web.Services.Configuration.
       WebServicesConfiguration, Microsoft.Web.Services,
       Version=1.0.0.0, Culture=neutral,
       PublicKeyToken=31bf3856ad364e35" />
   </configSections>

   <system.web>

    <!-- The rest of the web.config file -->

   </system.web>

</configuration>
```

You next need to add the code in Listing 8-3 to the `web.config` file within the `<system.web>` elements.

Listing 8-3: Defining the WSE SoapExtension

```
<system.web>
  <webServices>
    <soapExtensionTypes>
```

```
        <add type="Microsoft.Web.Services.WebServicesExtension,
          Microsoft.Web.Services, Version=1.0.0.0, Culture=neutral,
          PublicKeyToken=31bf3856ad364e35" priority="1" group="0"/>
      </soapExtensionTypes>
    </webServices>

    <!-- The rest of the web.config file -->

</system.web>
```

Now that you have the `web.config` file in place and ready to go, the next step is to create the WebMethod. Listing 8-4 shows you the code for the `GetImage` WebMethod contained within `Service1.asmx`.

Listing 8-4: The GetImage WebMethod

`[VB]`

```
Imports System.Web.Services
Imports Microsoft.Web.Services
Imports Microsoft.Web.Services.Dime

<WebService(Namespace:="http://www.wiley.com")> _
Public Class Service1
    Inherits System.Web.Services.WebService

    <WebMethod()> Public Function GetImage()
        Dim responseContext As SoapContext = _
            HttpSoapContext.ResponseContext
        Dim dimeAttachment As DimeAttachment

        dimeAttachment = New DimeAttachment("image/jpeg", _
            TypeFormatEnum.MediaType, "C:\Trees.jpg")

        responseContext.Attachments.Add(dimeAttachment)
    End Function

End Class
```

`[C#]`

```
using System;
using System.Collections;
using System.ComponentModel;
```

Continued

Listing 8-4 *(Continued)*

```
using System.Data;
using System.Diagnostics;
using System.Web;
using System.Web.Services;
using Microsoft.Web.Services;
using Microsoft.Web.Services.Dime;

namespace myGetImage
{
    public class Service1 : System.Web.Services.WebService
    {
        [WebMethod]
        public void GetImage()
        {
            SoapContext responseContext =
                HttpSoapContext.ResponseContext;

            DimeAttachment dimeAttachment = new DimeAttachment(
                "image/jpeg", TypeFormatEnum.MediaType,
                @"C:\trees.jpg");

            responseContext.Attachments.Add(dimeAttachment);
        }
    }
}
```

The XML Web service is now ready to be consumed by clients that can work with DIME records. Here's a quick look at what is going on in the code in this sample from Listing 8-4.

You first need to make sure that you have imported the proper namespaces into the application. The `Microsoft.Web.Services` and the `Microsoft.Web.Services.Dime` namespaces are imported to allow you to work with the WSE-specific classes in order to attach DIME records to your SOAP responses.

The Web Service class that is going to be consumed has a single WebMethod, `GetImage`. Notice that the `GetImage` method call doesn't actually return anything, because there is no return value mentioned. You will later see how this plays out in the SOAP response.

Inside the WebMethod, you need to first create an instance of the `SoapContext` object that will return the SOAP response to the users:

```
Dim responseContext As SoapContext = HttpSoapContext.ResponseContext
```

The next step is to create an instance of the `DimeAttachment` object. This is a class that you will end up using to specify DIME header and payload information.

You then need to provide `DimeAttachment` the settings for the DIME record that you will end up constructing:

```
Dim dimeAttachment As DimeAttachment

dimeAttachment = New DimeAttachment("image/jpeg", _
    TypeFormatEnum.MediaType, "C:\Trees.jpg")
```

The `DimeAttachment` object takes three parameters. The first is a string declaring the type that will be contained in the Data section of the DIME record. In this case, `"image/jpeg"`. The second parameter is the type format of the DIME record that you are creating. There are a number of options for the type format, but in this case, you are specifying that the type format should be `MediaType`. Table 8-2 describes the other type formats used for working with DIME records.

TABLE 8-2 TYPE FORMAT OPTIONS

Type Format Option	Description
TypeFormatEnum.AbsoluteURI	An absolute URI.
TypeFormatEnum.MediaType	A media type format.
TypeFormatEnum.None	No format is specified.
TypeFormatEnum.Unchanged	There is no change to the type format from the preceding record.
TypeFormatEnum.Unknown	The type format is not known.

The last parameter in our example is a string that points to the path of the image that we are going to end up attaching to the SOAP message in a DIME record. This path is represented as a string. You can also pass in a `Stream` object as a parameter instead of a string that represents the path to an object.

For this example, you should place a test image somewhere in your file structure where you can make a reference to it and use this path in place of the path specified in this example.

Now that you have the `DimeAttachment` object created and pointing to the object that you want to expose via the WebMethod, you can simply attach this object to the outgoing SOAP response by adding this DIME record to the outgoing `SoapContext` object:

```
responseContext.Attachments.Add(dimeAttachment)
```

This is the last line of the WebMethod. Your XML Web service is now ready for consumption. Now create the client application that will consume this SOAP response and any associated DIME records that come with the SOAP message.

Creating the client application

The next step is to create a client application that will invoke this XML Web service and retrieve the JPEG image that is sent in a series of DIME records. Once the client application takes a hold of this image from the DIME records, the image will be displayed.

To build this client application, you build a Windows Application in either C# or Visual Basic .NET. Start a new Windows Application called GetImageApp. Once your GetImageApp project is created, be sure that you make reference to the Microsoft.Web.Services.dll in your project. You will also need to make a Web reference to the XML Web service that is exposing the GetImage() WebMethod. Once the reference is made, you should make sure that the proxy class now derives from Microsoft.Web.Services.WebServicesClientProtocol. Also, since there is no web.config file in a Windows form application, you will have to make reference to the WSE within the app.config or machine.config file.

You should now be presented with a drawing surface form for your application. In order to create your application, you will simply need to place two controls on the form. The first step is to place a Button control in the upper-left corner of the form. Then place a PictureBox control on the form and stretch it out so that the image that you are going to display will have room in the form. Your Windows form should look similar to Figure 8-5.

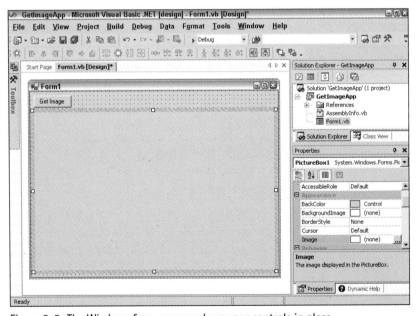

Figure 8-5: The Windows form once you have your controls in place

When the user clicks on the button, the XML Web service will be invoked and the Windows Form application will receive a SOAP response that will have a couple of DIME records associated with it. The client application will then take the information from the DIME records and display this JPEG image in the PictureBox control on the form.

The code-behind for the button-click event is shown in Listing 8-5.

Listing 8-5: The code-behind for the Windows Form application that will display an image that it receives in a series of DIME records

[VB]

```
Public Class Form1
    Inherits System.Windows.Forms.Form

Private Sub Button1_Click(ByVal sender As System.Object, _
    ByVal e As System.EventArgs) Handles Button1.Click

    Dim ws As New localhost.Service1()
    ws.GetImage()

    PictureBox1.Image = _
        New Bitmap(ws.ResponseSoapContext.Attachments(0).Stream)

    End Sub

End Class
```

[C#]

```
using System;
using System.Drawing;
using System.Collections;
using System.ComponentModel;
using System.Windows.Forms;
using System.Data;

namespace WindowsApplication1
{
    public class Form1 : System.Windows.Forms.Form
    {
        private System.Windows.Forms.Button button1;
        private System.Windows.Forms.PictureBox pictureBox1;

        private void button1_Click(object sender, System.EventArgs e)
```

Continued

Listing 8-5 *(Continued)*

```
    {
        localhost.Service1 ws = new localhost.Service1();
        ws.GetImage();

        pictureBox1.Image =
            new
Bitmap(ws.ResponseSoapContext.Attachments(0).Stream);
    }
  }
}
```

This little client application simply has a button that the user clicks. This button-click invokes the XML Web service, which returns a SOAP response with a series of DIME messages associated with the SOAP message.

Within the `Button1_Click` event in the code-behind for this Windows Form application, the first line of code creates an instance of the XML Web service. Then the `GetImage` WebMethod is called without the need to supply any parameters to the method call:

```
Dim ws As New localhost.Service1()
ws.GetImage()
```

This method call retrieves the DIME records along with the SOAP response. There can be any number of attachments contained within the DIME records and for that reason, the image that is assigned to the `PictureBox1` control is the first of the array of attachments that was retrieved. In this case, there was only one image retrieved from the DIME records. Even if there was more than one image retrieved, you are still just using the first attachment in the series of DIME records. The `Stream` property is used as it gets the stream for reading the attachment payload:

```
PictureBox1.Image = _
    New Bitmap(ws.ResponseSoapContext.Attachments(0).Stream)
```

When the user clicks the button, the client application displays a picture that was sent by the XML Web service. This image being displayed in the client application is shown in Figure 8-6.

Figure 8-6: The retrieved image shown in the client application

DIME Processing

The next logical point to cover is what happens when the DIME records are received by the client application. When a response is received that contains DIME records, the DIME records are handed to a DIME parser by the WSE. The DIME parser takes the first DIME record in the series and ensures that the version number specified in the Version section of the DIME header is one that the DIME parser can process. If the version contained within the DIME header is incompatible with the DIME parser, an exception is thrown.

If the version of the DIME record is compatible with the versions that are accepted by the DIME parser, the first record contained in the series of DIME records is flagged with a `Message Begin` flag. If the first message in the series is not properly flagged, the DIME records are considered to be malformed and are rejected and an exception is thrown.

If the DIME record contains a flag that specifies that the current DIME record is a Chunked Data record, its payload will be combined with the next in the series of DIME records until there are no more Chunked Data flags in place.

Once the DIME parser comes to the end of the series as specified with the Message End flag in the DIME header, the DIME parser stops reviewing the DIME records. If there are any additional records in the series of DIME records, they must be malformed and should be rejected.

If you use the SOAP Toolkit 3.0 to look at the SOAP and DIME messages that are being sent back and forth across the wire, you will see an XML representation of the DIME records that were sent along with the SOAP response.

Learn how to use the SOAP Toolkit 3.0 to be able to trace SOAP and DIME
messages. You will find this information in Appendix A.

The first thing to look at is the SOAP request that is sent from the client application to the XML Web service. This is shown in Listing 8-6.

Listing 8-6: The SOAP request

```xml
<?xml version="1.0" encoding="utf-8" ?>
   <soap:Envelope
xmlns:soap="http://schemas.xmlsoap.org/soap/envelope/"
xmlns:xsi="http://www.w3.org/2001/XMLSchema-instance"
   xmlns:xsd="http://www.w3.org/2001/XMLSchema">
      <soap:Header>
        <wsrp:path
         soap:actor="http://schemas.xmlsoap.org/soap/actor/next"
         soap:mustUnderstand="1"
         xmlns:wsrp="http://schemas.xmlsoap.org/rp">
        <wsrp:action>http://www.wiley.com/GetImage
        </wsrp:action>
        <wsrp:to>
            http://localhost:8080/myGetImage/service1.asmx
        </wsrp:to>
        <wsrp:id>
            uuid:45959441-4c08-4296-a427-ca77e8042b42</wsrp:id>
        </wsrp:path>
        <wsu:Timestamp
         xmlns:wsu="http://schemas.xmlsoap.org/ws/2002/07/utility">
            <wsu:Created>2002-12-14T19:44:26Z</wsu:Created>
            <wsu:Expires>2002-12-14T19:49:26Z</wsu:Expires>
        </wsu:Timestamp>
      </soap:Header>
      <soap:Body>
        <GetImage xmlns="http://www.wiley.com" />
      </soap:Body>
</soap:Envelope>
```

The SOAP request does not send any parameters, as you can see; it simply
invokes the XML Web service. The response from the XML Web service is the interesting action occurring in this message transfer. The SOAP Toolkit 3.0 shows the
SOAP response in a couple of ways. The first item it shows is the SOAP response,
shown in Listing 8-7.

Listing 8-7: The SOAP response

```
<?xml version="1.0" encoding="utf-8" ?>
<soap:Envelope
xmlns:soap="http://schemas.xmlsoap.org/soap/envelope/"
 xmlns:xsi="http://www.w3.org/2001/XMLSchema-instance"
 xmlns:xsd="http://www.w3.org/2001/XMLSchema">
 <soap:Header>
  <wsu:Timestamp
   xmlns:wsu="http://schemas.xmlsoap.org/ws/2002/07/utility">
    <wsu:Created>2002-12-14T19:44:33Z</wsu:Created>
    <wsu:Expires>2002-12-14T19:49:33Z</wsu:Expires>
  </wsu:Timestamp>
 </soap:Header>
 <soap:Body>
  <GetImageResponse xmlns="http://www.wiley.com" />
 </soap:Body>
</soap:Envelope>
```

As you can see from the SOAP response, there isn't too much to it. There is no data returned in the SOAP body. The only thing that this response contains is some timestamp information for the client to act on if need be.

The SOAP Toolkit 3.0 offers an XML view of the DIME records that are associated with an XML Web service's SOAP response. Listing 8-8 shows the DIME records as they are represented in the SOAP Toolkit.

Listing 8-8: The DIME records sent from the XML Web service

```
<DimePayload>
  <DimeRecord traceOffset="0x00000000">
    <Recordinfo Version="1" MB="1" ME="0" CF="0" IDLength="41" />
    <Typefield TNF="2" TypeLength="41" />
    <Options O="0" OptionLength="0" />
    <Datalength length="506" />
    <ID value="uuid:be798153-57a8-468c-80eb-6c5161e1f002" />
    <Type value="http://schemas.xmlsoap.org/soap/envelope/" />
  </DimeRecord>
  <DimeRecord traceOffset="0x00000260">
    <Recordinfo Version="1" MB="0" ME="1" CF="0" IDLength="41" />
    <Typefield TNF="1" TypeLength="10" />
    <Options O="0" OptionLength="0" />
    <Datalength length="114129" />
    <ID value="uuid:a7eaf13a-50d3-4155-9ab4-8b43edff4f68" />
    <Type value="image/jpeg" />
  </DimeRecord>
</DimePayload>
```

From this XML representation of the DIME records, notice that there are two DIME records in this response from the XML Web service. The first DIME record contains the SOAP response from Listing 8-7.

From the DIME header, you can see that the version of the DIME record is version 1 and that in the first record that the MB flag is set. Note also that each DIME record has its own unique ID value. The other item to notice is that each record has a different type. Having unique IDs allows you to work with DIME records on an individual basis. The first DIME record has a type of a SOAP envelope, meaning that the SOAP message is contained within this record. The second DIME record has a type of "image/jpeg". This is the DIME record that is encapsulating the JPEG image that was sent from the XML Web service.

The second record has some additional values that you should look at in this example. The first is that the ME flag is set, meaning that this is the last record in the series of DIME records and the DIME parser will not find any additional DIME records within the collection. The other interesting item here is the Datalength section that specifies the size of the DIME payload. You can see that the payload of the DIME record that contains the JPEG image is 114,129 bytes.

Modifying the Construction of DIME Records

Just as you can easily plug almost any kind of file type into your DIME records, you can just as easily control how these records are constructed before the DIME records are sent on their way.

Attaching multiple attachments

You are not limited to attaching just a single file to your outgoing responses from your XML Web service. You can attach as many attachments to an outgoing response as you want. The attachments that you place in DIME records are not required to be of the same type. Therefore, you can have attachments that include JPEG images alongside attachments that are Microsoft Word documents. Listing 8-9 shows an example of attaching multiple files to your outgoing XML Web services response.

Listing 8-9: An XML Web service that sends out multiple attachments of different types

[VB]

```
Imports System.Web.Services
Imports Microsoft.Web.Services
Imports Microsoft.Web.Services.Dime

<WebService(Namespace:="http://www.wiley.com")> _
```

```vb
Public Class Service1
    Inherits System.Web.Services.WebService

    <WebMethod()> Public Function GetImage()
        Dim responseContext As SoapContext = _
            HttpSoapContext.ResponseContext
        Dim dimeAttachment1 As DimeAttachment
        Dim dimeAttachment2 As DimeAttachment

        dimeAttachment1 = New DimeAttachment("image/jpeg", _
            TypeFormatEnum.MediaType, "C:\Trees.jpg")

        dimeAttachment2 = New DimeAttachment("application/msword", _
            TypeFormatEnum.MediaType, "C:\myDoc.doc")

        responseContext.Attachments.Add(dimeAttachment1)
        responseContext.Attachments.Add(dimeAttachment2)
    End Function

End Class
```

[C#]

```csharp
using System;
using System.Collections;
using System.ComponentModel;
using System.Data;
using System.Diagnostics;
using System.Web;
using System.Web.Services;
using Microsoft.Web.Services;
using Microsoft.Web.Services.Dime;

namespace myGetImage
{
    public class Service1 : System.Web.Services.WebService
    {
        [WebMethod]
        public void GetImage()
        {
            SoapContext responseContext =
                HttpSoapContext.ResponseContext;

            DimeAttachment dimeAttachment1 = new DimeAttachment(
```

Continued

Listing 8-9 *(Continued)*

```
            "image/jpeg", TypeFormatEnum.MediaType,
            @"C:\trees.jpg");

        DimeAttachment dimeAttachment2 = new DimeAttachment(
            "application/msword", TypeFormatEnum.MediaType,
            @"C:\myDoc.doc");

        responseContext.Attachments.Add(dimeAttachment1);
        responseContext.Attachments.Add(dimeAttachment2);
        }
    }
}
```

Listing 8-9 shows two attachments that are assigned to the SoapContext object that will be sending a response from the XML Web service. The neat thing about this example is that in addition to a JPEG image that is being included as an attachment, there is also a Microsoft Word document that is being attached right alongside the image – two completely different file types.

The series of DIME records that you receive from this XML Web service is shown in Listing 8-10.

Listing 8-10: A series of DIME records that contain multiple documents

```
<DimePayload>
  <DimeRecord traceOffset="0x00000000">
    <Recordinfo Version="1" MB="1" ME="0" CF="0" IDLength="41" />
    <Typefield TNF="2" TypeLength="41" />
    <Options O="0" OptionLength="0" />
    <Datalength length="506" />
    <ID value="uuid:fef00475-44d3-4262-96ec-f01c6a78cf9f" />
    <Type value="http://schemas.xmlsoap.org/soap/envelope/" />
  </DimeRecord>
  <DimeRecord traceOffset="0x00000260">
    <Recordinfo Version="1" MB="0" ME="0" CF="0" IDLength="41" />
    <Typefield TNF="1" TypeLength="10" />
    <Options O="0" OptionLength="0" />
    <Datalength length="114129" />
    <ID value="uuid:d2e03df8-726b-49b7-8e21-8eefeb5c4e24" />
    <Type value="image/jpeg" />
  </DimeRecord>
  <DimeRecord traceOffset="0x0001C078">
    <Recordinfo Version="1" MB="0" ME="1" CF="0" IDLength="41" />
    <Typefield TNF="1" TypeLength="18" />
    <Options O="0" OptionLength="0" />
```

```
      <Datalength length="19968" />
      <ID value="uuid:65388aa4-1df4-4a44-bc04-a12d0caa0408" />
      <Type value="application/msword" />
   </DimeRecord>
</DimePayload>
```

Note that there are three DIME records in total. The first is of type `http://schemas.xmlsoap.org/soap/envelope`, meaning that it is the SOAP response from the XML Web service and is using an absolute URI for the value of the type format.

The second DIME record here is the JPEG image, specified with a type format value of `image/jpeg`, and the third DIME record is the Microsoft Word document specified with a type format value of `application/msword`. You can tell that each attachment has its own unique identifier as well.

For an extensive list of type format values that you can use, refer to Appendix D.

Controlling the ID value of the attachment

Notice that by default, when the DIME records are constructed, the WSE gives each attachment that is encapsulated within a single or multiple DIME records a unique identifier that will distinguish this attachment from others (such as `uuid:a7eaf13a-50d3-4155-9ab4-8b43edff4f68`).

You can control this ID quite easily in the code of your XML Web service. Listing 8-11 shows you how to control the value given to the ID field.

Listing 8-11: Specifying the ID value for your attachments

[VB]

```
Imports System.Web.Services
Imports Microsoft.Web.Services
Imports Microsoft.Web.Services.Dime

<WebService(Namespace:="http://www.wiley.com")> _
Public Class Service1
    Inherits System.Web.Services.WebService

    <WebMethod()> Public Function GetImage()
        Dim responseContext As SoapContext = _
```

Continued

Listing 8-11 *(Continued)*

```
        HttpSoapContext.ResponseContext
    Dim dimeAttachment As DimeAttachment

    dimeAttachment = New DimeAttachment("image/jpeg", _
        TypeFormatEnum.MediaType, "C:\Trees.jpg")

    dimeAttachment.id = "Trees.jpg"

    responseContext.Attachments.Add(dimeAttachment)
End Function

End Class
```

[C#]

```
using System;
using System.Collections;
using System.ComponentModel;
using System.Data;
using System.Diagnostics;
using System.Web;
using System.Web.Services;
using Microsoft.Web.Services;
using Microsoft.Web.Services.Dime;

namespace myGetImage
{
    public class Service1 : System.Web.Services.WebService
    {
        [WebMethod]
        public void GetImage()
        {
            SoapContext responseContext =
                HttpSoapContext.ResponseContext;

            DimeAttachment dimeAttachment = new DimeAttachment(
                "image/jpeg", TypeFormatEnum.MediaType,
                @"C:\trees.jpg");

            dimeAttachment.id = "Trees.jpg";

            responseContext.Attachments.Add(dimeAttachment);
        }
    }
}
```

The bold line of code is the addition that allows you to control which ID is used for the attachment. By not specifying the ID, the WSE uses a unique GUID for the ID. It's possible to use whatever you want for the ID. In this case, the name of the file is used as the ID; this allows the client to make logical decisions about how to use attachments that are sent in DIME records based upon an expected ID value as opposed to a random GUID that the client will not know beforehand.

Listing 8-12 shows the exact DIME record that contains this image.

Listing 8-12: The DIME record after changing the attachment's ID value

```
<DimeRecord traceOffset="0x00000260">
  <Recordinfo Version="1" MB="0" ME="0" CF="0" IDLength="41" />
  <Typefield TNF="1" TypeLength="10" />
  <Options O="0" OptionLength="0" />
  <Datalength length="114129" />
  <ID value="Trees.jpg" />
  <Type value="image/jpeg" />
</DimeRecord>
```

Working with the Attachments You Receive

Because an XML Web service can send multiple DIME records, you might want to work with the DIME records as you receive them. Therefore, after retrieving the DIME records, you are in most cases going to want to apply some conditional logic the series of attachments that you receive. This section shows you of some of the possible options you can use when checking your DIME records.

Checking if any attachments exist

One of the first logical steps to take when you receive a response from an XML Web service that might contain attachments using DIME is to determine whether any DIME records actually exist. Listing 8-13 shows you how to determine whether you received any attachments in the series of DIME records.

Listing 8-13: Checking if you have received any DIME records

[VB]

```
Dim ws As New localhost.Service1()
ws.GetImage()

If ws.ResponseSoapContext.Attachments.Count = 1 Then
```

Continued

Listing 8-13 *(Continued)*
```
    ' Work with attachments here.
End If
```

[C#]

```
localhost.Service1 ws = localhost.Service1();
ws.GetImage();

if (ws.ResponseSoapContext.Attachments.Count == 1)
{
    // Work with attachments here.
}
```

This code determines whether there is at least one attachment in the series of DIME records. If an attachment is found, you can work with these attachments within the conditional statement.

Iterating through multiple attachments

Because it is possible to have multiple attachments within your series of DIME records, you will occasionally need to iterate through all of the attachments to work with them on an individual basis.

Listing 8-14 shows you how to iterate through the attachments that are included within the DIME records.

Listing 8-14: Iterating through multiple DIME attachments

[VB]

```
Dim ws As New localhost.Service1()
ws.GetImage()

Dim dimeAttachment as DimeAttachment

For Each dimeAttachment In ws.RequestSoapContext.Attachments
    ' Work with attachments here.
Next
```

[C#]

```
localhost.Service1 ws = localhost.Service1();
ws.GetImage();

foreach (DimeAttachment dimeAttachment in
```

```
ws.RequestSoapContext.Attachments)
{
    // Work with attachments here.
}
```

Working through each of the attachments individually is simple using the `DimeAttachment` object. The `DimeAttachment` object represents a generic attachment. Using the `For Each` statement, you can iterate through all of the `DimeAttachment` objects.

Working with the attachment's metadata in your client application

Along with the attachments that are sent by an XML Web service, the DIME records that contain these attachments also contain the attachment's metadata. It is easy to work with this metadata within your applications. Listing 8-15 shows the code-behind for an ASP.NET page that displays the metadata information about the attachments it receives from the DIME records.

Listing 8-15: Displaying a DIME record's metadata

[VB]

```
Imports Microsoft.Web.Services
Imports Microsoft.Web.Services.Dime

Public Class WebForm1
    Inherits System.Web.UI.Page

Private Sub Page_Load(ByVal sender As System.Object, _
    ByVal e As System.EventArgs) Handles MyBase.Load

        Dim ws As New localhost.Service1()

        ws.GetImage()

        Dim dimeAttachment As DimeAttachment

        For Each dimeAttachment In
ws.ResponseSoapContext.Attachments
            Response.Write("<b>File Type:</b> " & _
                dimeAttachment.Type.ToString() & "<br>")
            Response.Write("<b>File Type Format:</b> " & _
                dimeAttachment.TypeFormat.ToString() & "<br>")
```

Continued

Listing 8-15 *(Continued)*

```
            Response.Write("<b>Dime Record ID:</b> " & _
                dimeAttachment.Id.ToString() & "<br>")
            Response.Write("<b>Chuck Size:</b> " & _
                dimeAttachment.ChunkSize.ToString() & "<hr><p>")
        Next
    End Sub

End Class
```

[C#]

```csharp
using System;
using System.Collections;
using System.ComponentModel;
using System.Data;
using System.Drawing;
using System.Web;
using System.Web.SessionState;
using System.Web.UI;
using System.Web.UI.WebControls;
using System.Web.UI.HtmlControls;

namespace WebApplication1
{
    public class WebForm1 : System.Web.UI.Page
    {
        protected System.Web.UI.WebControls.TextBox TextBox1;
        protected System.Web.UI.WebControls.TextBox TextBox2;
        protected System.Web.UI.WebControls.Button Button1;
        protected System.Web.UI.WebControls.Label Label1;

        private void Button1_Click(object sender, System.EventArgs e)
        {
        localhost.Service1 ws = new localhost.Service1();

            ws.GetImage();

            foreach (DimeAttachment dimeAttachment in
                ws.ResponseSoapContext.Attachments) {

                Response.Write("<b>File Type:</b> " + _
                    dimeAttachment.Type.ToString() + "<br>");
                Response.Write("<b>File Type Format:</b> " + _
                    dimeAttachment.TypeFormat.ToString() + "<br>");
```

```
            Response.Write("<b>Dime Record ID:</b> " + _
                dimeAttachment.Id.ToString() + "<br>");
            Response.Write("<b>Chuck Size:</b> " + _
                dimeAttachment.ChunkSize.ToString() + "<hr><p>");
        }
      }
    }
}
```

From this example, you will notice that for each attachment that is sent in with the series of DIME records, the file type, file type format, ID, and chuck size can be retrieved from the attachment. Figure 8-7 shows what the ASP.NET page will look like after receiving a couple of attachments within the DIME records.

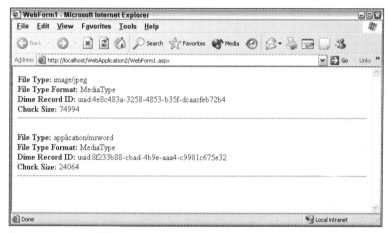

Figure 8-7: The ASP.NET page after execution

Being able to work with specific information about the attachments that are sent in with the DIME records is a powerful tool. It allows you to apply conditional logic to whether or not you are going to work with an attachment or how you might work with the attachment that you receive.

For instance, if you were only going to work with images that have a specific ID value, you could use a conditional statement as shown in Listing 8-16.

Listing 8-16: Working with a specific attachment

[VB]

```
Dim ws As New localhost.Service1()
```

Continued

Listing 8-16 *(Continued)*

```
ws.GetImage()

If ws.ResponseSoapContext.Attachments(0).Id = "Trees.jpg" Then
    ' Work with attachment here.
End If
```

[C#]

```
localhost.Service1 ws = new localhost.Service1();
ws.GetImage();

if (ws.ResponseSoapContext.Attachments[0].Id == "Trees.jpg")
{
    // Work with attachment here.
}
```

You can work with the attachments that you receive in a number of ways. Not only can you check the ID values of the attachments that you receive, but you can also compare the chunked data size or the type format of the attachment that is being sent.

Comparing Serialization to DIME Encapsulation

Now let's do a fun little experiment. In the beginning of this chapter, you looked at how to send documents directly in the SOAP payload of your SOAP messages. The image being sent in this example was serialized into XML and placed directly in the body of the SOAP message for transport.

Then using the WSE, you learned how to instead use DIME to keep from having to serialize the image. Keeping the image outside of the SOAP body *will* make the transport faster – but let's take a look at how much faster.

To compare these two different means for achieving the same goal, create a Windows form application that will allow you to send a series of images either using serialization or DIME encapsulation. Once the application is complete, run it using the both methods. You can then see for yourself the speed difference and actually experience the advantages of using DIME first-hand.

Creating the XML Web service

The XML Web service for this example has two WebMethods. To create this XML Web service, create a new ASP.NET Web Service project called `ImageTest`. After you have configured the XML Web service to work with the WSE, you are ready to create the two WebMethods that this class is going to expose in the end.

The first WebMethod for the `Service1` class is `GetImage1()` and the second WebMethod is called `GetImage2()`. `GetImage1()` will expose a series of three images in random order using the serialization process. These images as they are called by the client application will be serialized into XML and sent in the body of the SOAP message to the client. `GetImage2()` will expose the same three images in a random order, but instead of the serialization process, they will use DIME encapsulation to send the images to the client.

Listing 8-17 shows the code for the XML Web service.

Listing 8-17: The XML Web service with two WebMethods — GetImage1() and GetImage2()

[VB]

```
Imports System.Web.Services
Imports Microsoft.Web.Services.Dime
Imports Microsoft.Web.Services
Imports System.IO
Imports System.Drawing

<WebService(Namespace:="http://www.wiley.com")> _
Public Class Service1
    Inherits System.Web.Services.WebService

    <WebMethod()> Public Function GetImage1() As Byte()

        Dim myBitmap As Bitmap
        Dim myMemoryStream As MemoryStream

        myMemoryStream = New MemoryStream()

        Dim i As Integer = CInt(Int(3 * Rnd()))

        Try
            If i = 0 Then
                myBitmap = New Bitmap("C:\Trees.jpg")
            ElseIf i = 1 Then
                myBitmap = New Bitmap("C:\Car.jpg")
            ElseIf i = 2 Then
                myBitmap = New Bitmap("C:\Castle.jpg")
            End If

            myBitmap.Save(myMemoryStream, _
                System.Drawing.Imaging.ImageFormat.Jpeg)

            Return myMemoryStream.ToArray()
```

Continued

Listing 8-17 *(Continued)*

```
      Catch
          Return Nothing
      End Try
   End Function

   <WebMethod()> Public Function GetImage2()
      Dim responseContext As SoapContext = _
         HttpSoapContext.ResponseContext
      Dim dimeAttachment As DimeAttachment

      Dim i As Integer = CInt(Int(3 * Rnd())

      If i = 0 Then
         dimeAttachment = New DimeAttachment("image/jpeg", _
            TypeFormatEnum.MediaType, "C:\Trees.jpg")
      ElseIf i = 1 Then
         dimeAttachment = New DimeAttachment("image/jpeg", _
            TypeFormatEnum.MediaType, "C:\Car.jpg")
      ElseIf i = 2 Then
         dimeAttachment = New DimeAttachment("image/jpeg", _
            TypeFormatEnum.MediaType, "C:\Castle.jpg")
      End If

      responseContext.Attachments.Add(dimeAttachment)
   End Function

End Class
```

[C#]

```
using System;
using System.Collections;
using System.ComponentModel;
using System.Data;
using System.Diagnostics;
using System.Web;
using System.Web.Services;
using Microsoft.Web.Services;
using Microsoft.Web.Services.Dime;
using System.IO;
using System.Drawing;

namespace ImageTest
```

```
{
    public class Service1 : System.Web.Services.WebService
    {
        [WebMethod]
        public void GetImage1()
        {
            Bitmap myBitmap;
            MemoryStream myMemoryStream;

            myMemoryStream = new MemoryStream();

            try
            {
                System.Random r = new Random();
                int i = (r.Next(3));

                myBitmap = new Bitmap(@"C:\\Trees.jpg");

                if (i==1) {
                    myBitmap = new Bitmap(@"C:\\Car.jpg");
                }
                else if (i==2) {
                    myBitmap = new Bitmap(@"C:\\Castle.jpg");
                }

                myBitmap.Save(myMemoryStream,
                    System.Drawing.Imaging.ImageFormat.Jpeg);

                return myMemoryStream.ToArray();
            }
            catch
            {
                return null;
            }
        }

        [WebMethod]
        public void GetImage2()
        {
            SoapContext responseContext =
                HttpSoapContext.ResponseContext;

            System.Random r = new Random();
```

Continued

Listing 8-17 *(Continued)*

```
int i = (r.Next(3));

DimeAttachment dimeAttachment = new DimeAttachment(
      "image/jpeg", TypeFormatEnum.MediaType,
      @"C:\Trees.jpg");

if (i==1) {
   DimeAttachment dimeAttachment = new DimeAttachment(
      "image/jpeg", TypeFormatEnum.MediaType,
      @"C:\Car.jpg");
}
else if (i==2) {
   DimeAttachment dimeAttachment = new DimeAttachment(
      "image/jpeg", TypeFormatEnum.MediaType,
      @"C:\Castle.jpg");
}

responseContext.Attachments.Add(dimeAttachment);
      }
   }
}
```

You can see that there are two methods used in sending the image to the consumer. The next section creates a client application that will work with both of these WebMethods.

Creating the consumer

The consumer of this XML Web service is a Windows Form application that will allow you to work with both WebMethods. To create this Windows Form, open Visual Studio .NET and create a new Windows Application project. Name this project GetImage.

You will then be presented with a blank form to build your controls upon. It is assumed that you have made the necessary changes to the machine.config file so that you can work with the WSE.

On the blank form, place a Button, Label, Checkbox and PictureBox control. This is shown in Figure 8-8.

The idea of this form is that when the user clicks the button on the form, the XML Web service will be invoked in a loop of 50 invocations. After each call to the XML Web service, the image that is retrieved from the Web service will be displayed in the picture box and each picture retrieved will be counted with this number being displayed by the Label control.

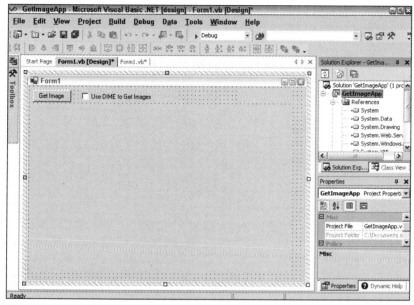

Figure 8-8: The Windows Form populated with the controls used for this comparison example

The code-behind for this form is illustrated in Listing 8-18.

Listing 8-18: The code-behind for the Windows form

[VB]

```vb
Imports System.IO
Imports System.Drawing
Imports Microsoft.Web.Services
Imports Microsoft.Web.Services.Dime

Public Class Form1
    Inherits System.Windows.Forms.Form

Private Sub Button1_Click(ByVal sender As System.Object, _
    ByVal e As System.EventArgs) Handles Button1.Click

        Dim ws As New localhost.Service1()

        Dim i As Integer = 1
        For i = 1 To 50
            If CheckBox1.Checked = True Then
```

Continued

Listing 8-18 *(Continued)*

```
            ws.GetImage1()

            PictureBox1.Image = _
              New Bitmap _
              (ws.ResponseSoapContext.Attachments(0).Stream)
            PictureBox1.Update()

            Label1.Text = i.ToString()
            Label1.Update()
        Else
            Dim myByte As Byte()
            Dim myImage As Bitmap
            Dim myMS As MemoryStream

            myByte = ws.GetImage2()

            myMS = New MemoryStream(myByte)
            myImage = New Bitmap(myMS)

            PictureBox1.Image = myImage
            PictureBox1.Update()

            Label1.Text = i.ToString()
            Label1.Update()
        End If
        Next
    End Sub
End Class
```

[C#]

```
using System;
using System.Drawing;
using System.Collections;
using System.ComponentModel;
using System.Windows.Forms;
using System.Data;
using System.Drawing;
using System.IO;
using Microsoft.Web.Services;
using Microsoft.Web.Services.Dime;

namespace GetImage
{
```

```
public class Form1 : System.Windows.Forms.Form
{
    private System.Windows.Forms.PictureBox pictureBox1;
    private System.Windows.Forms.Button button1;
    private System.Windows.Forms.Label label1;
    private System.Windows.Forms.CheckBox checkBox1;

    private void button1_Click(object sender, System.EventArgs e)
    {
        localhost.Service1 ws = new localhost.Service1();

        for (int i=1; i==50; i++)
        {
            if (checkBox1.Checked == true)
            {
                ws.GetImage1();

                pictureBox1.Image = new Bitmap
                    (ws.ResponseSoapContext.Attachments[0].Stream);
                pictureBox1.Update();

                label1.Text = i.ToString();
                label1.Update();
            }
            else
            {
                byte[] myByte;
                Bitmap myImage;
                MemoryStream myMS;

                myByte = ws.GetImage2();

                myMS = new MemoryStream(myByte);
                myImage = new Bitmap(myMS);

                pictureBox1.Image = myImage;
                pictureBox1.Update();

                label1.Text = i.ToString();
                label1.Update();
            }
        }
    }
}
```

Remember that you also have to make a reference to the XML Web service and configure the proxy class that is generated from the reference so that this proxy class inherits from `Microsoft.Web.Services.WebServicesClientProtocol`.

Compile and run this application. Without checking the checkbox that is on the form, click the Get Images button. This will run through 50 iterations of invoking the XML Web service in order to retrieve a random image. This image will be displayed in the form and the Label control will count the interactions as they happen. A picture of the result is shown in Figure 8-9.

Figure 8-9: The end result of the application

If you check the checkbox and then click the Get Image button, you instead invoke the WebMethod that uses DIME encapsulation. Right away you will see the power of using DIME encapsulation because this will be considerably faster than the method of serializing the image into XML. DIME is a powerful and wonderful tool to use when you are going to transport items that are best kept in their original format.

Summary

This chapter focused on how to send objects that cannot be easily serialized into XML and would benefit from having these images kept in their original format. This is possible using WS-Attachments and DIME for sending messages across the wire.

This chapter discussed many of the ways of working with DIME when sending images, and other types of documents as well. Whenever you need to send these types of files along with your SOAP messages, DIME is a quick and easy way to do this. Not only is it easy to use, but it is also a far better alternative to the previous ways of accomplishing this task.

Chapter 9

Using WSE Filters

IN THIS CHAPTER

- ◆ Understanding the WSE message flow
- ◆ Controlling filters

SO FAR, ALL OF THE CHAPTERS in this book have shown you how to use the WSE to build and consume advanced XML Web services that use some of the latest GXA specifications. This is due to the fact that you can send any outgoing or incoming SOAP messages through the WSE's various filters. This chapter takes a close look at these filters and shows you how you can control the filters to fine-tune and customize your SOAP messages.

Understanding the WSE Message Flow

When a SOAP request or SOAP response is sent from either the client application or the XML Web service, by using the WSE, this SOAP message is instead handed off to one of two new classes that the WSE provides — `Microsoft.Web.Services.SoapWebRequest` and `Microsoft.Web.Services.SoapWebResponse`.

Outbound SOAP messages

When a message is sent outbound from either the client application or the XML Web service, it is handed to an instance of the `SoapWebRequest` class. This class creates an instance of the `SoapEnvelope` class that contains the entire SOAP message. This `SoapEnvelope` instance then runs through a series of WSE outbound filters. The collection of filters as a whole is referred to as the *pipeline*.

This pipeline of filters makes additions and modifications to the contents of the SOAP header as well as the contents of the SOAP body. The outbound filters are controlled by the `SoapContext` class. Figure 9-1 shows the SOAP message path for an outgoing SOAP message using the WSE.

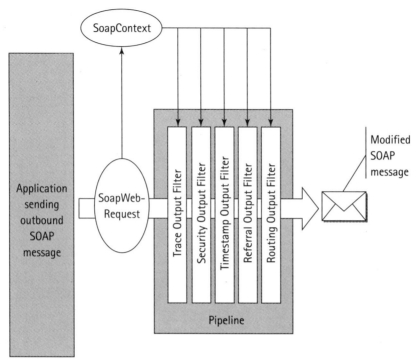

Figure 9-1: The WSE process of sending an outbound SOAP message

Once the outbound SOAP message passes through all of the available filters, it is sent on its way in the typical fashion.

As you can see from Figure 9-1, there are presently five filters provided through the WSE. Each of these five WSE output filters are described in Table 9-1.

So as a SOAP message is working through the filters present in the WSE, the SoapContext class controls the filters. The filters, in turn, perform operations such as adding timestamp information to the SOAP header, adding security credentials, encrypting SOAP payloads, and recording trace information.

TABLE 9-1 WSE OUTPUT FILTERS

Output Filter	Description
TraceOutputFilter	Logs trace information to a specified file.
SecurityOutputFilter	Writes security token information to the SOAP header. This output filter also works at encrypting the body of SOAP messages.

Output Filter	Description
`TimestampOutputFilter`	Records SOAP message activity times within the SOAP header.
`ReferralOutputFilter`	Allows for dynamic updating of routing paths that will be taken by the SOAP message.
`RoutingOutputFilter`	Processes the routing information of the SOAP message.

Inbound SOAP messages

SOAP messages that are inbound go through a similar path as outbound SOAP messages – but in reverse. Incoming SOAP messages are converted into an instance of the `SoapEnvelope` class. The WSE's input filters then take apart the SOAP message as it relates to the information that the particular filter is assigned.

The input filters also work with the `SoapContext` class to ensure that the elements are valid. The filters can dissect the SOAP headers and decrypt and encrypt SOAP payloads. In the end, an inbound SOAP message is handed to the application to work with. Figure 9-2 shows how the inbound SOAP messages flow into an application.

Similar to the output filters, there are five WSE input filters. These filters, controlled by the `SoapContext` class, work to decipher SOAP headers and SOAP payloads in order to deliver a SOAP message to an application. Table 9-2 describes each of the five input filters provided by the WSE.

TABLE **9-2 WSE INPUT FILTERS**

Output Filter	Description
`TraceInputFilter`	Logs trace information to a specified file.
`SecurityInputFilter`	Analyzes security token information from the SOAP header. This input filter also works at decrypting the body of SOAP messages.
`TimestampInputFilter`	Monitors SOAP message activity times within the SOAP header and records when SOAP messages were received.
`ReferralInputFilter`	Allows for dynamic updating of routing paths that will be taken by the SOAP message.
`RoutingInputFilter`	Processes the routing information of the SOAP message to allow you to route SOAP messages based upon your own custom logic.

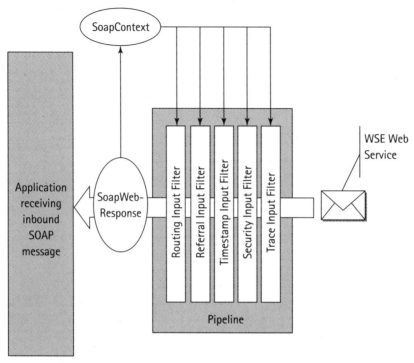

Figure 9-2: The WSE process of receiving an inbound SOAP message

The filters of the WSE work to analyze credentials, analyze and apply time-stamps, and record trace information. These filters are what make everything that has been described in this book thus far possible and being individually separated in this manner allows you to pick and choose the filters that you are going to use as well as how they are employed.

Controlling Filters

The great thing about the WSE is the granular control that it gives you. The WSE has the capability to automatically work with the various input and output filters to modify SOAP messages so that they are GXA-compliant. The developer can also control how the WSE uses these filters. This capability gives you a fine-grained control over the construction and processing of your SOAP messages.

One of the easiest ways to control the filters is to selectively turn them off for message processing. The reason for this is that you might not need all of the aspects that are provided by the WSE within your SOAP messages.

For instance, when sending a SOAP request from a client application to an XML Web service that contains a username and hashed password for login credentials, the SOAP message sent from the client takes the form shown in Listing 9-1.

Listing 9-1: A SOAP request sent from a client application

```
<soap:Envelope
xmlns:soap="http://schemas.xmlsoap.org/soap/envelope/"
 xmlns:xsi="http://www.w3.org/2001/XMLSchema-instance"
 xmlns:xsd="http://www.w3.org/2001/XMLSchema">
    <soap:Header>
      <wsrp:path
       soap:actor="http://schemas.xmlsoap.org/soap/actor/next"
       soap:mustUnderstand="1"
       xmlns:wsrp="http://schemas.xmlsoap.org/rp">
      <wsrp:action>http://www.wiley.com/HelloAuthenticatedUser
      </wsrp:action>

<wsrp:to>http://localhost/webservice1/wse_auth.asmx</wsrp:to>
        <wsrp:id>uuid:1db14135-3e2b-41b0-b776-1e3fdd1216d9</wsrp:id>
      </wsrp:path>
      <wsu:Timestamp
       xmlns:wsu="http://schemas.xmlsoap.org/ws/2002/07/utility">
        <wsu:Created>2002-12-27T21:16:00Z</wsu:Created>
        <wsu:Expires>2002-12-27T21:21:00Z</wsu:Expires>
      </wsu:Timestamp>
      <wsse:Security soap:mustUnderstand="1"
       xmlns:wsse="http://schemas.xmlsoap.org/ws/2002/07/secext">
        <wsse:UsernameToken
         xmlns:wsu="http://schemas.xmlsoap.org/ws/2002/07/utility"
         wsu:Id="SecurityToken-9ef53df7-e04f-46a0-bb49-
bb7cc949929d">
          <wsse:Username>BillEvjen</wsse:Username>
          <wsse:Password Type="wsse:PasswordDigest">
           HjQzp7X4SXxeOl4qOshxeKnb1rk=</wsse:Password>
          <wsse:Nonce>eLE5tGEvwCgFu9cpEnR48g==</wsse:Nonce>
          <wsu:Created>2002-12-27T21:16:00Z</wsu:Created>
        </wsse:UsernameToken>
      </wsse:Security>
    </soap:Header>
    <soap:Body>
      <HelloAuthenticatedUser xmlns="http://www.wiley.com/" />
    </soap:Body>
</soap:Envelope>
```

Notice that in addition to the important credential information included with the SOAP message there is also routing and timestamp information. This routing and timestamp information might not be required.

The routing information is really meant for routing scenarios in which a SOAP message moves through one or more SOAP intermediaries. This example includes a point-to-point SOAP request and therefore it's not vital for this routing information to be part of the header.

The timestamp information records when the SOAP message was created and there is a five-minute time span assigned to the SOAP message for its validity. As the routing information, the XML Web service may not be concerned with the time-stamp information, so it might be beneficial to remove this information from the SOAP header.

If the routing and timestamp information is not required, you can remove this information for transport. This can lead to an increase in performance because there are fewer elements to create and be digested on the receiving end.

There also may be moments where you are working with communicating SOAP messages across disparate platforms and these platforms or applications may understand only selected aspects of the GXA specifications. If you are communicating with a platform or application that understands the WS-Security specification but may not understand the WS-Routing, WS-Referral, and WS-Timestamp specifications, you are going to want to work through this process and construct your SOAP messages to be interoperable by removing the elements that will err when processed by the other system.

Now take a look at how you might process a SOAP message from a client application that includes only the security information in the SOAP header and not the routing and timestamp information.

Building a class to work with the pipeline filters

The first step in this process is to build a class that will interact with the pipeline filters. In this example, you build a simple class that removes the filters from the pipeline that you don't want to work with – the routing, referral, and timestamp filters.

In the Visual Studio .NET project of the client application that will send a SOAP message similar to the one shown in Listing 9-1 (this is from the application in Listings 3-14 and 3-15), you need to create a new class called `myOutputFilter.vb` or `myOutputFilter.cs`, depending on your language choice. You then must create a class that works with the WSE's output filters, because that's all you need at the moment.

The class is actually quite simple and is shown in Listing 9-2. It is explained following the listing. Remember, for this class to work within your application, your client application must be configured and ready to work with the WSE.

Listing 9-2: myOutputFilter.vb / myOutputFilter.cs

```
[VB]
```

```
Imports Microsoft.Web.Services
```

```
Imports Microsoft.Web.Services.Configuration

Public Class myOutputFilter
    Inherits SoapOutputFilter

    Public Overrides Sub ProcessMessage(ByVal envelope _
        As SoapEnvelope)

        Dim outputFilters As SoapOutputFilterCollection = _

WebServicesConfiguration.FilterConfiguration.OutputFilters

        outputFilters.Remove(GetType(Routing.RoutingOutputFilter))
        outputFilters.Remove(GetType(Referral.ReferralOutputFilter))

outputFilters.Remove(GetType(Timestamp.TimestampOutputFilter))
    End Sub

End Class
```

[C#]

```
using System;
using Microsoft.Web.Services;
using Microsoft.Web.Services.Configuration;

namespace WebApplication1
{
    public class myOutputFilter : SoapOutputFilter
    {
        public override void ProcessMessage(SoapEnvelope envelope)
        {
            SoapOutputFilterCollection outputFilters =

WebServicesConfiguration.FilterConfiguration.OutputFilters

            outputFilters.Remove(typeof(Routing.RoutingOutputFilter));
            outputFilters.Remove(typeof(Referral.ReferralOutputFilter));

outputFilters.Remove(typeof(Timestamp.TimestampOutputFilter));
        }
    }
}
```

The WSE provides you with a base class for defining output filters — SoapOutputFilter. There is also another base class for defining input filters — SoapInputFiter. For control over the pipeline filter process, you need to create a class that derives from one of these base classes. For this example, you need to derive a class (myOutputFilter) from SoapOutputFilter since you are going to be removing some of the WSE's output filters from the pipeline process.

Both SoapInputFilter and SoapOutputFilter contain a method that you can override. This method is called ProcessMessage; it takes a type of SoapEnvelope. The SoapEnvelope class is an extension of the XmlDocument class and represents a SOAP message.

In the class from Listing 9-2, an instance of the SoapOutputFilterCollection class is created that represents all the output filters that will be used in the pipeline of filters. Then it is as simple as removing from this collection the specific filters you don't need. In this case, you need to remove RoutingOutputFilter, ReferralOutputFilter, and TimestampOutputFilter.

Once the class is in place, recompile the application. It is then time to use the class within the WSE by referring to this class from the web.config file. This is described in the next section.

Using the web.config file

Now that a class is in place that will remove filters from the output filtering process, you need to make references to this class from the web.config file. Just as the web.config file has been used for much of the WSE's configuration settings, working with the WSE's filters is no different.

Listing 9-3 shows how you should work with the class that was just created in the web.config file.

Listing 9-3: The web.config file referring to the class that removes output filters from the SOAP message construction

```
<configuration>

    <microsoft.web.services>
        <filters>
            <output>
                <add
                type="WebApplication1.myOutputFilter, WebApplication1"
/>
            </output>
        </filters>
    </microsoft.web.services>

    <system.web>
```

```
    <!-- The rest of the web.config file -->

  </system.web>

</configuration>
```

To make a reference to the `myOutputFilter` class from the `web.config` file, you need to use the `<microsoft.web.services>` element to define your output filers. The class that you want the WSE to use for the output filter is specified using `<filters>` followed by `<output>`. The `<add>` element is where the class is referenced. In this case, it uses the following construction:

```
<add type="Namespace.Class, Assembly" />
```

Once your class is referenced in the `web.config` file, you are ready to send the SOAP request.

The result

Running the application will cause this client application to send a SOAP request to the XML Web service. Listing 9-4 shows what your SOAP request should look like after following the examples.

Listing 9-4: The modified SOAP request.

```
<soap:Envelope
xmlns:soap="http://schemas.xmlsoap.org/soap/envelope/"
 xmlns:xsi="http://www.w3.org/2001/XMLSchema-instance"
 xmlns:xsd="http://www.w3.org/2001/XMLSchema">
    <soap:Header>
      <wsse:Security soap:mustUnderstand="1"
        xmlns:wsse="http://schemas.xmlsoap.org/ws/2002/07/secext">
        <wsse:UsernameToken
          xmlns:wsu="http://schemas.xmlsoap.org/ws/2002/07/utility"
          wsu:Id="SecurityToken-6b6f4b9d-44da-457d-864c-
6be658b04e5f">
          <wsse:Username>BillEvjen</wsse:Username>
          <wsse:Password Type="wsse:PasswordDigest">
           8L7EFP14fRk8SP3/p2DnlvJZYs4=</wsse:Password>
          <wsse:Nonce>uga8tX274XAxXLMeVqSizA==</wsse:Nonce>
          <wsu:Created>2002-12-27T21:19:30Z</wsu:Created>
        </wsse:UsernameToken>
      </wsse:Security>
    </soap:Header>
```

Continued

Listing 9-4 (Continued)

```
    </soap:Header>
    <soap:Body>
      <HelloAuthenticatedUser xmlns="http://www.wiley.com/" />
    </soap:Body>
</soap:Envelope>
```

Notice that the routing and timestamp information has been removed from the SOAP header. The only information that is now contained within the SOAP header is the WS-Security information.

Summary

Hopefully you have seen the tremendous value of using the WSE to build your SOAP requests and responses so that they abide by the latest GXA specifications. Just remember that the idea is to promote a common language that disparate systems can use to communicate application logic and data. The WSE takes it one step further to allow you to use the common language model in defining your SOAP message's security and routing information, as well as in its ability to attach non-XML related items such as images and documents.

As stated in this chapter, it does this by running SOAP messages through a series of filters that modify SOAP messages before they are sent on their way as well as interpreting SOAP messages as they are received. This chapter gave you a brief introduction on the ability to also control how these filters work.

You can be assured that the ability to work with security, routing, and attachments is not going to be all the WSE is about. As the WSE goes into new versions, new functionality will be added based on the new specifications that are released by companies such as Microsoft and IBM.

Appendix A

Tracing

TRACING INVOLVES GATHERING copies of the SOAP requests and responses as they are sent and recording these instances for later review. This is a powerful capability that allows you to debug your XML Web services or the client applications that work with XML Web services.

It is already quite easy to look at the payload of some SOAP messages by simply invoking the XML Web service from the XML Web service's test page. For instance, if you invoke a simple Add method from an XML Web service, you can see the following results delivered from the XML Web service test page:

```
<?xml version="1.0" encoding="utf-8" ?>
<int xmlns="http://www.wiley.com">7</int>
```

What you see here is the SOAP payload that has been serialized into XML. But this may not be what you are looking for. You might instead need to see the entire SOAP message – including the entire SOAP envelope as has been shown with the many examples in this book.

There are a couple of ways to view the entire SOAP message when working with XML Web services on the .NET platform. One new way is provided with the WSE. This is by far the easiest way to accomplish the task of monitoring your SOAP messages, but this method doesn't track the DIME records that you might send. Besides this built-in capability within the WSE, the other option includes using the Microsoft SOAP Toolkit 3.0. The SOAP Toolkit is a powerful little application that allows you to see quite a bit about your SOAP messages. There are additional ways of accomplishing the task of monitoring your SOAP messages, but this appendix concentrates solely on these two options because they are the most productive.

Using the WSE to Monitor Your SOAP Messages

The WSE has the built-in capability to take your SOAP transmissions and record them to a file. It is very simple to do and will help you considerably when you need to debug your Web services or the client applications in their dealings with any SOAP messages.

One of the greatest features of the WSE's built-in tracing capabilities is that you can use this tracing functionality whether you are the client application or whether you are the XML Web service provider. To use this feature, you must have the capability to work with the WSE.

For instance, if you want to enable tracing for a client application, you have to take the following steps in your application:

1. Make a reference to the `Microsoft.Web.Services` DLL within the References folder. This is found in the Solution Explorer window within Visual Studio .NET.

2. After you make a reference to an XML Web service, you have to change the proxy class that is automatically generated by Visual Studio .NET. To find the proxy class, click the Show All Files button within the Solution Explorer.

3. Open the Web References folder (this folder is represented by a tiny globe in the Solution Explorer).

4. Expand the plus sign next to the `Reference.map` file; you will see the `Reference.vb` or the `Reference.cs` file (shown in Figure A-1).

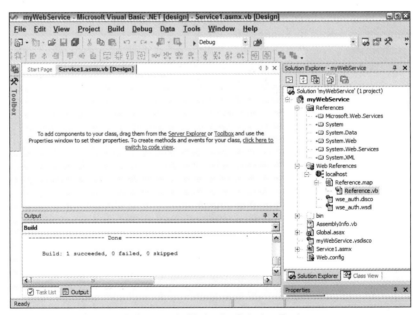

Figure A-1: Finding the Reference.vb file in the Solution Explorer

5. The `Reference.vb` or `Reference.cs` file is the proxy class that was generated by Visual Studio .NET. It takes care of marshaling the SOAP messages back and forth across the wire. In order for the WSE to record any of the SOAP requests or responses, you have to force these transmissions through the WSE by making the proxy class inherit from `Microsoft.Web.Services.WebServicesClientProtocol` instead of from `System.Web.Services.Protocols.SoapHttpClientProtocol`. Make this change and recompile the project.

6. Open the `web.config` file and make the following changes:

```
<?xml version="1.0" encoding="utf-8" ?>
<configuration>

    <microsoft.web.services>
        <diagnostics>
            <trace enabled="true"
             input="inputTrace.config"
             output="outputTrace.config"/>
        </diagnostics>
    </microsoft.web.services>

    <system.web>

        <!-- The rest of the web.config file -->

    </system.web>
</configuration>
```

Notice that the `<microsoft.web.services>` nodes are outside of the `<system.web>` elements but inside of the `<configuration>` elements.

7. Run your application.

The `<trace>` element can have three possible attributes, as described in Table A-1.

The file extension for the trace file should always be `.webinfo` or `.config`. This ensures a higher level of security. By using `.webinfo` or `.config`, the files won't be accessible via a browser. You should still make sure that there is limited access to the file beyond just typical browser access because this file can contain personal information due to the fact that the entire SOAP message is stored in the file as plain text. There are instances where your SOAP messages might contain information not meant for others.

Table A-1 POSSIBLE <trace> ELEMENT ATTRIBUTES

Attribute	Description
enabled	This attribute turns WSE tracing on or off. The two possible values include `true` or `false`. A value of `true` means that tracing is on, whereas `false` means that tracing is off. The default value is `false`.
input	This is an optional attribute that will assign a name to the file where the incoming SOAP message is stored. By default, the WSE will publish the value of the trace to a file named `inputTrace.webinfo`.
output	This is an optional attribute that will assign a name to the file where the outgoing SOAP message is stored. By default, the WSE will publish the value of the trace to a file named `outputTrace.webinfo`.

 For tracing to work, the ASP.NET worker process must take control of the file in order to write the SOAP message to the file. To allow this, you have to give the ASP.NET worker process full control over the files.

Using the Microsoft SOAP Toolkit to Monitor Messages

You can also use Microsoft's SOAP Toolkit 3.0 to record your SOAP messages. You can get a free copy of the SOAP Toolkit from Microsoft's MSDN site at http://msdn.microsoft.com/soap. After you install the toolkit, you will find a number of new abilities available for dealing with Web services such as a WSDL generator and the ability to send SOAP attachments.

Out of all these great tools, you need only one at the moment – the Trace utility. You can use the Trace utility within the SOAP Toolkit to trace the SOAP messages as they are being sent and received by an XML Web service's client application.

You must take a few steps in order to use the Trace utility. First, you need to have an XML Web service that you can consume. For the sake of this example, you can consume the XML Web service from Chapter 8 that exposed a single image using DIME (review Listing 8-4).

Next, you need to build an application that consumes this XML Web service and can make a request that causes the Web service to issue a response.

When building your consuming application, you need to take certain steps in order to work with the XML Web service. When using Visual Studio .NET, one of those steps is to make a Web reference to the XML Web service's WSDL file so that the IDE can create a proxy class for your application. Use the following steps to get at the Visual Studio .NET created proxy class:

1. Make a Web reference to the XML Web service's WSDL file. If you can't find the WSDL file and if the Web service is built upon the Microsoft platform, you can simply make a reference to the .asmx file itself.

2. Click the Show All Files button at the top of the Solution Explorer window.

3. Open the Web References folder (this folder is represented by a tiny globe in the Solution Explorer).

4. Expand the plus sign next to the Reference.map file; you will see the Reference.vb or the Reference.cs file (shown in Figure A-1).

5. The Reference.vb or Reference.cs file is the proxy class generated by Visual Studio .NET. In order to work with the Microsoft SOAP Toolkit's Trace utility, you need to manipulate this file so that the SOAP messages are sent through the same port that the Trace utility is using. If you are running the Trace utility to monitor a local XML Web service, in most cases you might want to set the Trace utility to monitor port 8080. Open the Reference.vb or Reference.cs file to tell the proxy class to send the SOAP messages through port 8080 so that the Trace utility can monitor these messages for you.

6. You only need to make one change within the proxy class in order to instruct it to use port 8080. Scroll down part way until you see the following lines of code:

[VB]

```
Public Sub New()
   MyBase.New
   Me.Url = "http://localhost/myGetImage/Service1.asmx"
End Sub
```

[C#]

```
public myGetImage() {
   this.Url = "http://localhost/myGetImage/Service1.asmx";
}
```

Change the code of the proxy class by inserting the port number that you want the proxy class to use when marshaling the SOAP messages. This is shown in the following code:

[VB]

```
Public Sub New()
   MyBase.New
   Me.Url = "http://localhost:8080/myGetImage/Service1.asmx"
End Sub
```

[C#]

```
public myGetImage() {
 this.Url = "http://localhost:8080/myGetImage/Service1.asmx";
 }
```

 Your XML Web service's path might be different from the one listed in the code.

7. Save the file and choose Build → Build Solution so that this file is recompiled.

8. Now you are finished with the proxy class, but before you run the XML Web service client application, you need to start the Trace utility application by choosing Start → All Programs → Microsoft SOAP Toolkit Version 3 → Trace Utility.

9. From the Trace utility application, choose File → New → Formatted Trace. The Trace Setup window opens and enables you to specify the local port number that you will use, as well as the destination host and port number. See Figure A-2.

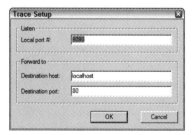

Figure A-2: The Trace Setup dialog window

Next, go back to the XML Web service client application that you are building in order to consume the `myGetImage` XML Web service.

10. Compile and run your client application.

Now both your XML Web service client application and the Trace utility should be open. The next step is to invoke the XML Web service from the client application. After you click on the application's button, the result from the XML Web service is returned and the value is placed into a control on the form.

Now comes the interesting part. If you go back to the Trace utility, you see that there is an entry in the left pane of the application. `127.0.0.1` is your local IP address. Expand the plus sign next to this IP address and you see `Message #1`. Highlight `Message #1` and you will then see the SOAP messages show up in the other two panes within the utility. Figure A-3 shows what the Trace utility should look like after you have taken these steps.

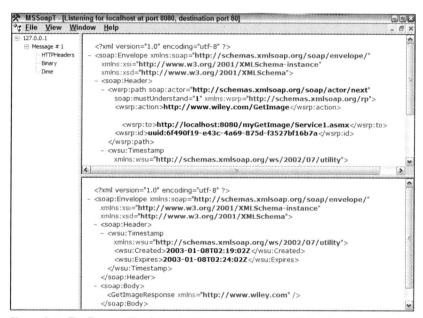

Figure A-3: The Trace utility from the Microsoft SOAP Toolkit Version 3 showing both the request and response SOAP messages

Not only does the Trace utility give you a view of the SOAP requests and responses that are being sent to and from the client application, but it also contains three other views of the information that is being sent.

Underneath the `Message #1` listing in the left pane of the Trace utility is a listing of sub-categories. These include HTTPHeaders, Binary, and Dime. Besides the ability to look at the SOAP requests and responses, probably the most interesting section is the DIME section. Here you have the ability to view an XML representation of the DIME records that are sent along with the SOAP requests or responses. This isn't possible to do with the built-in tracing means that are included with the WSE. Figure A-4 shows the Trace utility with the DIME category selected.

Figure A-4: The Trace utility showing DIME records

After completing all of these steps, you can now watch the SOAP messages that are sent to and from your XML Web services. This will be quite beneficial for debugging and for determining whether you are forming your SOAP messages as desired.

There are other tools that you can use to watch SOAP packets as they move across the wire, but the Microsoft SOAP Toolkit Version 3 will take care of most of your needs. Although it might not be as easy as using the built-in WSE capabilities, it is easy to use and allows you to look at DIME records, something that isn't possible with the trace abilities that accompany the WSE.

Appendix B

The Web Services Enhancements Settings Tool

As you probably noticed when working through the examples of this book, there are a number of repetitive changes that you are required to make to your XML Web services and the client applications that consume them. These changes are necessary in order for these applications to work with the capabilities that the Web Services Enhancements offers. Some of these include making changes to the `web.config` file in addition to changing the proxy class for any Web references that you have.

In light of this, Microsoft has released along with the WSE a little tool called the Web Services Enhancements Settings Tool. You can find the download for the Settings Tool on MSDN. This 525KB file is a quick download and installs to work with Visual Studio .NET, so you must be using Visual Studio .NET. At the time of this writing, the Settings Tool is an unsupported product and that is why it wasn't used as a way of configuring the WSE's configuration files throughout all the examples in this book.

So, what does this tool do for you? It saves time when building either client applications or XML Web services that will work with the WSE. It does this by providing you with a GUI-based dialog to modify the WSE settings that would need to be present in the `web.config` file as well as changing the way in which proxy classes are generated.

Configuration File Changes

Once you have installed the Web Services Enhancements Settings Tool, create a new ASP.NET Web Service project to see a demonstration on how to use it within Visual Studio .NET.

The Settings Tool makes it quite easy to configure your XML Web service to get you up and running rather quickly. To configure your XML Web service to work with the WSE by using the Settings Tool, right-click on the project name within the Solution Explorer and select WSE Settings. This process is shown in Figure B-1.

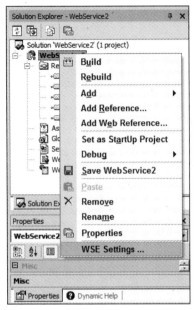

Figure B-1: Selecting the WSE Settings Tool within
the project's options from the Solution Explorer

Clicking on WSE Settings will pull up the Web Services Enhancements Settings
dialog box. This dialog box includes five tabs: General, Security, Customized
Filters, Routing, and Diagnostic (see Figure B-2).

To get started building an XML Web service that is going to work with the WSE,
you need to select the first check box of the General tab (Enable This Project for
Web Services Enhancements 1.0). This check box will enable the project to work
with the WSE. It does this by automatically making a reference to the
Microsoft.Web.Services DLL in your project.

The second check box on the General tab (Enable Microsoft Web Services
Enhancement SOAP Extensions) makes the appropriate changes to the web.config
file by adding the WSE SOAP Extensions elements and settings to the file.

The Security tab (shown in Figure B-3) allows you to make changes to the
web.config file through the GUI that deals with the WSE's security implementation. From this page, you can specify your Password Provider and Decryption
Provider classes as well as any settings you have for your X.509 certificates or any
binary security tokens.

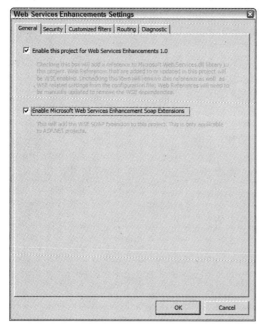

Figure B-2: The Web Services Enhancements Settings dialog box

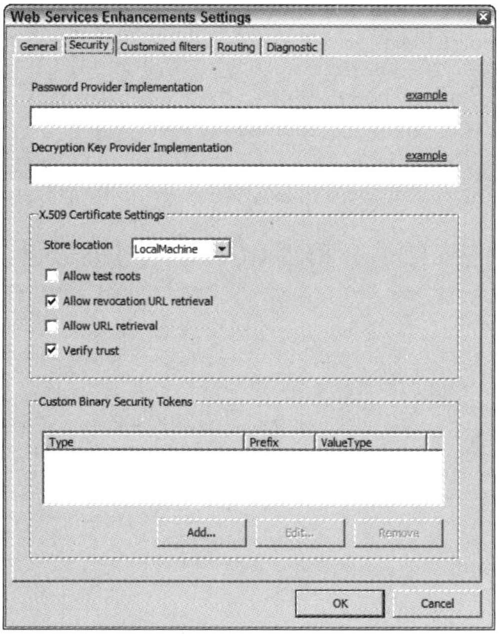

Figure B-3: The Security tab

The Customized Filters tab allows you to make settings to your WSE filters. The next tab, Routing, allows you to apply your references to the routing handlers and to the referral cache.

The final tab, Diagnostic, allows you to apply tracing and to specify where the trace information is saved. Remember that the file extension should be either .webinfo or .config for security reasons.

After you make all the changes you want to the Settings Tool GUI and click the OK button, Visual Studio .NET will make a reference to the Microsoft.Web. Services DLL for you. It will also make the appropriate configurations changes in the web.config file. This capability provided by the Settings Tool can be a great time saver and can keep you from making errors in the configuration file.

Proxy Class Changes

Without using the Settings Tool, whenever you make a reference to an XML Web service from your client application, you are required to go into the proxy class and change the class so that it inherits from Microsoft.Web.Services. WebServicesClientProtocol. Once you have this in place, you can then work with all the capabilities that the WSE offers you in your development.

After you have installed the Settings Tool, it will also take care of this process for you. Before you make a Web reference to an XML Web service, you need to make sure that there is a reference to the Microsoft.Web.Services DLL within your project. Then once you have this reference in place, whenever you make a Web reference to an XML Web service, the Settings Tool will cause Visual Studio .NET to create the proxy class in a different manner so that there is one class that inherits from the default System.Web.Services.Protocols.SoapHttpClientProtocol and another class that inherits from Microsoft.Web.Services. WebServicesClientProtocol. This allows you to choose whether or not you want to work through the WSE.

For example, you make a Web reference to an XML Web service with a URL address of Service1.asmx, and therefore have two proxy classes created for you, one called Service1 and another called Service1Wse. Instantiating the class Service1 as your proxy class will allow you to communicate with the XML Web service without using the WSE. Instantiating the class Service1Wse as your proxy class allows you to work with the XML Web service using everything that the WSE provides. Listings B-1 and B-2 show you how to make references to each of these classes.

Listing B-1: Instantiating the proxy class that does not work with the WSE

[VB]

```
Dim ws As New localhost.Service1()
```

[C#]

```
localhost.Service1 ws = new localhost.Service1();
```

Listing B-2: Instantiating the proxy class that works with the WSE

[VB]

```
Dim ws As New localhost.Service1Wse()
```

[C#]

```
localhost.Service1Wse ws = new localhost.Service1Wse();
```

The Settings Tool makes it easier to work with the WSE, because it takes care of configuring your applications as needed.

Appendix C

WSE Configuration Files

ONE OF THE IMPORTANT parts of working with the WSE is setting up the configuration files properly. The Web Services Enhancements Settings Tool does help you in setting up your configuration files, but even with this tool, you'll likely find yourself making changes to the configurations files to get the WSE to behave exactly how you want. This appendix takes a look at the structure of the configuration files that need to be in place for the WSE to work properly.

Configuring the web.config File

One of the main places that you have to make configuration settings in order to work with the WSE is within the `web.config` file that is located in your project. Listing C-1 shows a generic structure of all the WSE-related elements that can be contained within this configuration file.

Listing C-1: web.config settings

```
<configuration>

   <configSections>
      <section name="microsoft.web.services"
       type="Microsoft.Web.Services.Configuration.
       WebServicesConfiguration, Microsoft.Web.Services,
       Version=1.0.0.0, Culture=neutral,
       PublicKeyToken=31bf3856ad364e35" />
   </configSections>

   <microsoft.web.services>
      <security>
         <passwordProvider type="WebService1.myPasswordProvider,
          WebService1" />
         <decryptionKeyProvider
          type="WebService1.DecryptionKeyProvider, WebService1" />
         <binarySecurityToken
```

Continued

Listing C-1 *(Continued)*

```
            type="WebService1.BinaryKeyProvider, WebService1"
            xmlns:x="XML namespace"
            valueType="x:Name of token used in SOAP messages." />
         <x509 storeLocation="LocalMachine|CurrentUser"
            verifyTrust="true|false"
            allowTestRoot="true|false" />
      </security>
      <diagnostics>
         <trace enabled="true|false" input="ClientRequest.config"
            output="ServiceResponse.config" />
      </diagnostics>
      <referral>
         <cache name="referralCache.config" />
      </referral>
      <filters>
         <input>
            <add type="WebService1.customFilterClass, WebService1" />
         </input>
         <output>
            <add type="WebService1.customFilterClass, WebService1" />
         </output>
      </filters>
   </microsoft.web.services>

   <system.web>

      <webServices>
         <soapExtensionTypes>
            <add type="Microsoft.Web.Services.WebServicesExtension,
               Microsoft.Web.Services, Version=1.0.0.0,
               Culture=neutral,
               PublicKeyToken=31bf3856ad364e35" priority="1"
               group="0"/>
         </soapExtensionTypes>
      </webServices>

      <httpHandlers>
         <add verb="*" path="*.asmx"
            type="Microsoft.Web.Services.Routing.RoutingHandler,
            Microsoft.Web.Services,
            Version=1.0.0.0, Culture=neutral,
```

```
            PublicKeyToken=31bf3856ad364e35" />
        </httpHandlers>

    </system.web>

</configuration>
```

This listing shows all the elements that can be placed within the web.config file. Not all of them are required in order to work with the WSE; you can use specific WSE configuration settings here to accomplish the specific tasks from the WSE. These settings, which are explained in detail throughout the book, are laid out here for your quick reference.

Configuring the referralCache.config File

The other configuration file within the WSE is referralCache.config. This file configures the routing process within the SOAP router that you construct. Listing C-2 shows an example configuration file. The entire routing configuration file is explained in Chapter 7.

Listing C-2: The SOAP router's referralCache.config file

```
<?xml version="1.0" ?>
<r:referrals
 xmlns:r="http://schemas.xmlsoap.org/ws/2001/10/referral">
  <r:ref>
    <r:for>
      <r:exact>http://localhost/Router/Service1.asmx</r:exact>
    </r:for>
    <r:if />
    <r:go>
      <r:via>http://localhost/AddWS/Service1.asmx</r:via>
    </r:go>
    <r:refId>uuid:fa469956-0057-4e77-962a-81c5e192f2ae</r:refId>
  </r:ref>
</r:referrals>
```

Appendix D

MediaType Values

WHEN ENCAPSULATING ITEMS within DIME records, in some cases you will need to specify the MIME type as one of the parameters of the `DimeAttachment` object. This declaration identifies the data type of the data contained within the `Data` section of the DIME record. For instance, the code in Visual Basic .NET would look as follows:

```
dimeAttachment = New DimeAttachment("image/jpeg", _
   TypeFormatEnum.MediaType, "C:\Trees.jpg")
```

The following table lists some of the possible MIME type declarations that you can use for this parameter.

File Name Extension	MIME Type
.jpg	image/jpeg
.jpeg	image/jpeg
.jpe	image/jpeg
.gif	image/gif
.cod	image/cis-cod
.ief	image/ief
.pbm	image/x-portable-bitmap
.rgb	image/x-rgb
.dib	image/bmp
.cmx	image/x-cmx
.pnm	image/x-portable-anymap
.jfif	image/pjpeg
.tif	image/tiff

Continued

File Name Extension	MIME Type
.xbm	image/x-xbitmap
.ras	image/x-cmu-raster
.tsv	text/tab-separated-values
.xml	text/xml
.323	text/h323
.htt	text/webviewhtml
.stm	text/html
.html	text/html
.xsl	text/xml
.htm	text/html
.sct	text/scriptlet
.hta	application/hta
.isp	application/x-internet-signup
.crd	application/x-mscardfile
.pmc	application/x-perfmon
.spc	application/x-pkcs7-certificates
.sv4crc	application/x-sv4crc
.bin	application/octet-stream
.clp	application/x-msclip
.mny	application/x-msmoney
.p7r	application/x-pkcs7-certreqresp
.evy	application/envoy
.p7s	application/pkcs7-signature
.eps	application/postscript
.setreg	application/set-registration-initiation
.xlm	application/vnd.ms-excel
.cpio	application/x-cpio

File Name Extension	MIME Type
.dvi	application/x-dvi
.p7b	application/x-pkcs7-certificates
.doc	application/msword
.dot	application/msword
.p7c	application/pkcs7-mime
.ps	application/postscript
.wps	application/vnd.ms-works
.csh	application/x-csh
.iii	application/x-iphone
.pmw	application/x-perfmon
.man	application/x-troff-man
.hdf	application/x-hdf
.mvb	application/x-msmediaview
.texi	application/x-texinfo
.setpay	application/set-payment-initiation
.stl	application/vndms-pkistl
.mdb	application/x-msaccess
.oda	application/oda
.hlp	application/winhlp
.nc	application/x-netcdf
.sh	application/x-sh
.shar	application/x-shar
.tcl	application/x-tcl
.ms	application/x-troff-ms
.ods	application/oleobject
.axs	application/olescript

Continued

File Name Extension	MIME Type
.xla	application/vnd.ms-excel
.mpp	application/vnd.ms-project
.dir	application/x-director
.sit	application/x-stuffit
.*	application/octet-stream
.crl	application/pkix-crl
.ai	application/postscript
.xls	application/vnd.ms-excel
.wks	application/vnd.ms-works
.ins	application/x-internet-signup
.pub	application/x-mspublisher
.wri	application/x-mswrite
.spl	application/futuresplash
.hqx	application/mac-binhex40
.p10	application/pkcs10
.xlc	application/vnd.ms-excel
.xlt	application/vnd.ms-excel
.dxr	application/x-director
.js	application/x-javascript
.m13	application/x-msmediaview
.trm	application/x-msterminal
.pml	application/x-perfmon
.me	application/x-troff-me
.wcm	application/vnd.ms-works
.latex	application/x-latex
.m14	application/x-msmediaview
.wmf	application/x-msmetafile

File Name Extension	MIME Type
.cer	application/x-x509-ca-cert
.zip	application/x-zip-compressed
.p12	application/x-pkcs12
.pfx	application/x-pkcs12
.der	application/x-x509-ca-cert
.pdf	application/pdf
.xlw	application/vnd.ms-excel
.texinfo	application/x-texinfo
.p7m	application/pkcs7-mime
.pps	application/vnd.ms-powerpoint
.dcr	application/x-director
.gtar	application/x-gtar
.fif	application/fractals
.exe	application/octet-stream
.ppt	application/vnd.ms-powerpoint
.sst	application/vndms-pkicertstore
.pko	application/vndms-pkipko
.scd	application/x-msschedule
.tar	application/x-tar
.roff	application/x-troff
.t	application/x-troff
.prf	application/pics-rules
.rtf	application/rtf
.pot	application/vnd.ms-powerpoint
.wdb	application/vnd.ms-works
.bcpio	application/x-bcpio

Continued

File Name Extension	MIME Type
.dll	application/x-msdownload
.pma	application/x-perfmon
.pmr	application/x-perfmon
.tr	application/x-troff
.src	application/x-wais-source
.acx	application/internet-property-stream
.cat	application/vndms-pkiseccat
.cdf	application/x-cdf
.tgz	application/x-compressed
.sv4cpio	application/x-sv4cpio
.tex	application/x-tex
.ustar	application/x-ustar
.crt	application/x-x509-ca-cert
.gz	application/x-gzip
.z	application/x-compress
.ra	audio/x-pn-realaudio
.mid	audio/mid
.au	audio/basic
.snd	audio/basic
.wav	audio/wav
.aifc	audio/aiff
.m3u	audio/x-mpegurl
.ram	audio/x-pn-realaudio
.aiff	audio/aiff
.rmi	audio/x-pn-realaudio
.aif	audio/x-aiff
.mp3	audio/mpeg

Appendix E

Web Services Resources

THE FOLLOWING TWO books that will help you get up to speed quickly with the .NET Framework as well as XML Web services.

- *XML Web Services for ASP.NET,* by Bill Evjen (Wiley, ISBN 0-7645-4829-8).

- *Visual Basic .NET Bible,* by Bill Evjen (Wiley, ISBN 0-7645-4826-3).

 Browse through additional titles at the Wiley home page: `www.wiley.com/compbooks`.

Since the Internet is as large as it is, it can be rather difficult to find the proper resources on the Internet in regards to Web services. Below is a short list of some of the sites that I frequent the most. It is not by any means meant to be comprehensive, but these sites I rate as the best ones to get you all the information you need on this topic.

Web Site	Description
msdn.microsoft.com/webservices	Microsoft's Web services home page
www.vbws.com	Learn XML Web services
www.soapwebservices.com	News on Web services
www.xmethods.com	Web services directory
www.salcentral.com	Web services directory
www.xmlwebservices.cc	XML Web services
www.webservices.org	WebServices.Org

Continued

Web Site	Description
www.gotdotnet.com	GotDotNet (Microsoft)
www.asp.net	ASP.NET home page (Microsoft)
www.w3.org	W3C
www.oasis-open.org	OASIS
www.ws-i.org	Web Services Interoperability Group
www.ietf.org	Internet Engineering Taskforce (IETF)
www.uddi.org	UDDI, The Universal Description, Discovery, and Integration Project
msdn.microsoft.com/newsgroups	Microsoft newsgroups
www.aspadvice.com	Asp ListServes
www.dotnetjunkies.com	DotnetJunkies
www.xmlforasp.net	XML for ASP.NET
www.123aspx.com	Directory of .NET articles and resources
msdn.Microsoft.com/xml	Microsoft's XML Home page

Index

Symbols and Numerics

continued

continued